# AN

# APOSTOLIC

# JOURNEY

# AN

# APOSTOLIC

# JOURNEY

STEPHEN L RICHARDS AND THE
EXPANSION OF MISSIONARY WORK
IN SOUTH AMERICA

RICHARD E. TURLEY JR.
CLINTON D. CHRISTENSEN

Published by the Religious Studies Center, Brigham Young University, Provo, Utah, in cooperation with Deseret Book Company, Salt Lake City.
Visit us at rsc.byu.edu.

© 2019 by Brigham Young University. All rights reserved.

Printed in the United States of America by Sheridan Books, Inc.

DESERET BOOK is a registered trademark of Deseret Book Company.
Visit us at DeseretBook.com.

Any uses of this material beyond those allowed by the exemptions in US copyright law, such as section 107, "Fair Use," and section 108, "Library Copying," require the written permission of the publisher, Religious Studies Center, 185 HGB, Brigham Young University, Provo, UT 84602. The views expressed herein are the responsibility of the authors and do not necessarily represent the position of Brigham Young University or the Religious Studies Center.

Cover and interior design by Emily V. Strong.

ISBN 978-1-9443-9477-6

Library of Congress Control Number: 2019936538

# CONTENTS

| | |
|---|---|
| PREFACE | vii |
| PROLOGUE: LATTER-DAY SAINT MISSIONARY EFFORTS IN SOUTH AMERICA, 1851–1947 | xi |
| 1. THE RICHARDSES ARRIVE IN SOUTH AMERICA | 1 |
| 2. ARGENTINA | 9 |
| 3. URUGUAY | 75 |
| 4. BRAZIL | 105 |
| 5. REPORTS AND CONFERENCE TALK | 159 |
| EPILOGUE: LATTER-DAY SAINT MISSIONARY EFFORTS IN SOUTH AMERICA, 1948–2018 | 183 |
| APPENDIX: TIMELINE OF THE CHURCH IN LATIN AMERICA | 203 |
| BIBLIOGRAPHY | 211 |
| INDEX | 221 |
| ABOUT THE AUTHORS | 233 |

# PREFACE

During my eight-year tenure as assistant Church historian and recorder for The Church of Jesus Christ of Latter-day Saints in Salt Lake City, Utah, I taught a series of classes on the Church's global history for staff of the Church History Department. When I was teaching a section on the history of the Latter-day Saints in South America, Clinton D. Christensen, a student in the class, made me aware of a recent acquisition.

In November 2013, Clint was invited to the home of Lynn S. Richards Jr., a grandson of Apostle Stephen L Richards. The home was ready to be sold, and the family papers were boxed in the garage. Clint discovered many historical treasures, including papers of Elder Stephen L Richards, his wife Irene, and even the portraits of Irene's grandparents George A. and Bathsheba Smith that had hung in the celestial room of the Nauvoo Temple in 1846.[1] Among Irene's papers was a book of letters she wrote detailing her husband's three-month apostolic tour of South America in 1948. As luck would have it, Clint acquired the papers and brought Irene's letter book to the Church history class within a week of our discussion about Stephen L Richards's trip.

Given the importance of Stephen L and Irene Merrill Smith Richards's visit to Argentina, Uruguay, and Brazil in the history of the Church in South America, Clint and I decided to coauthor a volume on their travels, which marked a turning point for Latter-day Saints on that continent. Bookending the chapters on the experiences of Elder and Sister Richards are a prologue and an epilogue giving an overview of the history of the Church in South America up to 1948 and then from 1948 to 2018. Because a complete history of the Church in South America has yet to be written, the prologue and epilogue help fill a need by providing a solid introduction to the much larger story of Latin American Church history. Enhancing this historical overview is a timeline of key events in the history of the Church in Latin America.

The travel chapters include documents from Elder and Sister Richards, mission presidents, missionaries, mission records, journalists, and, to a lesser extent, local Church members. All letters replicate the originals, including nonstandard spellings and the omission of diacritical marks in Spanish and Portuguese, with the exception of spacing and other formatting details that have been adjusted for improved readability and presentation. Each documentary section begins with a daily summary describing the events of the apostolic tour followed by related documents containing bracketed clarifications and footnotes where deemed helpful. For space reasons, footnote references to the Church History Library in Salt Lake City, Utah, have been abbreviated to "CHL."

We are particularly grateful to my administrative assistant, Andrea Maxfield, and to Eileen Jenkins and Gretchen Becker, who prepared, typed, and reviewed the documents. Alison Gainer, Andrea Snarr, and Dan Holliday helped with initial editing of the manuscript. We thank the team at BYU's Religious Studies Center: publications director Scott C. Esplin; project editor Don L. Brugger and his assistants Ashlin Awerkamp, Sharai McGill, and Petra Javadi-Evans; production supervisor Brent R. Nordgren; and designer/typesetter Emily V. Strong. Gratitude also goes to the staff and senior missionaries of the Church History Department for their generous help: Matt Godfrey, Michael Landon, Matt Geilman, Jeremy Talmage, Jeff Crossley, Elena Lowe, and Richard and Rosalie Jones. LaMond Tullis and Mark Grover provided insightful reviews of the chapters on the history of the Church in Latin America. We are also grateful for the cooperation of the families of South American returned missionaries and for a few earlier missionaries who remember the Richardses' visit in 1948 and have shared their memories, scrapbooks, and journals with us while we prepared this book.

We hope that readers of this volume will not only get a clear sense of the history of the Latter-day Saints during the time of the Richardses' visit but will also see how their travels became a milestone in the development of what is now a multimillion-member church in South America.

—Richard E. Turley Jr. with Clinton D. Christensen

---

### NOTE

1. The paintings are on display in the "Heavens Are Open" exhibit at the Church History Museum in Salt Lake City, Utah.

## PROLOGUE

# LATTER-DAY SAINT MISSIONARY EFFORTS IN SOUTH AMERICA, 1851–1947

### AN ONGOING CHARGE TO PREACH THE GOSPEL WORLDWIDE

In concluding his forty-day postresurrection ministry, Jesus Christ commanded his disciples:

> Go ye therefore, and teach all nations, baptizing them in the name of the Father, and of the Son, and of the Holy Ghost: teaching them to observe all things whatsoever I have commanded you: and, lo, I am with you alway, even unto the end of the world. Amen. (Matthew 28:19–20)

When the American prophet Joseph Smith and his associates formally organized the Church of Christ on April 6, 1830, they understood it to be the restoration of Christ's ancient church and took seriously the New Testament charge to take the gospel to all nations and peoples.[1] Even before the Church's formal organization, believers spread word of the new movement to regions surrounding where Smith and his family lived in upstate New York and northern Pennsylvania.[2]

The Prophet Joseph Smith translated an ancient book of scripture that became known as the Book of Mormon. Before the book became available for sale in March 1830, believers with access to press galleys took portions for others to read, and a local journalist with after-hours access to the printshop began pirating major segments of the volume in his own newspaper.[3] When the book became available in its entirety, readers discovered that its title page represented the volume as a modern translation of an ancient book of scripture intended for "the convincing of the Jew and Gentile that Jesus is the Christ, the Eternal God, manifesting Himself unto all nations."[4]

Early efforts to take this restored gospel to all people included famous missionary forays by Smith's younger brother Samuel. His labors led to the conversion of Brigham Young, the man who would succeed Smith after the founding prophet's death at the hands of vigilantes in 1844.[5] During Smith's lifetime, Church members spread the gospel message throughout much of the United States, Canada, and the British Isles; to portions of continental Europe, the Middle East, and Australia; and even to the islands of what became French Polynesia.[6]

## EARLY MISSIONARY INTEREST IN SOUTH AMERICA

One of the most famous efforts to spread the latter-day gospel occurred just months after the Church's organization when a revelation received by Joseph Smith called his closest associate in the work, Oliver Cowdery, and ultimately three companions to preach to native peoples of the Americas.[7]

### A CALL TO TEACH NATIVE PEOPLES

One of Cowdery's companions was Parley P. Pratt, later dubbed by biographers "the Apostle Paul of Mormonism."[8] Pratt's mind was far-reaching, and he took seriously the revealed missionary charge that "he shall go . . . into the wilderness among the Lamanites," a Book of Mormon term for ancient peoples of America that Church members of his generation interpreted to mean America's Indians.[9] Cowdery, Pratt, and their companions endured bitter winter cold and other harsh conditions as they moved west to the frontiers of the organized United States to commune with Indian peoples who had been pushed to the nation's margins.¹⁰

The Latter-day Saint missionaries soon found themselves forced out of Indian territory by government agents tasked with protecting native peoples from the kind of exploitation that had marked centuries of interaction with colonial Europeans. But the mission journey was not a total failure: they found great success among Pratt's former associates in Ohio, many of whom joined the fledging Church.¹¹

## PARLEY P. PRATT'S 1851 JOURNEY TO CHILE

Pratt never forgot his original charge, and when he followed Brigham Young west to what became Utah and received responsibility over the Church's new mission in the Pacific, he studied Spanish and made plans to take the Latter-day Saint message to the native peoples of South America whose nations bordered the Pacific Ocean. To that end, Pratt left in 1851 on a cargo ship for Chile, accompanied by two companions: his ailing, pregnant wife Phoebe Soper Pratt and Rufus C. Allen.

This small missionary group suffered immensely before arriving in Chile, where they encountered language challenges, limitations on religious liberty, and soaring inflation. They also faced political challenges, ran out of money to support themselves, and failed to secure employment to replenish their stores. Most notably, Phoebe suffered through an excruciating labor, giving birth to a son, Omner, who died a few weeks later. The Pratts buried their son and returned with Allen to the United States in 1852, feeling their labors had failed.¹²

## FURTHER MISSIONARY SETBACKS

After Pratt and his companions arrived in the United States, but before they returned to Utah, Latter-day Saint leaders in Salt Lake City held a conference on August 29, 1852, in which Pratt's brother Orson officially announced the Saints' longtime practice of plural marriage. To offset the public relations firestorm they knew would ensue, and to gather believers as part of their millennial message, the leaders called some one hundred missionaries to take the message of the restored gospel throughout the world. The leaders assigned missionaries to serve in North America, South America, Europe, Africa, Asia, and Australia.[13]

The missionaries called to South America were directed to British Guiana on the northeast coast of the continent, apparently assuming that English influence on the colony would ensure that language and religious liberty would pose fewer problems than they had earlier for Parley P. Pratt and his companions in Chile. The two newly called missionaries, James Brown and Elijah Thomas, traveled to California and by sea to Panama, becoming the first Latter-day Saints known to reach Central America.[14]

The missionaries crossed the Panamanian isthmus and took a boat to Jamaica, which was then a British colony. In Jamaica they joined four fellow missionaries who had arrived by a different route.[15] The growing opposition to Latter-day Saints in the press, however, stopped Elders Brown and Thomas before they could reach their assigned field of labor. Unable to get passage directly to British Guiana, they planned to first go to the island of Barbados. "After paying their passages" to Barbados, a Church historian recorded, "they were not allowed to proceed thither; the prejudice was so great against the Elders [missionaries] that the harbor agent or naval officers would not allow them to be shipped to any English island."[16] By January 1853 formal efforts in the nineteenth century to take The Church of Jesus Christ of Latter-day Saints to South America had ended.

After Parley P. Pratt left South America in 1852, he wrote that he desired to go to Peru, where the political environment was more promising, but the missionaries had run out of funds. Pratt came to understand that Peru was more populated with native peoples than Chile was and thus more closely fit his original revelatory charge as a missionary. His plans to return to South America at some point were thwarted when he died at an assassin's hand in 1857.[17] It was not until the early twentieth century that the next known Latter-day Saint, Alfred William McCune, traveled to Peru. Although not an ardent believer in the restored gospel, McCune, a mining and railroad magnate, went to Peru in 1901 as part of a multiyear effort to develop mines there and build a railway that would transport mining products to the coast for shipping.[18]

## MEXICO: GATEWAY FOR EXPANDING THE WORK SOUTHWARD

Meanwhile, official Church efforts to reach Latin America focused on Mexico, which had been on the minds of ecclesiastical leaders during Joseph Smith's lifetime. Latter-day Saint newspapers in Nauvoo, Illinois, repeatedly carried articles on Mexico, especially its relationship with Texas.[19] In 1843 Joseph Smith formed the Council of Fifty, a confidential administrative body that he charged with exploring future settlement sites for the Saints. The council looked at Mexico as a place for both settlement and future missionary work.[20]

Latter-day Saints were interested in Mexico, and Mexicans were curious about the Saints. Within a month of Smith's death on June 27, 1844, a newspaper in Mexico reported his martyrdom as a subject of public interest.[21] Subsequent newspaper articles in Mexico featured Latter-day Saint history and scripture.[22] When Brigham Young led the famous Latter-day Saint pioneer company to the Great Basin in 1847, he settled the Saints at the foot of the mountains southeast of the Great Salt Lake and named the community after that body of water. At the time, the land where they settled (which later became the territory and then state of Utah) was in the Mexican territory of Alta, or Upper, California. After settling most of his party there, Young returned east, and for half a year the Saints in Great Salt Lake City worked on building their community in Mexican territory.[23] Before Young returned west in 1848, land ownership in the region shifted from Mexico to the United States with the signing of the Treaty of Guadalupe Hidalgo on February 2.[24] Later, when US president James Buchanan sent troops to Utah in 1857 to ensure the seating of new federal appointees among the Saints, who would rather have governed themselves, he had expansionist ideas that included nudging the Latter-day Saints into Mexico.[25]

During the Utah War, among the schemes to entice the Saints to move south of America's territorial borders were one to get them into Mexico and another to the Mosquito Coast.

> Recognizing that the Mormons would move again if they had to, "General" William Walker and a Colonel Kinney offered to sell to the church thirty million acres of land on the Mosquito Coast in

Central America. Another proposition came to settle Sonora, in northern Mexico. Some officials in Washington seemed to regard the proposals as offering means of disposing once and for all of America's "Mormon question" and were prepared to recommend that financial inducement be offered the Mormons to accept. But Brigham, determined if at all possible to remain in Utah Territory, did not carry these negotiations to the advanced stage.[26]

The Utah War of 1857–58 ended after questions posed by Congress about Buchanan's military plans led to a resolution and peace commission.[27] However, before federal troops entered the Salt Lake Valley following a negotiated peace, Brigham Young and most of the Saints temporarily left Salt Lake for points farther south, and thereafter Young kept open an escape route in that direction, a pathway to travel in the event persecution forced him and his people to flee, as it had previously done in New York, Ohio, Missouri, and Illinois.[28]

The Saints returned to their homes after the Utah War, but Young kept looking south, especially after the completion of the transcontinental railroad in 1869 led to an influx of people who were not members of the Church to the greater Salt Lake region. In 1873 Young ordered pioneering missionaries to cross the Colorado and move deeper into Arizona. The first efforts at settling the region failed, though later efforts proved successful.[29]

In 1875 Latter-day Saint missionaries published extracts of the Book of Mormon in Spanish and soon traveled to Mexico.[30] By 1876 Brigham Young saw Mexico as the key to preaching the latter-day gospel throughout all of Latin America and establishing settlements there. "I look forward to the time when the settlements of the Church of Jesus Christ of Latter day Saints will extend right through to the City of Old Mexico," he wrote, "and from thence on through Central America to the land where the Nephites [a Book of Mormon people] flourished in the Golden era of their history, and this great backbone of the American Continent be filled, north and south, with the cities and temples of the people of God."[31]

Young died the following year in 1877, but his successor, John Taylor, authorized missionary work to Mexico City in 1879 and settlement in northern Mexico during the mid-1880s. Soon a Latter-day Saint mission sprang up, along with several colonies of immigrant Saints of many nations who worked the soil and sold goods in an effort to establish themselves on sound financial footing. They worked at learning Spanish, and many of the next generation learned it fluently. The Spanish language had proved an impediment during Parley P. Pratt's first trip to Latin America, but subsequent generations of Saints living in Mexico, including many who descended from Pratt, would speak the language well and thus be able to communicate their missionary message throughout much of Latin America.[32]

Between 1885 and 1912, the Church grew among the Latter-day Saint immigrants to Mexico, if less so among the native-born Mexicans outside the colonies. In 1912 political problems forced most Anglo Latter-day Saints from Mexico. Some of them later returned to Mexico, where their descendants live to this day. Others remained in the United States and retained their ability to speak Spanish.[33]

Rey L. Pratt, a grandson of Parley P. Pratt, grew up in the Latter-day Saint colonies in Mexico and used his language abilities to steer the Mexican Mission for twenty-four years until 1931. During times of revolution and political problems, President Pratt's contact with Mexican members kept the Church moving forward in a struggling country.[34] The Latter-day Saint colonies in Mexico eventually became a rich resource for missionaries and leaders with language skills to further the work in Mexico and serve throughout Latin America.[35]

## TWENTIETH-CENTURY MISSIONARY DEVELOPMENTS IN SOUTH AMERICA

### ANDREW JENSON'S CENTRAL AND SOUTH AMERICAN TOUR

The catalyst for establishing a permanent Latter-day Saint presence in South America was a Latin American tour taken unofficially by assistant Latter-day Saint Church historian Andrew Jenson, originally of Denmark. Jenson had become the Church's most traveled official and had visited numerous countries. But he had yet to visit South America when he sought permission and Church sponsorship to do so in 1923.[36]

When Church leaders declined to sponsor his trip, he elected to go anyway, taking the trip as a vacation experience with the financial aid and companionship of a well-to-do sponsor, Thomas Page. Their travels from January to May 1923 took them coast-to-coast in the United States and through much of Latin America.[37]

"On my recent tour to Central and South America," Jenson reported to senior Church leaders in July 1923, "I visited eleven different countries, namely Mexico, Guatemala, Salvador, Nicaragua, Panama, Peru, Bolivia, Chile, Argentina, Uruguay, and Brazil, and while traveling I also obtained important information concerning other countries near the line of my journeyings, including Honduras, British Honduras, and Costa Rica in Central America, and Venezuela, Colombia, Paraguay, and Ecuador in South America, and the West Indies."[38]

Two of the major problems that plagued Parley P. Pratt and other early missionaries to Latin America—the language barrier and lack of religious freedom—now seemed solvable in Jenson's mind. Nearly a half century of missionary work and settlement in Mexico showed that Latter-day Saints now possessed the necessary language skills. And fortuitously, in all the Latin American countries, Jenson noted with simplicity, "the Spanish language is the prevailing tongue, with the exception of Brazil, where the Portuguese is the national tongue, though Spanish is understood there also by most of the inhabitants."[39]

As for the lack of religious freedom, Jenson wrote, "Though the Roman Catholic religion prevails in nearly all parts of Mexico, Central America, and South America, and on many of the islands in the West Indies, there is perfect religious liberty in all, and I have reason to believe that, at least in some of the republics in both Central and South America, Latter-day Saint missionaries would be well-received."[40]

Jenson went on to provide statistics on each country, "knowing, as I do," he wrote, "that the Lord has commanded the Latter-day Saints to preach the gospel to every nation, kindred, tongue and people."[41]

Besides pursuing a scriptural mandate and following Jenson's recommendation, Church leaders had another reason for sending missionaries to South America. Latter-day Saint converts from Europe had migrated there, providing natural seedbeds for Church growth and expansion on the continent. In Argentina, German members had begun holding meetings, doing missionary work, and publishing articles about the Church. They had also opened correspondence with the Church's Presiding Bishop in Salt Lake City, Charles Nibley, who spoke German and encouraged their efforts.[42]

In May 1925 Nibley became a member of the Church's First Presidency, who had been talking about South America for months and now discussed how to respond to requests from the Argentine members for missionaries. "We have taken up with the Presidency the matter of sending missionaries to the Argentine, but so far nothing definite has been decided," Nibley's successor as Presiding Bishop, Sylvester Q. Cannon, informed his South American correspondent. "However, we are making inquiry with regard to suitable men who can speak the German and Spanish languages."[43] Though the immigrant Church members in Argentina at the time spoke German, Church leaders were well aware that significant expansion of membership there would also require preaching in Spanish.

In their quest for the right people to send to South America, Church leaders counseled with linguist Gerrit de Jong Jr., who had just been named dean of the College of Fine Arts at Brigham Young University and professor of modern languages. Ultimately, they decided to send a member of the Church's Quorum of the Twelve Apostles, the group who had been responsible for opening new missions since the first decade of the Church's history. They also decided that "two men be sent along with the member of the Quorum of the Twelve, one to speak German and one to speak Spanish."[44]

From among the Church's Apostles, the First Presidency chose Melvin J. Ballard, a junior member of the Twelve who had been a mission president among native peoples in Montana.[45] To accompany him, the leaders chose two members from the next tier of Church leadership, the First Council of the Seventy: Rulon S. Wells and Rey L. Pratt.[46] Nearly a generation older than Ballard, Wells had substantial missionary experience that included missions to Germany and Switzerland, so his language ability was valuable.[47] Pratt, who had moved to Mexico with his family at age nine, was a former missionary and mission president in Mexico who later oversaw all of the Church's Spanish-speaking entities before being called to the First Council of the Seventy in early 1925. He was the obvious choice for the Spanish-speaking member of the group.[48]

In November 1925, Ballard, Wells, and Pratt traveled eastward to New York and boarded a steamship bound for South America. During the ocean voyage, Ballard studied Spanish and South American history. The missionaries crossed the equator on November 25 and five days later docked at Rio de Janeiro, Brazil. "I was the first one to put my feet on South American soil," Ballard recorded in his journal.[49] After spending the day touring, they left at midnight for Buenos Aires. They paused for half a day in Montevideo, Uruguay, on December 5 and early the next morning arrived at their destination in Argentina, where the local German-speaking Saints welcomed them. After getting settled in their hotel that afternoon, the visiting missionaries held a meeting in which each of them spoke. They had begun their work in South America, a labor that would finally succeed on that continent.[50]

The three missionaries quickly made history. On December 12, 1925, within a week of their arrival, Ballard recorded in his journal, "Just as the sun was going down, I baptized six people in the Rio de la Plata, near the German electric plant here, the first in this generation in South America."[51] The converts were all of German descent.[52] The next day, the missionaries confirmed those who were baptized, ordained two priests and a deacon, and administered the sacrament of the Lord's Supper for the first time.[53]

Soon they visited the mayor of Buenos Aires, with whom they were able to communicate effectively because of Pratt's considerable fluency in Spanish. The mayor guaranteed them complete religious liberty and said the government would not interfere in their work.[54]

## DEDICATING THE LAND FOR PREACHING THE GOSPEL

Finally, early on Christmas morning 1925, the missionaries visited a park to dedicate the continent of South America for missionary work. They sang hymns, read scriptures, and then knelt under a weeping willow as Ballard offered a dedicatory prayer.[55] He expressed gratitude for being chosen "to come to this great land of South America, to unlock the door for the preaching of the gospel to all the peoples of the South American nations, and to search out the blood of Israel that has been sifted among the Gentile nations, many of whom, influenced by the spirit of gathering, have assembled in this land."[56]

The prayer was lengthy, in part expressing gratitude, in part imploring further blessings. "We thank thee," he said, "for the few who have received us and for those we have had the joy of taking into the waters of baptism in this land. May they be the first fruits of a glorious harvest."[57]

Two days after the dedication, the missionaries began holding meetings in Spanish, a portent of the harvest they expected to achieve among the native Spanish-speaking population.[58]

These early successes and the hope they inspired for continued success did not mean the way was easy for the missionaries. Sadly, Wells became dizzy to the point of incapacitation the day they arrived in Buenos Aires, and on January 14, 1926, he returned home with what turned out to be hemorrhaging in the brain. That left Ballard and Pratt without the translator they had brought to communicate with the German Church members.[59]

## THE ACORN-TO-OAK-TREE PROPHECY

After several more months of struggles and some successes, Ballard and Pratt finally returned to the United States in July 1926, but not before Ballard uttered what later Latter-day Saints looked upon as a noteworthy prophecy. During his last meeting in Buenos Aires that month, Ballard spoke of the future of the Church in South America. "The work will go forth slowly for a time," he predicted, "just as the oak grows slowly from an acorn. It will not shoot up in a day as does the sunflower that grows quickly and thus dies. Thousands will join here. It will be divided into more than one mission and will be one of the strongest in the Church. The work here is the smallest that it will ever be. The day will come when the Lamanites here in South America will get the chance. The South American Mission will become a power in the Church."⁶⁰

The 1925–26 visit to South America of Melvin J. Ballard, Rulon S. Wells, and Rey L. Pratt took on even greater significance in the years to come. Frederick Salem Williams, who was born in one of the Latter-day Saint colonies in Mexico, heard Elder Ballard speak a few months after his return to the United States and, deciding to follow in his footsteps, requested to go to South America. Williams became a missionary in Argentina in 1927 and president of the Argentine Mission in 1938.⁶¹ Williams noted that when he served in South America, "the members and investigators I knew always spoke of him [Elder Ballard] in reverent tones. Many of them would show me their right hands and say, 'I shook hands with Apostle Ballard with this hand!'"⁶²

The Church grew much as Elder Ballard had predicted, eventually being divided into Brazilian and Argentine missions. Elder Ballard's visit to South America as a senior Latter-day Saint leader was not followed by another such visit until J. Reuben Clark, former US ambassador to Mexico and newly called second counselor in the First Presidency, traveled to South America late in 1933 at the behest of US president Franklin D. Roosevelt to attend the International Conference of American States in Uruguay. Clark also visited briefly with the Church's members in a stopover in Buenos Aires on January 2, 1934.⁶³

### OPENING THE WAY FOR ANOTHER APOSTOLIC VISIT

Knowing how important it was for the South American Saints to receive an extended visit from an eminent Church leader, Williams wrote to the First Presidency in 1941 to recommend an extended visit from one of the Church's General Authorities:

> President Bowers of the Brazilian Mission and I feel that it would be of immense worth to us if one of the Authorities could come and visit us. Then the Church would know at firsthand what our problems are. Then too, the visit would be a great stimulation to the

missionaries and to the saints. There are hundreds of saints who are eagerly looking forward to the time when they can meet one of the Authorities. It is true that we have been visited by Brother Ballard, President Clark and Wells, but this was a long time ago. There are less than twenty saints that knew Brother Ballard, and perhaps about fifty that were fortunate enough to hear President Clark. Since then our mission has changed as from day to night.

Williams went on to list other challenges in the mission and then pleaded:

I realize how busy you all are and that the time involved is great, but if the airlines were used one can be in Buenos Aires from Salt Lake City in less than a week's time. And between the Brazilian and the Argentine Missions I feel a great work could be accomplished by said visit. But I would ask that at least a month be spent in Argentina so that one could become thoroughly conversant with the conditions and the wonderful promises for the future.[64]

Later that month, the First Presidency replied in a letter that expressed sympathy for the mission's challenges but also a desire to balance Williams's wishes with the Church's resource restraints:

Your first suggestion is that one of the General Authorities visit you and the Brazilian Mission at the earliest opportunity. We know from the results of other missions that official visits by members of the First Presidency or of the Council of the Twelve to the Missions result in a great deal of good. Direct observation is far more enlightening than information obtained by correspondence, especially is this true when conditions in the Mission are more or less unfamiliar. At present, however, the prospects of such a visit to South America are somewhat remote.[65]

Besides seeking a visit from a senior Church leader, Williams had requested an automobile to help in traveling over the immense area of the mission and permission to establish a printing operation for publishing Church literature in Spanish. The leaders granted his request for the car and would look further into the need for published literature.[66]

"I got the car; one out of three isn't bad," Williams later quipped.⁶⁷ He remained convinced, however, that a General Authority visit and a printing operation were also important, and over time both became realities.

The US entry into World War II following the bombing of Pearl Harbor, three months after Williams made his request, not only postponed any visit from a senior Church leader but also led to a reduction in the number of Latter-day Saint missionaries in Argentina.⁶⁸ During the war, after concluding his term as president of the Argentine Mission, Williams worked under the US State Department in Washington, DC, and then for the Institute of Inter-American Affairs in Venezuela and later in Uruguay. After the war, he returned to the United States to work in California.⁶⁹

In August 1946 Williams went with family members to Utah to attend a wedding. He took advantage of his time there to hold a reunion with some of the missionaries who served with him in Argentina. Williams later recalled what happened at the reunion:

> After reliving our experiences in South America and reaffirming our commitment to and love for the people, we began wondering why the Church wasn't expanding into new South American countries. At that time only the Argentine and Brazilian missions existed. It seemed to us that Europe and the United States had received far more attention over the past twenty years. After some discussion we came to the conclusion that we should do something about it, for no one was in a better position to bring the matter to the attention of the Brethren. We felt we could point out to them in a forceful yet loving manner the tremendous proselyting opportunities existing to the south.⁷⁰

One of the former Argentine missionaries who engaged with Williams in this discussion was Don Smith, nephew of George Albert Smith, who at the time was the Church's President. Don Smith phoned his uncle and set up a meeting with him and the former missionaries the next morning. Williams, the designated speaker for the group, started by saying the missionaries felt that "because no General Authorities had ever lived in South America, with the exception of those who opened the work there under Elder Melvin J. Ballard (who died in 1939), [the group] felt perhaps [Church leaders] were not sufficiently acquainted with the conditions."⁷¹ Williams also justified the need for this meeting by recounting the dearth of Church leader visits to South America:

> I pointed out that Elder Ballard had opened the South American Mission in 1925, some twenty-one years before. Since then, the only General Authority to visit had been President J. Reuben Clark, Jr., of the First Presidency; he had been there less than a week to represent the United States Government in Uruguay and had visited with the Saints in Buenos Aires for only a matter of hours.⁷²

As Williams went on recounting the history and condition of the Church in South America, George Albert Smith sat quietly, neither commenting nor asking questions. At the end of Williams's presentation, which lasted about an hour, the President excused himself without comment and left.

"Because he had made no observations we felt that we had displeased him and began thinking to ourselves, 'Well, it was wonderful being a member of the Church while it lasted,'" Williams recalled. President Smith surprised them, however, by returning with David O. McKay, his second counselor, who had a well-deserved reputation of being among the most traveled of all Church leaders at the time, a man whose tenure included visits to many countries.⁷³

"I asked David to leave the meeting he was attending and come back with me," Smith explained. "Please repeat to him what you have told me, President Williams."

Williams rehearsed what he had already said and added a few further ideas. When he finished talking, a long period of silence ensued. "Our hearts fell" once again, Williams recalled.

Finally, Smith turned to his counselor and asked, "David, what do you think of all this?"

"I'm impressed with it," McKay replied. "I'm happy they came and brought it to our attention; I think we should do something about it."

"I do too," Smith concurred.

The two senior Church leaders thanked their visitors and told them to reduce their thoughts to paper. The former Argentine missionaries agreed to do so and left ebullient.

"We felt we were walking on air," Williams recorded.[74]

As spokesperson for the group, Williams wrote the requested report to the First Presidency. In it he related the history and conditions of each country of interest and recommended an order in which the Church should enter the nations, with Uruguay leading the list. "I also respectfully recommended that someone, preferably a General Authority, be called to live in South America to supervise and coordinate the activity of the various missions after they were established," Williams wrote in a letter that accompanied the report.[75]

The letter and report, which Williams forwarded to the First Presidency on September 28, 1946, after he returned to California, ran several pages. "It is lamentable that it is so voluminous," Williams apologized, "but to show a complete picture it was felt necessary to present one this length." Williams expressed his love and support of his Church leaders and wrote that "in no sense of the word is there any criticism impl[i]ed." Instead, he and his fellow returned missionaries offered their help "because," he wrote, "we feel we are more familiar with conditions and peoples of Central and South America" than others.[76]

The report began with a background section that emphasized the importance of Latin America. It listed the total population of the area and the major language groups, particularly Spanish. "The Spanish language," the report explained, "is spoken by more Christians, with the exception of English, than any other language in the world today."[77]

"The peoples of Latin America have much in common with the inhabitants of the United States," it pointed out. For example, people in both areas "are living in choice lands, they are living in Zion"—a reference to the Latter-day Saint belief that God would establish his people in this region. The report noted that like many people in the United States, many in Latin America descended from European roots. As for native Indian peoples, believed by the Saints to be descendants of Book of Mormon peoples,[78] the report posited, "we feel that the day of redemption for the Lamanite people will only come as fast as we are prepared to make it come about."[79]

"We feel we should devote time and energy to prepare ourselves to rede[e]m these people," Williams wrote on behalf of the returned missionaries. "To begin the work among the Indians does not necessarily mean going into the mountains and devoting all of our time to the pure races," many of whom spoke neither Spanish nor English. Instead, he suggested, work could begin "among the inhabitants of the Central and South American republics," many of whom were mixed "descendants of the Indians and also . . . some of the best blood of Europe that has immigrated to America." Over time, "our activities can fan out to embrace all of the Indian people."[80]

The report then went on to divide the countries according to where missionary work should begin. It recommended not starting in "Bolivia, Ecuador, Paraguay, Venezuela, and the three Guianas," giving reasons ranging from illiteracy and "low moral standards" to malaria. In this period more than three decades before the landmark 1978 revelation on priesthood that opened priesthood ordination and temple blessings to all Latter-day Saint men regardless of race, a key factor in why Williams and his companions sought to avoid some areas was "the great mixture" with people of African heritage."[81] Gratefully, in the 1970s the faithfulness of black Saints in South America would be a catalyst in the pondering that led to the 1978 revelation.[82]

Given Williams's experience in Uruguay, it was no surprise that he recommended that country as a place to start a mission. The report called Uruguay "the most democratic country and the most pleasant one in which to live in South America."[83]

In his cover letter, Williams wrote, "Our only wish and hope is to further the missionary work and to ask the Church to look Southward toward the great opportunities there awaiting our efforts."[84]

## PERSISTENCE PAYS OFF

Williams had high hopes the report would lead to action. "I sent the document off," he later wrote, "but never heard of it again."[85] Yet the letter did have an effect on Church leaders. In April 1947, about eight months after the missionaries met with George Albert Smith and David O. McKay, Williams received a telegram asking him to phone McKay the next morning.

When he did so, McKay asked, "Do you remember recommending opening a mission in Uruguay?"

Williams acknowledged that he did.

McKay responded, "How would you like to go down and open it?"⁸⁶

By the end of August 1947, Williams had arrived in Uruguay to do just that.⁸⁷ But before he left for South America, he renewed his request for a high-ranking Church leader to tour the missions on that continent. "While in Salt Lake City preparing to leave for Uruguay to open the mission," he remembered, "I took occasion to invite the Brethren to visit the South American missions, so that they might know the conditions first hand." McKay, whose son served under Williams in the Argentine Mission, responded, "It would be wonderful if one could be spared; we'll see what can be done."⁸⁸

After Williams arrived in Uruguay, he renewed the invitation in a letter to McKay, repeating the benefits that would follow from such a visit. McKay answered Williams's letter cordially, saying such a tour "would be most delightful" to him and "very informative." He noted that his son and other former missionaries to South America had been urging him to take such a trip. "Of this I am convinced," McKay concluded, "that one of the Presidency should visit these missions in the very near future. We should then be in a position to render clearer judgment regarding the matters that come before us from time to time."

By "near future," however, McKay did not mean very soon. He told Williams, "We have the matter under consideration, but prospects for a visit this year are very dim."⁸⁹

Undeterred, Williams wrote a long letter to Spencer W. Kimball, who was then serving in the Quorum of the Twelve Apostles, the second tier of Church leadership, but who would later become President of the Church, a world traveler, and the prophet who announced the 1978 revelation on priesthood that helped overcome barriers to the Church's expansion in Latin America and elsewhere. Williams predicted that the "future missionary field is in South America" and expressed his hope that a senior Church leader would visit. "What the South American missions need more than anything else is the visit of one or more of the General Authorities," Williams asserted. "Won't you please come and see?"⁹⁰

## STEPHEN L RICHARDS APPOINTED
## FOR SOUTH AMERICAN MISSIONS TOUR

Finally, after years of pleading, Williams received the hoped-for reply. On December 10, 1947, Stephen L Richards of the Quorum of the Twelve Apostles wrote him a letter explaining that the First Presidency had appointed him "to visit the South American missions" with his wife, Irene Smith Merrill Richards.[91] Elder Richards was one of the most respected of all Church leaders in his day. Born in 1879 in Mendon, Utah, to parents with prominent Latter-day Saint pioneer ancestry, Stephen grew up imbued with the culture and doctrine of The Church of Jesus Christ of Latter-day Saints and a love of the outdoors, sports, and recreation.[92] Also being a man of the mind, he attended the University of Utah, where he excelled in debate, drama, and literature. Science courses favoring evolution over creationism shook his "pre-conceived ideas" of religion, and "for a period of time," he later said, "I suffered from doubt and uncertainty." Unsure how to handle his doubts in a culture of belief, Stephen kept them to himself.[93]

*Stephen L Richards's official photo that was given to the press to use in news articles throughout South America. Courtesy of Church History Library (hereafter "CHL").*

Irene Smith Merrill was born in 1876 in Fillmore, Utah. Like Stephen, she was descended from notable Latter-day Saint ancestors. Stephen's senior in age by three years, Irene shared his interest in literature and drama. When they fell in love and Stephen asked her to marry him, she agreed, provided they could marry in a Latter-day Saint temple.[94] This condition brought to the forefront Stephen's simmering spiritual doubts. In Latter-day Saint culture, only devout members are permitted to marry in the temple. A man of integrity, Stephen would not feign belief in order to marry Irene. "He was a student at the U[niversity] of U[tah] and didn't really know what he believed," Irene recalled, and "so he began to study, debate, consider, and pray."⁹⁵

Stephen talked with family members and friends about his doubts. But in the end, he turned to God to resolve his problems. "I finally decided I would appeal to a higher source of wisdom in the solution of my difficulties," he later explained. In the process, filled with what Irene called "real desire," Stephen "finally decided that he really knew that the Gospel was true."⁹⁶

"My approach was very humble and I suppose many would say very naive," he later acknowledged. Yet Irene noted in her journal, "The richness of his study and convictions gave him a marvelous foundation for his whole life's work and accomplishments." "Never since then," he wrote of his conversion, "have I experienced any doubt as to the reality of spiritual forces nor have I had difficulty in correlating all that I have been able to learn with spiritual philosophy in my life."⁹⁷

Stephen and Irene married and began their life together, a life that over the course of decades focused on family, community, church, and recreation. They sacrificed so Stephen could begin a graduate program in law at the University of Michigan and complete it at the University of Chicago in the first graduating class of that law school. In time he became successful in law, business, and politics. He also served on the law faculty of the University of Utah. His successful career, coupled with Church service at both the local and general levels, led to a call to serve as an Apostle of The Church of Jesus Christ of Latter-day Saints in 1917 at age thirty-seven.⁹⁸

Elder Richards threw himself into his new calling with the same energy that characterized much of the rest of his life. Although his heavy duties kept him away from home much of the time, he and Irene continued to grow together as they raised their family and enjoyed vacations that took them outdoors. One of the heaviest responsibilities he bore was service on the Church Missionary Committee. It was this assignment that made him a natural choice to tour the missions of South America in 1948.

Irene looked at the trip as an adventure that would put her literary skills to work. "Papa will do all the work," she wrote in a letter to her children, "and I'll look at the scenery and do the writing."⁹⁹ Although Elder Richards would receive most of the attention on the trip, Irene's writing would preserve their historic journey for future readers. Indeed, she was the one who, over time, kept the most complete and interesting record of their lives.

Overjoyed to learn that the Richardses were coming to visit, mission president Frederick S. Williams wrote a two-page letter of gratitude and travel tips for them, expressing thanks "that after twenty years of waiting, the South American Saints 'would have the privilege of hearing an Apostle of the Lord.'"[100]

## NOTES

1. See Dean C. Jessee, Mark Ashurst-McGee, and Richard L. Jensen, eds., *Journals, Volume 1: 1832–1839*, vol. 1 of the Journals series of *The Joseph Smith Papers*, ed. Dean C. Jessee, Ronald K. Esplin, and Richard Lyman Bushman (Salt Lake City: Church Historian's Press, 2008), xxiii; James B. Allen and Glen M. Leonard, *The Story of the Latter-day Saints*, 2nd ed. (Salt Lake City: Deseret Book, 1992), 56. The restored Church of Christ was formally named The Church of Jesus Christ of Latter-day Saints in 1838; see Doctrine and Covenants 115:4.
2. See Solomon Chamberlain autobiography (1856), L. Tom Perry Special Collections, Harold B. Lee Library, Brigham Young University; John Taylor Journal, 50–54, CHL; Larry C. Porter, "The Book of Mormon: Historical Setting for Its Translation and Publication," in *Joseph Smith: The Prophet, the Man*, ed. Susan Easton Black and Charles D. Tate Jr. (Provo, UT: Religious Studies Center, Brigham Young University, 1993), 58–59.
3. See Chamberlain autobiography, 9–11; Porter, "Book of Mormon," 58–59; "The First Book of Nephi," *Palmyra (NY) Reflector*, January 2, 13, 1830, CHL; Richard E. Turley Jr. and William W. Slaughter, *How We Got the Book of Mormon* (Salt Lake City: Deseret Book, 2011), 32; Russell R. Rich, "The Dogberry Papers and the Book of Mormon," *BYU Studies* 10, no. 3 (Spring 1970): 315–20.
4. *The Book of Mormon* (Palmyra, NY: E. B. Grandin, 1830).
5. See *The Life of Brigham Young* (Salt Lake City: George Q. Cannon and Sons, 1893), 14; Leonard J. Arrington, *Brigham Young: American Moses* (New York: Alfred A. Knopf, 1985), 19; Richard E. Turley Jr. and Brittany A. Chapman,

eds., *Women of Faith in the Latter Days* (Salt Lake City: Deseret Book, 2011), 1:130n3.

6. See Steven C. Harper, "The Restoration of Mormonism to Erie County, Pennsylvania," *Mormon Historical Studies* 1, no. 1 (Spring 2000): 4–5; Richard Price and Pamela Price, "Missionary Successes, 1836–1844," *Restoration Voice* 26, no. 14 (November/December 1982): 14–16; John Devitry-Smith, "William James Barratt: The First Mormon 'Down Under,'" *BYU Studies* 28, no. 3 (1988): 53–66; Donald Q. Cannon and Richard O. Cowan, *Unto Every Nation: Gospel Light Reaches Every Land* (Salt Lake City: Deseret Book, 2003), 29–30; Arnold K. Garr, "Latter-day Saints in Tubuai, French Polynesia, Yesterday and Today," in *Regional Studies in Latter-day Saint Church History: The Pacific Isles*, ed. Reid L. Neilson, Steven C. Harper, Craig K. Manscill, and Mary Jane Woodger (Provo, UT: Religious Studies Center, Brigham Young University, 2008), 2–4.

7. See Doctrine and Covenants 28:8; Richard Lyman Bushman, *Joseph Smith: Rough Stone Rolling* (New York: Alfred A. Knopf, 2005), 122.

8. See Terryl L. Givens and Matthew J. Grow, *Parley P. Pratt: The Apostle Paul of Mormonism* (New York: Oxford University Press, 2011), 5–8.

9. Doctrine and Covenants 32:2.

10. See *Autobiography of Parley Parker Pratt*, ed. Parley P. Pratt Jr. (New York: Russell Brothers, 1874), 54–55; Givens and Grow, *Parley P. Pratt*, 45–46.

11. See Givens and Grow, *Parley P. Pratt*, 37–39, 46–47.

12. See Givens and Grow, *Parley P. Pratt*, 290, 306–12; A. Delbert Palmer and Mark L. Grover, "Hoping to Establish a Presence: Parley P. Pratt's 1851 Mission to Chile," *BYU Studies* 38, no. 4 (1999): 115–28; Frederick S. Williams and Frederick G. Williams, *From Acorn to Oak Tree: A Personal History of the Establishment and First Quarter Century Development of the South American Missions* (Fullerton, CA: Et Cetera, Et Cetera Graphics, 1987), 1.

13. See David J. Whittaker, "The Bone in the Throat: Orson Pratt and the Public Announcement of Plural Marriage," *Western Historical Quarterly* 18, no. 3 (July 1987): 293–314; *Deseret News Extra*, September 14, 1852, Mormon Publications: 19th and 20th Centuries, Harold B. Lee Library Digital Collections, Brigham Young University.

14. See George A. Smith, *The Rise, Progress and Travels of the Church of Jesus Christ of Latter-day Saints*, 2nd ed. (Salt Lake City: Deseret News, 1872), 36.

15. See Aaron F. Farr to George A. Smith, June 2, 1865, Correspondence, Missionary Reports, 1831–1900, CHL. The missionaries to Jamaica were Aaron Farr, Jesse Turpin, Darwin Richardson, and Alfred B. Lambson.
16. Smith, *Rise, Progress and Travels*, 36.
17. See Parley P. Pratt to Brigham Young, March 13, 1852, Incoming Correspondence, Brigham Young Office Files, CHL; reprinted in *Autobiography of Parley P. Pratt*, ed. Parley P. Pratt Jr., 4th ed. (Salt Lake City: Deseret Book, 1985), 367–68; Palmer and Grover, "Hoping to Establish a Presence," 129; Givens and Grow, *Parley P. Pratt*, 382–84.
18. See Orson F. Whitney, *History of Utah* (Salt Lake City: George Q. Cannon and Sons, 1904), 4:508.
19. See *The Wasp* 1, no. 1 (April 16, 1842): 3; no. 6 (May 21, 1842): 23; no. 12 (July 2, 1842): 45; no. 36 (January 7, 1842 [1843]): 141.
20. See Matthew J. Grow, Ronald K. Esplin, Mark Ashurst-McGee, Gerrit J. Dirkmaat, and Jeffrey D. Mahas, eds., *Administrative Records: Council of Fifty, Minutes, March 1844–January 1846*, vol. 1 of the Administrative Records series of *The Joseph Smith Papers*, ed. Ronald K. Esplin, Matthew J. Grow, and Matthew C. Godfrey (Salt Lake City: Church Historian's Press, 2016), 17, 47–48, 140–42.
21. *El Siglo Diez y Nueve*, July 27, 1844, in private possession of Fernando Gomez; copy located at Museum of Mexican Mormon History.
22. According to Fernando Gomez, "the official newspaper of the Mexican Government called *Diario Oficial del Supremo Gobierno* as early as the 1850s printed articles from *The Herald of New York*," which included content about Latter-day Saints. Fernando R. Gomez and Sergio Pagaza Castillo, *Benito Juarez and the Mormon Connection of the 19th Century* (Mexico City: Museo de Historia del Mormonismo en México, 2007), 10, 27n56.
23. See John G. Turner, *Brigham Young: Pioneer Prophet* (Cambridge, MA: Belknap Press of Harvard University Press, 2012), 123, 170; Allen and Leonard, *Story of the Latter-day Saints*, 257–58; Arrington, *Brigham Young*, 146–47.
24. See Turner, *Brigham Young*, 174; Tom Gray, "The Treaty of Guadalupe Hidalgo," National Archives, updated April 25, 2018, https://www.archives.gov/.
25. See William P. MacKinnon, "'Not as a Stranger': A Presbyterian Afoot in the Mormon Past," *Journal of Mormon History* 38, no. 2 (Spring 2012): 26–33.
26. Arrington, *Brigham Young*, 265–66. See also "The Utah Expedition: Its Causes and Consequences," part 3, *Atlantic Monthly*, May 1859, 583–84.

27. See Norman F. Furniss, *The Mormon Conflict, 1850–1859* (New Haven, CT: Yale University Press, 1960), 168–76; Will Bagley, ed., *Kingdom in the West: The Mormons and the American Frontier*, vol. 10 of *At Sword's Point, Part I: A Documentary History of the Utah War to 1858*, ed. William P. MacKinnon (Norman, OK: Arthur H. Clark, 2008), 479–81; LeRoy R. Hafen and Ann W. Hafen, eds., *The Utah Expedition, 1857–1858* (Glendale, CA: Arthur H. Clark, 1958), 327–28; Allen and Leonard, *Story of the Latter-day Saints*, 315–17.
28. See Eugene E. Campbell, *Establishing Zion: The Mormon Church in the American West, 1847–1869* (Salt Lake City: Signature Books, 1988), 246–48; John D. Lee to Emma B. Lee, December 9, 1876, HM 31214, John D. Lee Collection, Huntington Library, San Marino, CA.
29. See Donald Levi Gale Hammon, *Levi Byram and Martha Jane Belnap Hammon: Gold Medal Pioneers* (Chapel Hill, NC: Professional Press, 1996), 59–60; Kevin H. Folkman, "'The Moste Desert Lukking Plase I Ever Saw, Amen!' The 'Failed' 1873 Arizona Mission to the Little Colorado River," *Journal of Mormon History* 37, no. 1 (Winter 2011): 115–50.
30. See Daniel W. Jones, *Forty Years among the Indians* (Salt Lake City: Juvenile Instructor Office, 1890), 219–332; Helaman Pratt Journal, 1875–78, CHL; Anthony Woodward Ivins Diary, Anthony W. Ivins Collection, CHL.
31. Brigham Young to Wm. C. Staines, January 11, 1876, letterpress copybook, 14:125–26, Brigham Young Office Files, CHL.
32. See F. LaMond Tullis, *Mormons in Mexico: The Dynamics of Faith and Culture* (Logan: Utah State University Press, 1987); Thomas Cottam Romney, *The Mormon Colonies in Mexico* (1938; repr., Salt Lake City: University of Utah Press, 2005); LaVon Brown Whetten, *Colonia Juarez: Commemorating 125 Years of the Mormon Colonies in Mexico* (Bloomington, IN: AuthorHouse, 2010).
33. See Tullis, *Mormons in Mexico*; Romney, *Mormon Colonies in Mexico*; Whetten, *Colonia Juarez*.
34. See Andrew Jenson, comp., *Latter-day Saint Biographical Encyclopedia* (Salt Lake City: Andrew Jenson Memorial Association, 1901–36), 4:348; Dale F. Beecher, "Rey L. Pratt and the Mexican Mission," *BYU Studies* 15, no. 3 (1975): 293–307.
35. See Jason Swensen, "Mexican Colonies Offering Fruits of Leadership," *Church News*, May 11, 2001.

36. See *Autobiography of Andrew Jenson* (Salt Lake City: Deseret News, 1938), 547; Justin R. Bray and Reid L. Neilson, *Exploring Book of Mormon Lands: The 1923 Latin American Travel Writings of Mormon Historian Andrew Jenson* (Provo, UT: Religious Studies Center, Brigham Young University, 2014), 1–26.
37. See Bray and Neilson, *Exploring Book of Mormon Lands*, 21–24, 31n10.
38. Bray and Neilson, *Exploring Book of Mormon Lands*, 291.
39. Bray and Neilson, *Exploring Book of Mormon Lands*, 291.
40. Bray and Neilson, *Exploring Book of Mormon Lands*, 291.
41. Bray and Neilson, *Exploring Book of Mormon Lands*, 292.
42. See Williams and Williams, *From Acorn to Oak Tree*, 18–20.
43. Williams and Williams, *From Acorn to Oak Tree*, 20.
44. Bryant S. Hinckley, *Sermons and Missionary Services of Melvin Joseph Ballard* (Salt Lake City: Deseret Book, 1949), 89; Williams and Williams, *From Acorn to Oak Tree*, 20–21. On the role of the Quorum of the Twelve in opening missions, see *Record of the Twelve*, February 14, 1835, CHL; also available at the Joseph Smith Papers, https://www.josephsmithpapers.org/paperSummary/record-of-the-twelve-14-february-28-august-1835.
45. See Melvin R. Ballard, *Melvin J. Ballard—Crusader for Righteousness* (Salt Lake City: Bookcraft, 1966), 54–57.
46. See Ballard, *Crusader for Righteousness*, 54–57, 75–76; Jenson, *Latter-day Saint Biographical Encyclopedia*, 1:419–20.
47. See Jenson, *Latter-day Saint Biographical Encyclopedia*, 4:212–14.
48. See Jenson, *Latter-day Saint Biographical Encyclopedia*, 4:348; Arnold K. Garr, Donald Q. Cannon, and Richard O. Cowan, eds., *Encyclopedia of Latter-day Saint History* (Salt Lake City: Deseret Book, 2000), 942–43.
49. Hinckley, *Sermons*, 92. Elder Ballard's original journals were lost after his death. Bryant Hinckley had access to them, and so excerpts appear in his book.
50. See Hinckley, *Sermons*, 91–93.
51. See Hinckley, *Sermons*, 94.
52. To better understand Latter-day Saint German migration to South America, see Mark L. Grover, "The Mormon Church and German Immigrants in Southern Brazil: Religion and Language," *Jahrbuch für Geschichte von Staat, Wirtschaft und Gesellschaft: Lateinamerikas* (1989), 26:302–5.
53. See Hinckley, *Sermons*, 94.
54. See Hinckley, *Sermons*, 94.
55. See Williams and Williams, *From Acorn to Oak Tree*, 23–25.

56. Hinckley, *Sermons*, 94–95.
57. Hinckley, *Sermons*, 95.
58. See Williams and Williams, *From Acorn to Oak Tree*, 25.
59. See Hinckley, *Sermons*, 93; Williams and Williams, *From Acorn to Oak Tree*, 25.
60. Williams and Williams, *From Acorn to Oak Tree*, 30.
61. See Williams and Williams, *From Acorn to Oak Tree*, 3, 79; obituary of Frederick Salem Williams, *Deseret News*, October 10, 1991.
62. Williams and Williams, *From Acorn to Oak Tree*, 30.
63. See *The Diaries of J. Reuben Clark, 1933–1961, Abridged* (Salt Lake City: privately printed, 2010), 8–10; Frederick S. Williams to the First Presidency, September 1, 1941, in Williams and Williams, *From Acorn to Oak Tree*, 187. See also Buenos Aires Branch, January 2, 1934, in South American Mission Manuscript History and Historical Reports, vol. 2, Branch Histories, 1925–1935, CHL.
64. Williams to First Presidency, September 1, 1941, 187–89.
65. First Presidency [Heber J. Grant, J. Reuben Clark Jr., and David O. McKay] to Frederick S. Williams, September 17, 1941, in Williams and Williams, *From Acorn to Oak Tree*, 191.
66. First Presidency to Frederick S. Williams, September 17, 1941.
67. Williams and Williams, *From Acorn to Oak Tree*, 191.
68. See Mark L. Grover, "Argentina: Building the Church One *Bloque* at a Time," in *A Land of Promise and Prophecy: Elder A. Theodore Tuttle in South America, 1960–1965* (Provo, UT: Religious Studies Center, Brigham Young University, 2008), 186–231; Frederick S. Williams Oral History, interviewed by William G. Hartley, 1972, 25–33, CHL.
69. See Williams and Williams, *From Acorn to Oak Tree*, 195.
70. Williams and Williams, *From Acorn to Oak Tree*, 201.
71. Williams and Williams, *From Acorn to Oak Tree*, 201.
72. Williams and Williams, *From Acorn to Oak Tree*, 201.
73. Williams and Williams, *From Acorn to Oak Tree*, 201–2; Hugh J. Cannon, *To the Peripheries of Mormondom: The Apostolic Around-the-World Journey of David O. McKay, 1920–1921*, ed. Reid L. Neilson (Salt Lake City: University of Utah Press, 2011).
74. Williams and Williams, *From Acorn to Oak Tree*, 202; Keith McCune to the First Presidency, November 30, 2005, in Frederick S. Williams et al., "Proposed Plan for Activating and Extending the Missionary Work in Latin Amer-

ica," September 28, 1946, CHL. The last page of the report states that returned missionaries J. Vernon Graves, Robert R. McKay, Don Hyrum Smith, Edgar B. Mitchell, and Keith N. McCune assisted Williams with the report.

75. Williams and Williams, *From Acorn to Oak Tree*, 202–3.
76. Frederick S. Williams to the First Presidency, September 28, 1946, in Williams et al., "Proposed Plan," 1.
77. Williams et al., "Proposed Plan," 3.
78. For a geneticist's discussion of the complications inherent in attempts to reconstruct the genetic structure of ancient Native American populations, see Ugo A. Perego, "The Book of Mormon and the Origin of Native Americans from a Maternally Inherited DNA Standpoint," in *No Weapon Shall Prosper: New Light on Sensitive Issues*, ed. Robert L. Millet (Provo, UT: Religious Studies Center, Brigham Young University, 2011), 171–217.
79. Williams et al., "Proposed Plan," 3.
80. Williams et al., "Proposed Plan," 3.
81. Williams et al., "Proposed Plan," 4.
82. See Edward L. Kimball, "Spencer W. Kimball and the Revelation on Priesthood," *BYU Studies* 47, no. 2 (2008): 5–78; Jeremy Talmage and Clinton D. Christensen, "Black, White, or Brown? Racial Perceptions and the Priesthood Policy in Latin America," *Journal of Mormon History* 44, no. 1 (January 2018): 119–45; Mark L. Grover, "The Mormon Priesthood Revelation and the São Paulo, Brazil Temple," *Dialogue: A Journal of Mormon Thought* 23, no. 1 (Spring 1990): 42–44.
83. Williams et al., "Proposed Plan," 5.
84. Williams to First Presidency, September 28, 1946.
85. Williams and Williams, *From Acorn to Oak Tree*, 203. Decades after Williams and his fellow missionaries submitted their report, one of the missionaries wrote to a later First Presidency: "It is of interest that our recommendations were adopted by the brethren, pretty much as presented, over the following years." McCune to the First Presidency, November 30, 2005.
86. Williams and Williams, *From Acorn to Oak Tree*, 203.
87. See Williams and Williams, *From Acorn to Oak Tree*, 219.
88. Williams and Williams, *From Acorn to Oak Tree*, 237.
89. David O. McKay to Frederick S. Williams, October 28, 1947, Stephen L Richards Papers; Williams and Williams, *From Acorn to Oak Tree*, 238.

90. Williams and Williams, *From Acorn to Oak Tree*, 238; Kimball, "Revelation on Priesthood."
91. Williams and Williams, *From Acorn to Oak Tree*, 238–39; Stephen L Richards to Frederick S. Williams, December 10, 1947, Frederick S. Williams Papers, CHL.
92. See W. Dee Halverson, *Stephen L Richards, 1879–1959* (n.p.: Heritage Press, n.d.), 1–34.
93. See Halverson, *Stephen L Richards*, 34–40.
94. See Halverson, *Stephen L Richards*, 39, 42–53.
95. Halverson, *Stephen L Richards*, 39.
96. Halverson, *Stephen L Richards*, 39, 40.
97. Halverson, *Stephen L Richards*, 40.
98. See Halverson, *Stephen L Richards*, 55–116.
99. Halverson, *Stephen L Richards*, 141.
100. Williams and Williams, *From Acorn to Oak Tree*, 238–39.

CHAPTER ONE

# THE RICHARDSES ARRIVE IN SOUTH AMERICA

### HISTORICAL BACKGROUND

With family Christmas festivities concluded for 1947, Stephen L and Irene Richards prepared to leave Utah's freezing winter for the warmer climes of South America. They had letters from the governor of Utah, bankers, and businessmen that would be useful in securing travel visas and passports and in introducing them to prominent people and organizations when they arrived at their destinations.

Before leaving Salt Lake City, Elder and Sister Richards received priesthood blessings from the First Presidency on December 30, 1947. Church President George Albert Smith, assisted by his counselors J. Reuben Clark and David O. McKay, set Elder Richards apart on a "special mission to the Southland," reminding him of the "millions of our Father's children in that part of the country who are eligible to receive the gospel." Elder Richards was also encouraged to "investigate conditions," "make friends," and "advise those in charge." Central to his apostolic tour would be his role in "teaching the Gospel of Jesus Christ wherever you go."[1]

On a personal note, the blessing also mentioned Elder Richards's health and well-being on the trip. He suffered from heart problems, and although time on the ship would be relaxing, a rugged three-month trip for a man in his late sixties would prove challenging.

President David O. McKay then set Sister Richards apart "as a special missionary to South America to accompany her husband." She was admonished that when meeting the sisters, she would counsel them and have a "spirit of discernment and wisdom." She would also convey a "good impression" of the Church to businessmen, politicians, and influential leaders in the countries she and her husband visited.[2] She was promised health and also that she would be uninhibited in her expressions. That particular blessing likely reassured her since a previous throat surgery had affected her vocal cords so that her voice strained at times. As a result, she spoke softly or in a whisper and could no longer sing.[3]

The Church was in its infancy in Argentina, Brazil, and Uruguay with some twelve hundred members in all of South America and only two hundred missionaries.[4] Many more countries awaited their time for the restored gospel to come to their doors. Elder Richards's blessing had stated that "there is a great opening there."

Travel path of the SS Argentina from New York to South America. Courtesy of Moore-McCormack.

The Richardses departed Utah by train on a frigid New Year's Eve and crossed the country to Washington, DC, where they stopped for several days to obtain departure documents and meet with government officials. Then they traveled to New York City, where they set sail on the SS *Argentina* on January 15, 1948, accompanied by seven missionaries. During almost two weeks at sea, the group traced nearly the same path that Elder Melvin J. Ballard took in 1925, making stops in Trinidad, Rio de Janiero, Montevideo, and Buenos Aires.[5]

SS Argentina *at dock in Rio de Janeiro, Brazil. Courtesy of Moore-McCormack.*

## THE DOCUMENTS

Throughout Elder Richards's apostolic tour, Irene Richards wrote letters to her children detailing their trip and providing insights into their experiences. In one such letter before leaving Utah, she wrote in anticipation, "Papa will do all the work, and I'll look at the scenery and do the writing for him, and incidentally maybe I won't be able to look a banana or an orchid in the face by the time I return."[6]

It is important to note that Sister Richards, though more widely traveled than most Latter-day Saints of her day, had never been to Latin America, except for one trip to Cuba in the 1920s with her husband. Her writing showed appreciation for the scenery of the countryside and bustle of the cities and a love for the Latter-day Saints. However, at times her letters in this volume reflect a pro–North American perspective common to the era that is insensitive to growing economies and the Latin culture. Readers will do well to recognize both the strengths and weaknesses of those writing in the late 1940s.

## ON BOARD THE SS *ARGENTINA*, DOCKED AT RIO DE JANEIRO, BRAZIL

**Wednesday, January 28, 1948**

**Daily Summary**
*Toured Rio de Janeiro with President Harold Rex of the Brazilian Mission and returned to the ship*

### IRENE M. RICHARDS LETTER[7]

Rio de Janeiro
Jan. 28, 1948

Dear Lois and Frits:[8]

We arose at 5 to be on deck when we sailed into harbor. I think they are right when they claim that Rio is the most beautiful harbor in the world. As the dawn came the silhouette of peaks jutting out on every side with the "Christus" on the tallest one, made an unusual, and unforgettable impression on us. The harbor is very wide and there are several islands, covered with verdure, and the water goes back maybe 25 miles with lovely beaches in scallops. During the day we had opportunity to go into a private yacht club and sit on a lawn where the breeze sways the soft branches of the trees (trimmed just right) while Papa went the rounds to inspect the beautiful cruisers about. The playground and lovely hotels are on the water's edge and the trees, parks and flowers are lovely here. We lunched at "Cococaban".[9]

The President of the National Bank was first one to come aboard and offer his services to Papa. He was a very gracious gentlemen. Then President [Harold M.] Rex of the Brazilian mission came with Larson[10] (Mormon boy) who is in the Government here, and could get a pass to come aboard. We went with President Rex and Larson (his auto) who showed us about. Two missionaries (local) took care of the 7 boys aboard, so all had the chance to see Rio. We all died of the excessive heat and were glad to get back to our boat (which was like home) and the air conditioned dining room. Papa brought a light suit and a panama.[11] I did not suffer so, with a thin waist and a big hat, but my feet were so big I couldn't get my shoes

*Tourists at the Christ statue known as the Corcovado in Rio de Janeiro, Brazil. Courtesy of CHL.*

*View of Rio de Janeiro from the Corcovado. Courtesy of CHL.*

back on. But we were fairly comfortable with a fan (electric) and no gowns on, all night. I guess this is the hottest place in our travels.

Papa is visiting men and so I am resting on board. There is some breeze somewhere. I move around to find it. I am enjoying the light dress you let me take and am going to wear your little hat this afternoon as we are being taken up on one of the elevations where it's supposed to be cool, and a beautiful view, and wonderful hotel. We leave here tomorrow and stop at Santos, and then at B.A. [Buenos Aires], as they all call it here. There we, no doubt, will receive some mail from home.

We have held two Sunday services on the boat and have made many friends, I don't know how many enemies. Anyway, the missionaries have made a hit. They have sung, prayed and spoken and have attracted much attention. They are a fine bunch of boys. Two of them get off here and 5 go to Buenos Aires.

It's interesting to see the men load and unload this ship with the use of cranes and machinery. Mike[12] would be thrilled to watch them and he would understand all about it. Most of our crew are foreigners and most of them are refined, unusual persons. Some beautiful and proper. No man on the streets yesterday had his coat off. They can carry their pants on their arms, but they must wear a coat.

We are going to have the privilege of inviting a friend or two to lunch on the boat today; no doubt it will be expensive, but delightfully cool in our dining room. The boat is good. We appreciate it the more since we have been off on the hot streets and been in crowds. The harbor was pretty, lighted up last night, from deck, and the moon was grand in this soft climate. I think it helps my vocal cords[13] the same way it does my skin and hair.

We hope you are all well and happy. We are. We need Frederick[14] with his knowledge of languages, but I'm not so bad at talking with my face and hands.

Lovingly,
Father and Mother.

## SANTOS, BRAZIL, TO SÃO PAULO, BRAZIL

**Friday, January 30, 1948**

**Daily Summary**
*Arrived in Santos, took a jeep ride to São Paulo, and reboarded ship to Argentina*

### BRAZILIAN MISSION, SANTOS MISSIONARY RECORD[15]

Apostle and Sister Stephen L. Richards arrived [in Santos, Brazil] from New York on the S. S. Argentina. Elders Gerald Lee Little and H. Grant Kunzler accumpanied Elder Richards and they will labor in the Brazilian Mission. President and Sister Rex met the ship and escorted Apostle Richards and his wife to São Paulo in the mission's jeep. Returning from São Paulo the Richardses sailed at midnight, continuing their trip to Argentina.

---

**NOTES**

1. George Albert Smith, blessing to Stephen L Richards, December 30, 1947, Stephen L Richards Papers, 1921–59, CHL.
2. David O. McKay, blessing to Irene Smith Merrill Richards, December 30, 1947, Stephen L Richards Papers.
3. See Irene Louise Richards Covey and Cynthia Louise Covey Haller, *A Tribute to Irene Smith Merrill Richards, 1876–1969* (June 1988), Lynn Stephen and Annette Richards Family Papers, CHL.
4. Statistical information, South American Missions, December 30, 1947, Stephen L Richards Papers.
5. See Melvin R. Ballard, *Melvin J. Ballard—Crusader for Righteousness* (Salt Lake City: Bookcraft, 1966), 77.
6. Irene Richards, letter to children, December 24, 1947, Irene Richards Letters, CHL.
7. Irene Richards, *Dear Children*, January 28, 1948, Richards Family Papers, 1879–2004, CHL. Irene's letters to family members written during her trip were compiled and printed by her daughter Georgia R. Olson in 1950.
8. Lois Bathsheba Richards Hinckley was the Richardses' third child and was married to Frederick R. Hinckley, who was nicknamed "Frits."
9. They dined in the area of the Copacabana beach near Rio de Janeiro.
10. The person mentioned is Rolf L. Larson. See Frederick S. Williams and Frederick G. Williams, *From Acorn to Oak Tree: A Personal History of the Establishment and First Quarter Century Development of the South American Missions* (Fullerton, CA: Et Cetera, Et Cetera Graphics, 1987), 242.
11. A "panama" is a wide-brimmed hat made from the fibers of the toquilla tree.
12. Michael R. Hinckley was the son of Lois and Frederick Hinckley and a grandson of the Richardses.
13. Corraine Williams, wife of President Frederick S. Williams of the Uruguayan Mission, said of Sister Richards during her trip to South America, "She didn't

have any voice; she never did speak all the time that we were in the mission; she never spoke at any of the meetings. And I was really surprised at this because I felt like it could have been a help to the women if she had. But I think she had surgery or something, but anyway she spoke very softly." Corraine S. Williams Oral History, interviewed by Frederick G. Williams, 1975–76, 22, CHL.

14. Frederick R. Hinckley Jr. was the son of Lois and Frederick Hinckley and a grandson of the Richardses.

15. January 30, 1948, Santos Missionary Record, 1947–59, CHL.

CHAPTER TWO

# ARGENTINA

### HISTORICAL BACKGROUND

The SS *Argentina* wended its way around the bulge of South America, making brief stops in Brazil and Uruguay before concluding its journey in Buenos Aires, often described as the "Paris of South America." First on the Richardses' mission-tour itinerary was the Argentine Mission—heir to the South American Mission founded in 1925 by Elder Melvin J. Ballard. The ensuing two decades of Church expansion brought membership to nine hundred, with most Argentine Latter-day Saints being of Italian, Spanish, and German descent. During that early period, new branches of the Church emerged from the major cities throughout the country.

Notwithstanding a grueling schedule and traveling twenty-six hundred miles by car during February 1948, Elder Richards encouraged members and missionaries and witnessed the baptism of a family in Argentina. He also made time to meet the media and strengthen the image of the Church. Active in civic groups like the Rotary Club, the Apostle also delivered speeches at the invitation of businessmen during his stay.

## THE DOCUMENTS

Besides Sister Richards, the principal authors reporting on the Argentina trip were Howard J. Marsh, the mission secretary, and Argentine Mission president W. Ernest Young. Quite a few local newspapers also carried the story of a Latter-day Saint Apostle arriving in South America, capturing Elder Richards's views and shedding light on perceptions of the Church in 1948. In the glow of the pro–North American era following World War II, Latin American news writers were favorable toward the Church and sought to accurately explain its teachings and beliefs.

Interspersed in the next chapter are letters and journal entries of missionaries thrilled at the opportunity to have an Apostle visit them and meet the members. Periodically, Elder Richards corresponded with the First Presidency, giving them informative observations and remarking on the status of his health; some of this correspondence has been reproduced herein. Also included are articles that the South American missions mailed to Salt Lake City so the *Church News* could keep its readers updated on the nature and impact of the Apostle's visit.

### BUENOS AIRES, ARGENTINA

**Tuesday, February 3, 1948**

**Daily Summary**
*Arrived in Buenos Aires, met by President and Sister W. Ernest Young of the Argentine Mission, photographed and interviewed by reporters*

#### ELDER HOWARD J. MARSH, ARGENTINE MISSION HISTORICAL REPORT[1]

Elder Stephen L. Richards and his wife, Irene Merrill Richards, arrived this morning aboard the Moore-McCormick passenger ship "S/S/ Argentina", on her maiden run from New York. (After renovation from service as an Army Transport.) On hand to meet Brother and Sister Richards were President and Sister Young, ten of the Elders, and two local members. Photographs were taken aboard the ship by representatives of the local newspapers. Interviews were given by both Brother and Sister Richards and Brother and Sister Young.

After a two hour delay in the aduana (customs house), Elder and Sister Richards were allowed ashore without any future difficulties. On the way home a stop was made at the Moore-McCormick agency, where negociations were made, although not confirmed, for Elder Richard's return aboard the "S/S/ Argentina" on her next trip (due to leave Buenos Aires March 21, 1948).

After lunch and a brief rest Elder and Sister Richards were interviewed by a reporter from "LA CRÍTICA." The evening was spent in recuperation from "the

*The Richardses' arrival in Buenos Aires, Argentina. Courtesy of CHL.*

*Stephen and Irene Richards with W. Ernest and Cecile Young, February 3, 1948. Courtesy of CHL.*

exasperating ordeal" of the aduana, and in formulating plans for the rest of the visit.

Newspaper articles, plus photos, appeared in the evening editions of LA RAZÓN,[2] which was slightly unfavorable in vein, LA CRÍTICA,[3] which was quite favorable, and NOTICIAS GRÁFICAS,[4] which was just a brief announcement of the arrival.

### NEWS ARTICLE: *LA CRÍTICA*[5]

#### Apostle Richards

Apostle Richards has a venerable appearance, adequate to his elevated dignity. Scant in his declarations to the newspapermen, he expressed only that he had come to pass his vacation in Argentina and that he will observe the work of the various members of this religion, which number in the world more than a million initiates and was founded in 1830, in the United States by Joe Smith, prophet of the revelations from a celestial spirit, Moroni, who in life was the son of the last prophet of the ancient Americans, called Mormon, who arrived to this continent with the Jaredites several thousand years ago.

As you know, more than fifty years ago the Mormon Church excluded from its members the customs of polygamy. From Salt Lake City, Utah, the creed has extended to all parts of the world because of the work of its numerous missionaries.

In our country, relatively a few years ago, two hundred young Mormons established twenty-one missions.[6] Actually, in Buenos Aires the Mormon religion numbers more than a thousand members.

The Mormons, who believe in God, in Jesus, and the Holy Ghost, do not dress in ecclesiastical clothes nor adore images, flee from pomp and ostentation, and understand how to interpret, with simplicity and kindness, the Christian precepts contained in the Book of Mormon, which they do not consider in opposition to the Bible, but complementary.

They live a life healthful and natural. They practice sports, diffuse their teachings and beliefs. They abstain from tobacco, coffee, tea, and alcoholic drinks, and they live in accord with the norms that promise on

# Ha Llegado uno de los Doce Apóstoles Mormónicos

HOY a las 9 arribó a la dársena norte del puerto de la capital el vapor Argentina, procedente de Nueva York, habiendo efectuado escalas en Río de Janeiro, Santos y Montevideo. Dicha nave, al mando del capitán Thomas M. Simmons, integró junto con sus gemelos Uruguay y Brasil la flota de buena vecindad que unía antes de la guerra los principales puertos americanos. Las autoridades norteamericanas lo utilizaron luego como transporte de fuerzas del ejército, devolviéndolo hace unos meses a la firma Moore-McCormick, que antes de ponerlo nuevamente en circulación realizó en él diversas obras de refección que ampliaron su capacidad en 54 pasajeros más. Sus salones fueron decorados con motivos folklóricos argentinos, algunos de ellos notables, por artistas norteamericanos de vanguardia.

◆ **Directores de la compañía**

El Argentina partió de Nueva York el 15 de enero con 475 pasajeros. Llegaron hoy, entre ellos, tres destacadas personalidades de la importante compañía propietaria de la nave, los señores Eugen F. Moran, Emmet T. McCormick y E. P. Clarendon, vicepresidente fundador, vicetesorero y gerente general, respectivamente, quienes tienen el propósito de estudiar las condiciones de nuestro puerto y supervisar posteriormente la construcción de nuevos vapores que han de sumarse a la línea.

Viene también a conocer nuestra ciudad el señor Stephen Richards, que tiene en su país la dignidad de Apóstol de la Iglesia Mormónica, algunos de cuyos fieles figuran entre los miembros de la colectividad norteamericana en el nuestro.

Mr. Thomas W. Simmons es un conocido turfman de Los Angeles, cuyo Jockey Club preside actualmente. Amigo de los actores hollywoodenses Tyrone Power y Bing Crosby, que como se sabe adquirieron en sus respectivas visitas algunos caballos argentinos de carrera, expresa que ha llegado aquí en viaje de placer, pero que seguramente observará las condiciones en que se desarrolla nuestro turf, y comprará para su stud dos o tres posibles "cracks".

Nuestros 'pingos', como dice el Sr. Simmons, son muy apreciados en Los Angeles, sobre todo luego de los éxitos alcanzados por los que se llevara el popular Bing.

APOSTOL MORMON. — Mr. Stephen Richards, uno de los doce apóstoles de la religión mormónica, poco después del arribo, en compañía de su esposa

*The Richardses' visit was covered extensively by news articles. Courtesy of CHL.*

the average an existence of more than eight years longer than the average mortal.

The creed is essentially spiritual and has for a purpose the betterment, dignification, and elevation of the conditions of humanity. Its faith and its noble goals remind of the words of Mahatma Gandhi,[7] "All the religions are good, because they are looking for the same God."

## BUENOS AIRES, ARGENTINA

**Wednesday, February 4, 1948**

**Daily Summary**
*Lunched with the Rotary Club, shopped in the afternoon, and attended welcome social at the Liniers chapel*

### IRENE M. RICHARDS LETTER[8]

Buenos Aires<br>
Mission Home<br>
Feb. 4, 1948

Dear Phil:[9]

So we are in the tropics. Bananas everywhere. The fields stretch from the roads out farther than one can see to the jungle. And it is a jungle, but these people are rapidly ploughing it up into productive land. The banana bush just produces one stick, then they are picked green and the plant cut down, and grows up again. There seems to be lots of fruit here but the potatoes are scarce and expensive.

All the ports were beautiful, tall white houses, lovely beaches, parks, and statuary especially artistic. I suppose our America is still young in art. This is so delicate and expressive.

It was a thrill to dock and leave each time. Hundreds of people all pursuing their own ways. Coming and going, and greeting and saying good-bye. It is fine how good we feel when we spy some missionary looking for us. We can usually pick them out in a crowd. Sister Young had a beautiful bouquet of flowers for me. But before we could meet they were pretty well faded. We were three hours going thru the customs. Just because there were so

*The Argentine mission home. Courtesy of CHL.*

*The Richardses and the Youngs (pictured on right) in front of the Argentine mission home. Courtesy of CHL.*

many coming off the ship for Buenos Aires. But we were photographed and appeared in the headlines along with the McCormack President and I think he is sorry he didn't invite us to his dinner on the boat today, after he found out how important we are!! Sour grapes.

Well, everyone is so kind to us, and anxious to meet Papa. Tonight there will be a party of greeting for him, here in Buenos Aires, by the saints. Now he has gone to a Rotary luncheon and to meet some of those Bankers whose friends are Orval Adams and the New York City Bank, etc. At every port someone from the Bank has met us and extended a wish to be of service to us. Good will for our church, I guess.

On arriving here we have a letter from Allie, Dick and Louise,[10] and we expect others soon from you all. . . . We are fine.

Love from,
Mother and Father.

### IRENE M. RICHARDS LETTER[11]

Mission Home
Feb. 4, 1948

Dear Allie:[12]

We have finished our water travel for a while and the land still keeps coming up to meet us. Buenos Aires is also a pretty harbor, but the river water is red like the Colorado and the surrounding soil. The houses, mostly (apartment) along the beaches are new and quite severely modern. Papa has gone to a big hotel to Rotary Lunch and to meet some Bankers. Now, don't laugh. I am washing and ironing. But the servant at the mission won't let me do much, so I am really writing some letters. Your letter was one here to greet us. Thanks for it gave us a thrill from you so far away. Glad you are well.

We were three hours going thru the customs yesterday, unnecessarily. When will we all speak one language and treat each other like neighbors?

It was good to meet the missionaries and so many from home. Richards, Smiths, Biglars and Harvey Glade, our home neighbor, who is one of the winning basket ball team. There are half a dozen silver trophies here in our room won by our boys. They gain attention that way and make friends and enemies, I guess.

The mission home is a typical Spanish home, once elegant, now somewhat run down. If it were furnished and renewed I would love it, a very decorative exterior, with high wall and iron gates and fence, a beautiful garden, wonderful pines and shrubbery. Paved walks in tile, balconies and patio in tile. Marble floors, tall doors and windows and ceilings out of sight. With Spanish furniture, drapes, lamps, etc., it would be gorgeous. But it is not practical and the plumbing is no good. So I wish they could have a modern, no architectural pattern but convenient place like the President in Montevideo has. These beautiful old places are being replaced by ugly modern stuff very fast.

The beaches are crowded right now and it is really hot, but tomorrow they say it may be cool. We are going to attend a greeting party for Papa here tonight. I hope he won't be too tired when he gets home. We are fine and interested in what we are going to do next. Will try to drop a card or note as often as possible.

The statuary here is superior. All done in Italy I presume. The high class is ultra. I enjoy it all and am seeing things that Pap[a] doesn't because he is wrapped up in his work. Keep well and we know your garden will be lovely for Knight's[13] efforts.

Lovingly,
Mother and Father.

*Howard J. Marsh, the mission secretary, (middle) traveled with the Youngs and Richardses throughout Argentina. The* Church News *caption for this photo stated they "drove 2,600 miles of country roads" in this car. Courtesy of CHL.*

### ELDER HOWARD J. MARSH, ARGENTINE MISSION HISTORICAL REPORT[14]

At noon the President and Elder Richards dined with the local Rotary Club at the Plaza Hotel.

The afternoon was spent in "window shopping" on Florida Street.

At night the official "Bienvenida"[15] was held in the Liniers chapel. The program started at 8:15 p.m., and lasted until 10:05. . . .

There were 353 in attendence, and a deep spiritual influence was felt. The audience was especially appreciative of the fact that an Apostle could laugh and enter so thoroughly into the festivities. In his remarks Elder Richards expressed his thanks for the welcome rendered and dwelled for a short while on the theme "the Gospel makes brothers of us all."

The translation done by Elder Young followed in rapid order so that not one iota of the meaning or feeling was lost to the audience.

Many of the Saints in attendance were priviledged in meeting Bro. and Sis. Richards after the meeting.

Many of them expressed the idea that "tonight heralds a new future for the Argentine Mission."

Newspaper articles (all favorable) appeared in today's editions (all of them accompanied by photos) of <u>LA CRITICA</u>, <u>CLARIN</u>, <u>DEMOCRACIA</u>, <u>STANDARD</u>, <u>HERALD</u>, and <u>EL MUNDO</u>.

### NEWS ARTICLE: *LA CRÍTICA*[16]

**Mormon Apostle, Who Has Just Arrived in Buenos Aires, Admires Gandhi**

*Caption: Sent from God—Stephen Richards, one of the twelve apostles of the Mormon sect, who has just arrived in our capital, spoke to <u>LA CRÍTICA</u> on the mysteries of the order over which he presides, and he demonstrated a sincere admiration of Gandhi,*[17] *who—he expressed—defended the peace of the world in his own way.*

Very few inhabitants of this immense Buenos Aires know that in a moderate "petit-hotel" in the burrough of Flores, behind the rusty gates which lead into a small garden, is the seat of episcopal power of the "Church of Jesus of the Latter-day Saints", better known by the masses by the name of the "Mormon Sect."

Nothing in the house indicates that its occupants could render tribute to a religious faith. It appears more like a commercial office, with its necessary typists and its employees in charge of the books. Not a single symbol. All is internal and dwells in the hearts of these men and women; serene, gentle, and affable, who speak of the revelation of their miraculous book with a contagious security.

We went there in search of one of the twelve Apostles of the church, Stephen Richards, in order that he might illuminate us on the secrets and mysteries of the order over which he presides.

### With the Apostle

Apostle Richards arrived yesterday morning aboard the steamship Argentina. We must sincerely confess that his apostolic profession made us feel as if we were in the presence of a man who had something in common with those who are usually found in the common fantasies about a man who is in permanent contact with divine powers. Perhaps it was his dress, perhaps the visage, perhaps the amazement of a strange doctrine. None of these: Richards is a common man, plain, without appearances which would distinguish him from any ordinary North American of average excellence. This yes, stripped of all pretense in his manners, and placed on the same plane as the interlocutor, even though the writer was not born under the starry flag.

Apostle Richards received us in one of the offices of the "Church of Jesus Christ of the Latter-day Saints," in the midst of the hustle of the place. With him was the President of the Argentine Mission, W. Ernest Young, and the wives of the two.

Let us now listen to the smooth-flowing serene words from the lips of a man sent from Christ.

—I have visited Brazil, Uruguay and now Argentina.[18] I am very satisfied with the work of our missions. The work in Argentina dates from 1925, it is the longest established, and I will dedicate the largest part of my time to it. I will tour the country and come into contact with my brothers.

### The Book of Mormon

Our church—continued the apostle—is absolutely separated from politics. We honor and obey the laws of all countries. We respect, likewise, all religions. Our object is to extend the doctrine of Christ in the world, and we do not maintain ties with other churches.

We asked apostle Richards to explain his doctrine. He replied—

—Our doctrine is founded on the "Sacred history of the ancient Americans", compiled by the Apostle Mormon some 1500 years ago, and discovered in the north of the State of New York in the year 1823, on some plates of gold, during dome [some] archeological excavations. It was written in refined Egyptian, and already has been translated into the majority of the languages. The first part of the Book of Mormon corresponds to the

Bible, since the origin, unto the time of Isaiah, 600 years before Christ, and later continues with the American part.

We inquire—With the American part?

—Yes, because 600 years before Christ there was an emmigration of Hebrews from Jerusalem to South America. Here they established and founded a civilization very superior to the one which the Spaniards encountered during the epoch of discovery. Later they passed to Central America, and from there to North America, where internal wars consumed them until they disappeared. The Hebrews, on emmigrating to our continent, brought the Bible printed on plates of bronze. Mormon continued the American relation. And in his book he transmits the following message to the Americas: while you obey the laws of Jesus Christ you will prosper and be free forever.

—Could Mormon have known of the existence of Christ?

—His "history" demonstrates that he did. The archeological proofs are irrefutable.

### *The Greatness of Gandhi*

The Apostle preferred not to talk of international politics. Nevertheless, before saying farewell, we asked him this question.

—What do you think of the assassination of Mahatma Gandhi?

—We have lost a man of God. He defended the peace of the world in his own way, in a manner highly peculiar.

And the man sent from God extended his hand and awarded us with a smile full of kindness and condescension.

Trans. by Elder H. J. Marsh

## ELDER HOWARD J. MARSH, UNPUBLISHED NEWS ARTICLE[19]

Buenos Aires-----February 5, 1948

... Upon their arrival (Tuesday morning February 3$^{rd}$.) Brother and Sister Richards were the recipiants of a semi-formal welcome on the part of a small group of the local brethern. The official reception was held that

*Liniers chapel dedication, April 9, 1939. Courtesy of CHL.*

night in the chapel at Liniers (the only church owned and built chapel in Argentina).

Stretching the normal seating capacity of 300 to a number somewhat higher than 350, the large audience was highly pleased by the congenial spirit evidenced by Brother and Sister Richards. His infectious smile won the hearts of all—the majority of whom had come expecting to see a man of overpowering sobriety. (If this is hard to picture; remember that the visit of Elder Richards is the first visit of an authority of the church since the mission was dedicated in 1925, for this reason few of the local brethern had ever seen an general authority.)

During the program of "bienvenida" (welcome), which consisted in large part of native songs and dances, Elder and Sister Richards were presented with flowers and similar tokens from the local sisters.

In addressing the audience, through the interpretive ability of President Young, Elder Richards dwelled shortly on the theme "the Gospel makes Brothers of us all."

The feelings of all who were present is perhaps best typified by this remark which was voiced by several—"this night marks the beginning of a new era for the Argentine Mission." We all feel this deeply, that the Argentina Mission has finally outgrown its infancy, and has become of age. We trustfully look forward to a future period of increased missionary activity, reaping its harvest as it must.

This Sunday (February 8, 1948) a special conference will be held in Buenos Aires, after which Elder Richards plans to depart for a two-week inspection trip through the interior of Argentina.

Elder H. J. Marsh

## BUENOS AIRES, ARGENTINA

**Thursday, February 5, 1948**

**Daily Summary**
*Visited the Florida Branch, shopped, met with bank executives and businessmen*

### ELDER HOWARD J. MARSH, ARGENTINE MISSION HISTORICAL REPORT[20]

Elder Richards, accompanied by his wife, Bro. and Sis. Young, and Elder H. J. Marsh visited the Rama[21] of Florida in the morning. The afternoon was spent in the central part of town—shopping and establishing amicable relations with various men of importance in the financial and business world (First Nat'l Bank of New York). Rested at night. (i.e. the Apostle rested)

## BUENOS AIRES, ARGENTINA

**Friday, February 6, 1948**

**Daily Summary**
*Wrote letter to the First Presidency about arrival and attended opera in the evening*

## IRENE M. RICHARDS LETTER[22]

Mission Home
Buenos Aires
Feb. 6, 1948

Dear Lois and Louise and all:[23]

I think you see each other often and I am rather crowded just now for time. We are getting more involved every minute. They are holding a conference here and there are about 200 members and there will be 50 missionaries to meet. It takes a long time to hear each one, and that's the only real way to get to know how they feel and their plans and aspirations. One can usually read their spirits and dispositions. It is very interesting. We are in the old section of town, a very romantic setting. I expect to see a pretty Senorita coming out of her gate, or peeping out of the iron fence in her garden. . . .

. . . The press was sensational, but after interviewing Papa they spoke better of the Mormons. Evidently there is a lot of ignorance about, but everyone is interested in U.S.A.

The branch gave us a real welcome and flowers, a cake, sweater for Papa made by Relief Society sisters, etc. This town is beautiful and I have some pictures to bring home of it. Last night we went to hear "Butterfly"[24] given in an open air stadium. The singers, all Italian, were lovely and the setting enchanting. We sat on the last row but they let us down at the last act to the front, for which Papa was disappointed because it brought him down to realities. I was glad to see the costumes close, but it made the players fat. We are fine. Hope you all are. Thank you for your lovely letter.

Lovingly,
Mother and Father.

## STEPHEN L RICHARDS LETTER[25]

Dear Brethren:

On arrival here, I have sent you a cablegram, "Arrived, well, notify folks." We have received the most generous welcome, and I am sure that we are among a most hospitable congenial people.

We will begin holding conferences tomorrow. Our schedule takes us through all the districts and most of the branches of the mission. When we have made the tour we will be in a better position to crystalize our observations.

We are in good health and the report is that all the missionaries here are also. I will be glad to keep you advised of any items of moment. We hope that this will find you all well.

Faithfully and Affectionately yours,

[26]

SLR/pr

## BUENOS AIRES, ARGENTINA

**Saturday, February 7, 1948**

**Daily Summary**
*Missionary conference at Liniers*

### W. ERNEST YOUNG, ARGENTINE MISSION PRESIDENT[27]

February 7 a missionary report and testimony meeting was held for all elders in the Capital area at the Liniers chapel. There were forty-nine present including Elder and Sister Richards and Brother and Sister L. Pearce [Pierce] Brady.[28] The first session was at 10:15 a.m. and ended at 1 p.m., given for reports and testimonies. The second session began at 3:05 p.m. and ended at 7 p.m. with more reports and testimonies. After a ten-minute recess the meeting time was given to Elder Richards, who elaborated on the following

*Members prepare an "asado," a feast of meat. Courtesy of CHL.*

*Mission conference, March 1947. Courtesy of CHL.*

subjects: (1) Missionaries must adapt themselves to the different conditions in this field. (2) In this Church, the right of nomination has been given to the President of the Church. (3) He admonished all to follow the counsel of the Authorities. (4) The missionary responsibility is to present the gospel in such a manner so that the recipient of the missionary's message may be judged as having accepted or rejected it. After the meeting the missionaries went to the mission home where "North American" refreshments were served.

*Meeting of mission presidents and missionaries, with Frederick S. Williams, W. Ernest Young, and Stephen L Richards in the front row and their wives standing immediately behind them. Courtesy of CHL.*

## BUENOS AIRES, ARGENTINA

Sunday, February 8, 1948

**Daily Summary**
*Conferences at the Liniers, Ramos Mejía, Haedo, and Ciudadela Branches*

### ELDER HOWARD J. MARSH, ARGENTINE MISSION HISTORICAL REPORT[29]

Feb. 8, 1948. 8:30 a.m. attended priesthood meeting in Liniers. Elder Richards spoke on the theme "You have the responsibility of advancing yourselves in the priesthood so that you can receive the higher blessings." The party then proceeded to Ramos Mejía.[30] Elder Richards' theme—"The pure and simple spirit—the essence of the true Gospel of Jesus Christ." Then to Haedo.[31] Elder Richards spoke of "Participation in the work of Christ brings happiness. Lack of participation brings sorrow to the soul. Death is a part of the plan, not to be feared, but we look forward to the reunion of our loved-ones in the hereafter. We fear sin because this could keep us out of the happiness of the heavens.—One-third of the world now profess Christianity, but don't know Him very well—our duty is to teach them the true Gospel—the stone (of Daniel's dream) has started to roll.

*The Richardses visit the Ramos Mejía (left) and Haedo (right) Branches in Buenos Aires. Courtesy of CHL.*

Testimony of Elder Richards." And lastly of all to the Ciudadela Branch,³² where the theme of "Save the Children first", was developed.

At night a special district conference was held at Liniers. 338 were present.

---

## TRES ARROYOS, ARGENTINA

### Monday, February 9, 1948

**Daily Summary**
*Traveled to Tres Arroyos and held conferences with missionaries serving in Tres Arroyos, Bahía Blanca, Tandil, and Coronel Suárez*

### W. ERNEST YOUNG, ARGENTINE MISSION PRESIDENT³³

**Visit to Southern Branches of Mission**

February 9 Elder and Sister Richards, Cecile and I, and Elder Howard J. Marsh left early enroute to Tres Arroyos.³⁴ We arrived in mid-afternoon, and in the evening a missionary report meeting was held with the elders from Tres Arroyos, Bahia Blanca, Tandil, and Coronel Suarez.³⁵ As usual very good instructions were given to the missionaries, and testimonies and reports by the elders were good.

### ELDER EDWIN J. RICHARDSON LETTER³⁶

In Tres Arroyos there was nothing definitely planned so we had to wait till Pres. Young came at 4:00. Apostle Richards and his wife came too. They decided to hold the missionary meeting that night as two of the B.[ahía] B.[lanca] missionaries had to return the next morning for a picnic they had planned for the branch before they left. So the missionary meeting was held at 8:00 Monday night. These missionary meetings are the ones that are remembered longest by the missionaries. I think I told you about the one that lasted nine hours in the Capital (B. A.) last conference. Well, this one didn't last quite that long, but it was really inspirational. Each one of the missionaries spoke, including Hno. Costantini who doesn't understand any English and the meeting was held in English for the benefit of Elder Richards. Pres. Young translated Hno. Costantini's talk into English for Elder Richards. Then Brother Looney, our member here in Bahia, gave the account of his conversion and his testimony. That meeting was the only part of the conference he could attend as his wife was sick and he had to be back the next day. But he felt very highly repaid for his trip, Having had the opportunity to see and shake hands with an apostle. And too, Elder Richardss he complimented him quite highly and thanked him for his testimony. Then, of course, Elder Richards was the last speaker. He gave us some very fine and timely instructions. He was tired from his trip and had talked in several meetings the day before in Buenos Aires, and so, as he said he had a lot to tell us but since he was under the necessity of guarding his health he could not tell all. Nevertheless he gave us some very good instructions.

## TRES ARROYOS, ARGENTINA

**Tuesday, February 10, 1948**

**Daily Summary**
*Baptism of the Maldonado family and evening member meeting*

### ELDER EDWIN J. RICHARDSON LETTER[37]

Tuesday about noon we all went out in the country a mile or so where there was a small creek where we could hold some baptisms. The Tres Arroyos missionaries have done a fine job in converting an entire family. Seven of one family, including both parents, and a young girl from another family were baptized and afterward confirmed on the banks of the stream. Elder Richards made the statement after witnessing all this, or rather asked the question: "Who knows but what in a hundred years there will be over a thousand members in the church descendents of this family?" Then he said that in a reunion in Utah of the descendents of a man who joined the church 100 years ago there were more than 2000 people, descendents of that man. This will be one of the high lights of my mission because I

Above: The Youngs and the Richardses sit with the Maldonado family and young girl who were baptized. Elders Carroll and Marble are standing. Courtesy of CHL.

Musical number at the baptismal service. Courtesy of CHL.

Brother and Sister Maldonado with Elder Carroll at the site of their baptism. Courtesy of CHL.

*President W. Ernest Young translates for Elder Richards at the baptismal service. Courtesy of John R. Wall.*

confirmed one of the members of that family.

The conference session, only one was held, took place in the back end of the lot of the Tres Arroyos branch in the open air. It was a little cool for Elder Richards bald head so the session didn't last more than an hour and a half, but at that it was really worthwhile. Pres. Young spoke for about thirty minutes about the Apostasy, Restoration, the nearness of the Second Coming of Christ, a few other things pretty well linked together. Only one of the missionaries spoke and his was an extemporaneous speech. Elder Carrier gave a very humble testimony. Sister Young gave a few words and one of the member women from Tres Arroyos bore her testimony. Elder Richards talk of course came last and was the highlight of the Conference. He spoke of world conditions and the reason why they are in such a state, namely wickedness, lack of love for one another, greed and selfishness. Pres. Young translated for him. In that way we who had a knowledge of both English and Spanish got double benefit from the talk.

---

## BUENOS AIRES, ARGENTINA

**Wednesday, February 11, 1948**

**Daily Summary**
*Return trip to Buenos Aires and Irene's reflections on missionaries and Argentina*

## IRENE M. RICHARDS LETTER[38]

Buenos Aires, Argentina
February 11, 1948

Dear Ellen and Lloyd:

Having met your nephew[39] in this mission, inspires us to write a line to tell you how glad we were to discover he was yours. He surely is a fine Elder and is an inthusiastic and interesting as can be. He is well and very happy here. Its hard to understand just how much good a missionary can do here, until one sees them in action. We came upon them in Sunday School teaching the children in spanish. We attended a baptism where 6 or more were taken down into a clear stream by the Elders, heard them sing and preach in spanish. And we saw how they were regarded by the members of their branches. They stand out apart from the usual crowd. They are in very deed Saviors on Mount Zion.

Your boy is one of about 200 and an outstanding one. By the way he has a small mustache, which rather gives him distinction, and is becoming.

This is an entirely different country than ours, and it is hot summer now although it is cooler than usual they say. We traveled a distance of some 300 miles to meet this group, of missionaries. Tomorrow we are going in another direction to meet another group. And to hear them all speak and its a thrill to listen to their experiences and testimonies. They all say they have the best parents in the world, and I agree with them, and these parents have the best boys in the world.

There are no mountains in sight, just fields and meadows, some trees and hundreds of cattle. I have had some lovely bananas but no <u>tender</u> beef yet. I think they dont know how to cook here. I am sure the boys get along better doing their own cooking. There are lots of vegetables and fruit. I see melons but we have not tried them yet. I have not seen orchids yet. They say they are in Brazil.

The beautiful thing here is the tile side walks and floors. Everyone has them The patios and halls and walled in gardens are beautiful. Sometimes the boys can't find places to rent on the paved streets though. The middle class of people are fine looking and intelligent. I am sure the missionaries are attracting attention. They are outstanding among these South Americans. They need equipment and all the help we can give them. This is a big rich land and some day it may be o.k. if it can arrange its politics to be a true democaracy. The Argentinae's are envious and suspicious of North Americans and our boys have to convince them that they did'nt come to rob them, but want to help them. Weell, they seem earnest and willing to stand anything; so I'm sure they can succeed. Your nephew sends greetings and we do also. Hope all is weell with you.

Sincerely,<br>
Bro. & Sister Richards.

## IRENE M. RICHARDS LETTER[40]

Buenos Aires, Argentina<br>
Feb. 11, 1948

Dear Lynn:[41]

We have just returned from a trip to "Three Rivers". I won't attempt to tell it in Spanish.[42] . . .

On our trip we saw some ostrich, some llamas, some huge vultures feeding among the cattle and sheep. There seem to be some fine horses, also. . . .

I surely sympathize with the elders, who are so young and unused to this food. I think they do better preparing their own, but they are enthusiastic and interesting. The saints love them and that's enough. . . . We have met about 60 elders so far and expect to see the rest as we travel on. Lee [Richards][43] will be with the next bunch. There will be a basketball game next trip also. They are enthusiastic about this arrangement and think they meet more young people and a better class, than in tracting. Some business men, who sponsor sports, notice them also. I wish they could attract some better class than heretofore. These people don't know much about the Bible, they have grown to don't care, but it may be the reason for the best time to acquaint them. One man who just joined said he had waited for 30 years for a religion like this. Many are disgusted with the Catholics, especially the younger generation. The saints give us flowers every time we go to another meeting. The house is surely filled with lovely bouquets.

Papa has gone to town to do some business with President Young. I am glad to rest and do some pressing so we can go in another direction tomorrow. We went south yesterday, now we are going west and north. I think Papa is getting a fair idea of the people and country and conditions. They surely need equipment and all the help they can get. It is rather difficult to speak and put your message over, and have an interpreter, but they say Bro. Young is the best ever, and seems to give it out readily and well, and the audience is so attentive and considerate. . . .

Well, the time is passing and your winter will change to spring, and our summer will turn to spring and we will be home again. We find that no regular mail will ever get to us, so we send it all airmail. Louise's came in 7 days. Maybe Lois and Fritz will be going east when we arrive at New York the first part of April. Georgia[44] said possibly they would meet us there also. We shall see.

When we return in two weeks, we will write another letter to someone, and we may know by then just when we are coming.

Love to you all,<br>
Mother and Father Richards.

## BUENOS AIRES AND PERGAMINO, ARGENTINA

### Thursday, February 12, 1948

**Daily Summary**
*Visited US Ambassador and bank executives and held meetings in Pergamino*

### W. ERNEST YOUNG, ARGENTINE MISSION PRESIDENT[45]

February 12 in the morning two interviews were held with American ambassador James Bruce, who was very affable and interested in meeting Apostle Richards. Then an interview was held with the president of the Buenos Aires branch of the City National Bank of New York. The Church has business connections with this bank, and the president was cordial and interested in meeting Elder Richards.

In the afternoon the party left for the west, arriving at Pergamino[46] in time to hold a meeting at the branch with seventy-three in attendance.

An elders' meeting was held at Hotel Roma with the elders of Pergamino with good results.

---

## PERGAMINO AND ROSÁRIO, ARGENTINA

### Friday, February 13, 1948

**Daily Summary**
*First Presidency letter to Elder Richards, dedication of Pergamino chapel, travel to San Nicolás and Rosário, and evening program and missionary basketball game in Rosário*

### FIRST PRESIDENCY LETTER[47]

Dear Brother Stephen L:

We were most happy to get the cable report of your safe arrival in Buenos Aires and later to receive your letter of February 6 confirming the fact that you and Sister Richards are well and telling us of your plans.

We are sure that you will find a hearty welcome with the saints there and that you will enjoy your labors. We should be glad if you would please convey to the saints our affectionate greetings and our prayers that the Lord will help them so to live that He can pour out upon them His richest blessings.

President McKay is in Mexico visiting that mission and will be dedicating a new meeting house at Cuatla on Sunday.

Our great anxiety is that you shall not overwork yourself, and we urge you to be extremely cautious in this respect.

Again with our affectionate greetings to the saints, to President Young, his wife and staff, to the missionaries generally and to yourself and Sister Richards, we are

Faithfully yours,<br>
THE FIRST PRESIDENCY<br>
By: /s/ George Albert Smith<br>
/s/ J Reuben Clark Jr

## NEWS ARTICLE: *TRIBUNA*[48]

### There Will Arrive Today to This City a Mormon Apostle

*Caption: Apostle — D. Stephen L. Richard, Mormon Apostle who will be a guest of our city.*

There will arrive today to our city Apostle Stephen L. Richards of the Church of Jesus Christ of Latter-day Saints, commonly called the Mormon Church.

Mr. Richards, who has been sent by the First Presidency of the church, with headquarters in Salt Lake City, Utah, North America, will attend the Rosario District conference, which will be held next Sunday at 10 a.m. in the Sorrento "local,"[49] 1004 Zelaya St., and 7 p.m. at 4055 Córdoba St.

In the organization of the church, one finds apostles, prophets, seers, and revelators who have been called by God to the perfection of the Latter-day Saints.

### *The Second Time*

This is the second time in 22 years that the Argentine Mission is privileged with the visit of an apostle of the church. The first time was when Apostle Melvin J. Ballard came to dedicate the mission in December of 1925, in Buenos Aires. During this time the Argentine Mission has seen great advancement because there are 26 branches or groups of missionaries; in total there are 93 missionaries. President of the mission W. Ernest Young, together with his wife, Cecille S. Young, has been doing an intense labor during the last three years to advance the missionary work in Argentina, and also in the period 1935–1938.

## NEWS ARTICLE: *LA CAPITAL*[50]

### The Mormon Leader E. L. Richards in Our City Today

With the motive of assisting in the festivities organized by the Rosario District of the Church of Jesus Christ of Latter-day Saints, there will arrive in our city today the Mormon leader Stephen L. Richards, who has been sent to Argentina by the First Presidency of the aforementioned cult, with headquarters in Salt Lake City, Utah, U.S.A.

Mr. Richards was born in 1879 in the state of Utah, dedicated his best years to the faculty, and, after having acted as director of the public schools in Malb [Malad], Idaho, left the post of Professor of Law of the University of Utah.

The aforementioned leader has completed an intense and valorous labor as integrant of the Church of Jesus Christ of the Latter-day Saints, in which he was named second counselor to President Joseph Fielding Smith, after the death of George Reynolds. He married Irene Merril in 1900. Stephen Richards started from that date a forceful existence and dedicated himself to the tasks of an agriculturist, meanwhile he alternated the sacrifices of the rural life with the propagation of his cult.

The leader that is visiting us is a figure who enjoys extraordinary prestige in the scene of his church, by virtue of his directing position and being an eloquent preacher. Gifted with a profound versatility in Mormon material, his has been the motive of respect for a great number of the sustainers of his cult.

Taking opportunity of his visit, there will be completed an extensive and interesting program in which the following acts will take place:

Today at 7 p.m., concert in the salons of the "Centro Progresista,"[51] situated at 3638 San Juan St., there will perform a chorus of missionaries and the pianist Elder Leland Wakefield; at 9:30 p.m. a game of basketball in the "Club Policial"; Saturday, at 8 p.m., a special meeting in the salon at 4061 Córdoba St; Sunday, at 10 a.m., first session of the general conference in the Sorrent "local"; at 5 p.m. meeting of the priesthood and a meeting of the Relief Society; at 7 p.m., second general session of the conference in the "local"; Monday, at 8:30 p.m., a special affair in the "Club Intercambio,"[52] situated at 4740 Córdoba St.; at 11 p.m. a transmission by the air waves of radio station LT8.

### ELDER HOWARD J. MARSH, ARGENTINE MISSION HISTORICAL REPORT[53]

In the morning Elder Richards dedicated the newly acquired Pergamino chapel[54] (Excerpts attached). The group then travelled to Rosario, stopping at San Nicholas. Lunched with the "Travelling Elders", and the Elders from the Rosario District. At night attended a program and basketball game of the "Travelling Elders" (who unfortunately lost—before a crowd of 500—but made many friends).

## DEDICATORY PRAYER FOR PERGAMINO CHAPEL[55]

Excerpts from the Dedicatory Prayer on the L.D.S. Chapel at Pergamino, Argentina.

> By Apostle Stephen L. Richards.
> February 13, 1948. (9:15 a.m.)

Our Father who art in Heaven, we gather this morning, as a few of Thy servants, to present unto Thee this building, which has been acquired as a meeting place for the Saints, and as a place for the dissemination of Thy word. We thank Thee for the restoration—We pray that the work may go forward. We thank Thee for our understanding of Thy truth. We thank Thee for the missionary work—for past missionaries—for the future prospects of this mission; for the people who are learning the Gospel. We thank Thee for the priviledge to progress unto this point. We thank Thee for the purchase—thank Thee for the people who have made the purchase possible.

In the name of the Holy Priesthood, we dedicate this building and its surroundings, the grounds, to Thy service; to a place where the Holy Spirit may dwell, a place where Thee may manifest Thyself. That the people who come here may feel Thy spirit. That they may feel a spirit here that they may not feel elsewhere. That their testimonies may be strengthened.

Father Thou knowest the capacities of each of us—we pray that the capacities of the people who enter here may be expanded, that they may seek after intelligence.

We pray that those who minister here may be aided in their ministry.

We pray that Thou will cast out all sinister adversaries. We rebuke all evil spirits from here.

We call on the light of the universe to light the hearts of all who worship here.

Now we dedicate this house, humble as it may be, unto Thee. This we do humbly by the authority of the Holy Priesthood that has been given to us. This we do in the name of Thy Son Jesus Christ. Amen.

SLR/hjm

---

## ROSÁRIO, ARGENTINA

**Saturday, February 14, 1948**

**Daily Summary**
*Missionary conference and special program by Travelling Elders*

### IRENE M. RICHARDS LETTER[56]

Rosario, Argentina
Feb. 14, 1948

Dear Georgia:[57]

Today we received your two letters. We are miles inland visiting branches. There is a conference and the elders, about twenty of them, are here from parts around. We met Lee Gill Richards[58] here. He is quite thin and in investigating we find the weather is very depressing and hot right now; also he has been playing basket ball. We saw them play; they have taught these South American boys the game. They won one game and lost one. They also give concerts like Phil's Millenium Chorus did and sing the same songs (Mormon) and please many civic clubs and societies with their fine harmony. There are two boys who sing very well together and an excellent pianist. They are allowed and advertised to use the big civic hall free and have big audiences. I am using the inside of your envelopes to write on. There has been a carnival for a whole week, and every evening the streets are filled with people in costumes, especially children, some dressed beautifully. These people turn night into day. They rise during the forenoon and have breakfast at noon, then have a "siesta" until 3 o'clock, then do business until about 5, when the stores close, then have dinner at 9 and on until 1 or 2 and repeat. "Early to bed and early to rise and you meet no prominent people"—exactly. We got up at 6 this morning and no one but ice men, garbage men, street sweepers, etc., were about. Well, you have to give them a chance. When you consider the weather is so hot no one wants to move, just sit under a cactus, with a great "sombrero" and sleep. . . . There are fine looking people here who, when educated, will make a wonderful race. They don't know anything about religion, they have given up any idea about worship. They are tired of being presided over by priests, so they say, which shows the first signs of intelligence. Lee is travelling with us until we get back to Buenos Aires at the last of the week. There are no mountains in the scene and we have decided not to go to Chile. The plane goes too high, the train is too rough, and the auto is not feasible, and we haven't the time. But we may see the Andes from Minadosa[59] [Mendoza].

Feb. 15—I suppose this is the first time we haven't sent valentines, and today I received Louise's letter and a valentine from Irene Allen and Allie. I haven't had any time to shop and they won't let any article leave the country, so that saves a lot of time and money and when we get home things will be as ever, I hope. Everything seems to come from U.S. or England or France and only alligator bags are really Argentinian. There is no paper around and I haven't seen or spent any money since I left Salt Lake. We have been in three different countries and they all have different money so we just let the mission presidents take care of us and pay them when we leave their countries. . . . Hope you don't freeze to death this winter. We just can't sense being cold. This last week has been really hot. We could close our eyes and

**HOPE LIES IN YOUTH**—Elder Stephen L. Richards of the Council of the Twelve and Mrs. Richards admire a beautiful crocodile purse presented to her while they toured the three missions in South America. The great hope for the southern hemisphere countries, as well as for activities of the Church, is in its youth, Elder Richards commented.

*The Richardses admire a crocodile purse that was presented to them during their tour. Courtesy of CHL.*

imagine we were near Pocatello on the way to the Hebgen[60] in July. And here we are riding along in Argentina. Now the low hills are in view and tomorrow we will see some mountains. It's the rule here to honk at every intersection. You can imagine the mad noise with the cobble streets added. Well, we are still well and I think Papa will last out. He is learning self control. He can't just say do this and that as he is wont, for these people have their ideas also. It is surely interesting at least. Keep well, and excuse this paper and all.

Lovingly,<br>Mother.

### ELDER HOWARD J. MARSH, ARGENTINE MISSION HISTORICAL REPORT[61]

The morning was devoted to a missionary report and testimony meeting for the Elders of the Rosario District. 33 were present including 12 Elders from the district, Elder and Sister Richards, President and Sister Young, and the "Travelling Elders". Started at 10:15 a.m., finished at 1:00 p.m. Elder Richards delivered a few words on developing our talents.

Elder Richards rested in the afternoon, and at night attended a special program in the central branch of Rosario (Given by the "Travelling Elders"—105 in attendance). He delivered a few words of greeting.

---

## ROSÁRIO, ARGENTINA

### Sunday, February 15, 1948

**Daily Summary**
*Rosário District conference held at the Sorrento Branch*

### ELDER HOWARD J. MARSH, ARGENTINE MISSION HISTORICAL REPORT[62]

In the morning was held the first session of the Rosario District Conference—at the Sorrento Branch.[63] 103 in attendance. Elders Brady, Young, and Richards occupied the majority of the time. The general theme was the magnitud of the work in spite of the humble surroundings. Elder Richards (assisted by President Young) blessed a young baby—giving it the name of Maria Julia. During the evening Priesthood and the Relief Society held their sessions, followed by the second general session. 110 in attendance. Speakers were Elder Lee Richards,[64] President Young, and Elder Stephen L. Richards. Theme the restored church of Christ.

## CÓRDOBA, ARGENTINA

**Monday, February 16, 1948**

**Daily Summary**
*Traveled to Córdoba and held branch and missionary meetings*

### CÓRDOBA BRANCH MINUTES[65]

Feb. 16, 1948—Monday
Special Meeting

Today at 4:30 PM., <u>President & Mrs. Young</u> together with <u>Elder & Mrs. Stephen L. Richards</u> of the Council of the Twelve Apostles. Accompanying them were Elders Howard Marsh & Lee Richards.

This morning, Elders Bowman & Hawkins arrived from Villa María for a special district meeting with Elder Richards.

At 8:30 this evening, we held a meeting in the Local to which all of our members able to come as well as the general public were invited. Elder Jesse N. Hawkins, Pres. Young, Sister Young, preceded Elder Richards who spoke on the "message of Mormonism," while Pres Young translated. A very fine spirit prevailed, and the meeting was attended by approximately 60 people.

After the general meeting, a special district elders meeting was held. Each elder bore his testimony, as well as discussing the particular problems encountered by him, & suggestions for improvements in existing missionary aids, viz., literature, projectors, phonographs. Elder Richards concluded the meeting by giving us words of encouragement, beseeching us not to despair in the face of seeming defeat or difficulty; also stressed the missionaries should seek to be more dignified in bearing, speech, & relations with members & investigators.—Further questions were discussed & answered by Brother Richards & Pres. Young.

The party left Tues. morning for Rio Cuarto.—This is the second time in 22 years that a member of the Quorumn of the Twelve Apostles has visited Argentina!

s/s Russell Cannon

## RÍO CUARTO, MENDOZA, AND BUENOS AIRES, ARGENTINA

### Tuesday, February 17, to Thursday, February 19, 1948

**Daily Summary**
*Traveled to Río Cuarto, Mendoza, and Buenos Aires and held branch and missionary meetings*

#### W. ERNEST YOUNG, ARGENTINE MISSION PRESIDENT[66]

February 17 the party traveled to Rio Cuarto about 75 miles to the south of the city of Cordoba, where the first event was an elders' meeting held for four elders in Rio Cuarto at the Hotel Roma in Apostle Richards' room, and later in the evening a meeting was held at the branch[67] local with eighty-one persons attending.

#### W. ERNEST YOUNG, ARGENTINE MISSION PRESIDENT

February 18 the mission group drove west to Mendoza, at the foot of the Andes, and held an elders' meeting with the four missionaries in that city. This was followed with a variety program and a branch conference at which twenty-nine were in attendance. At the Grand Hotel there was some difficulty to find suitable rooms; also Elder and Sister Richards had intended returning to Buenos Aires on the train as a special experience on the English Railway, but the schedule of trains was too delayed for them.

## ELDER HOWARD J. MARSH, ARGENTINE MISSION HISTORICAL REPORT[68]

<u>Feb. 19, 1948</u>. Travelled the 1100 kilometers[69] to Buenos Aires, arriving late at night. No stop-overs en route.

## BUENOS AIRES, ARGENTINA

**Friday, February 20, 1948**

**Daily Summary**
*Business visits and dinner at home of L. Pierce Brady*

### W. ERNEST YOUNG, ARGENTINE MISSION PRESIDENT[70]

February 20 I accompanied Elder Richards to the downtown business center of Buenos Aires, and inspected the money exchange houses for Traveler's and other checks, and the exchanges of the banks, etc. Also Elder Richards ordered a tailormade suit at the James Dry Goods Co. Mr. James, an Englishman, was sociable and told us about his cattle ranch and winning prizes at the fairs for his good breed of cattle, saying, "Yes, I make a damn good living." In the evening Elder and Sister Richards were entertained and dined at the home of the mission's first counselor, L. Pierce Brady and wife. Brother Brady is in the brokerage import business.

## LA PLATA, ARGENTINA

**Saturday, February 21, 1948**

**Daily Summary**
*Relief Society bazaar and surprise party in La Plata for the Richardses' wedding anniversary*

## W. ERNEST YOUNG, ARGENTINE MISSION PRESIDENT[71]

February 21 the group traveled to La Plata,[72] where they attended a Relief Society bazaar. Special honors were extended to Elder and Sister Richards in commemoration of their forty-eighth wedding anniversary, with an attendance of 105 people.

---

## LA PLATA, ARGENTINA

### Sunday, February 22, 1948

**Daily Summary**
*Conference in La Plata and Irene's contemplations in Buenos Aires on mission tour so far*

### NEWS ARTICLE: *EL DIA*[73]

### The Mormon Church Will Speak Today in the La Plata Mission

*The Richardses with some members of the La Plata Branch. Courtesy of CHL.*

Mormonism, represented in all the world by the Church of Jesus Christ of Latter-day Saints, which has been functioning since 118 years ago, having commenced its activities in the United States under the inspiration of its founder Joseph Smith. The principles of the said religion are based on the revelations made by a celestial spirit named Moroni, who was in his material existence the son of Mormon, the last prophet of the ancient Americans, descendant, and the same time from the pre-Flood[74] prophet Jared.

The Mormons believe in God, in Jesus Christ, and in the Holy Ghost; contrary to other religions, they consider that men will be punished for their own sins and not for Adam's transgression; they admit the precepts of the Bible as fundamental, besides the teachings of the Book of Mormon or Book of Gold: their organization has been based on the primitive Christian church and its integrants do not receive pay. Mormonism abandoned in a definite manner polygamy many years ago; it had characterized them since their beginning, having adapted themselves to the exigencies of the modern life.

*Elder Richards gave a priesthood blessing to Dora Lencina when she was ill. Courtesy of CHL.*

A chief of the said sect, Mr. Stephen L. Richards, who is visiting our country, proceeding from the United States and has just realized an interesting tour of all of the principal Argentine cities, will preach today, at 10 o'clock, in the temple that the aforementioned cult has established at 1169 63rd St. Mr. Richards will arrive accompanied by the president of the mission in Buenos Aires, Mr. W. Ernest Young, and will be received by the integrants of the local branch, Mss'rs. Gorton, Ogden, Bruce, and Marsh.

### ELDER HOWARD J. MARSH, ARGENTINE MISSION HISTORICAL REPORT[75]

Feb. 22, 1948. Conference at La Plata. Remarks by Elders Pierce Brady, H.J. Marsh, President Young, and Elder Stephen L. Richards. 81 in attendance. Elder Richards' theme—"The dignity of man."

Dined at noon in the home of the Salvioli family. Visited a sick member, Dora Lencina, and returned to the Capital in the afternoon.

### ELDER H. CLAY GORTON MISSIONARY JOURNAL[76]

Sunday Pres. Young & Bro. Brady came for Priesthood Meeting & at 10:00 we held a Special Conference for Apostle Richards. . . .

There are certain conditions existing in the Branch on which a certain amount of advice is necessary. If Apostle Richards had known all these conditions he could not have spoken better or more to the Subject.[77] or written policy for [the] District.

### IRENE M. RICHARDS LETTER[78]

Buenos Aires
Feb. 22, 1948

Dear Lynn:[79]

We have been traveling for nearly two weeks south to Rosario and west to Mendosa and are now back in B.A. It's good to return to the mission home after trying anything once. We enjoyed the auto, although it has been hot and not very good roads. There are always some parks, hotels, shops which are special about each town and we have been staying in the Palace, the Plaza and all the best hotels, which are old and "passe". When we finally got one with good plumbing, there was no water for it. So I enjoy the old Spanish romance of the beauty of the past and Papa endures the accommodations and hopes for the better one next place. The best is none too good. Oh, how this country needs a little freedom. There is such a richness to the soil and so much of it, that democracy would make it grow fast.

*Baptisms (left) and baptismal service (right) in La Plata, Argentina, on March 22, 1947. Courtesy of CHL.*

We nearly met "Peron".[80] He ran across us on a street. All of a sudden the sirens blew and all policemen ordered our car to the side; and apast us whizzed about a dozen cars. He was coming home to his palace on the River after his official day in the "Pink House". I guess Pink is to distinguish it from our "White House" in U.S. and it is tinted pink.

Now, we have met all of the missionaries in Argentina. They are all fine and enthusiastic and efficient and rather an unusual number of them talented in music. This helps most in the concerts they give, whereby they meet the more cultured citizens. If they just tract, the contacts are very lowly and unintelligent. So many are uneducated, and it is to the youth we must look for future members. They have no religion, ordinarily, and are hoping for freedom in education. Some don't even know what the Bible is. The Mutual and Primary seem to do a fine work for after 10 years the children remember some good things and are attracted to the missionaries when they meet them. By one means and another, they are hopeful and energetic in their jobs, preaching, teaching Eng. [English] classes, singing, playing basket ball, cottage meetings, etc.

At every "locale"[81] (which means branch) the saints have given us a great welcome. They have put on programs and dances, in Spanish, so we really don't know what has been said about us. I can recognize some words and know when they are addressing us by their expressions and motions. It's quite disconcerting, and (tiresome) to sit at attention, and try to look intelligent. Papa always speaks for me, and does a very good job. They have showered us with flowers, cakes, sweaters, doilies, handkerchiefs, scarfs, and even a toothpick holder. They have the deplorable habit

*The Youngs and the Richardses in front of the monument "Hill of Glory" in Mendoza, a tribute to the army of the Andes. Courtesy of CHL.*

here of picking teeth, but maybe that is not the worst thing. The saints and all are killing us with kindness. We will have finished with Argentina by Friday, when we take the boat for Uruguay. Papa has some special work here with the branch and mission home for two or three days to finish up. That gives me an opportunity to wash my hair and clean up in general. What is the advice in the Testament, "When you leave a city shake the dust off your feet"?

Well, we are not going to Chile. It's too high for Papa, and there is plenty to do here. . . .

After a very long drive on our way home, Papa was somewhat tired, but by resting a day he recovered. The weather is very hot and we are not accustomed to it. The nights are cool and the people don't go to bed until after midnight, so by morning it is more pleasant. As soon as the evening comes, everyone seems to be either sitting in doorways, or on sidewalks, or walking in parks and on beaches. They rest in their dark houses during the heat. I guess they know what they are doing when they take a "siesta" thru the heat of the day, but we kept on traveling, which was a mistake. There are no screens or windows or doors and in order to keep insects out and their houses cool, places are kept dark. Maybe that's why so many have poor eyesight?

*Catholic cathedral in La Plata visited by the Richardses. Courtesy of CHL.*

At "La Platte"[82] we saw the museum where is displayed many prehistoric monsters. We also saw a Cathedral of great beauty inside.

At Mendosa we were near the Chilean border. The Andes were wonderful, with snow. They seemed rugged and about as our Rockies look. The soil is red like Bryce and the streams are red, although there have been no storms lately.

Papa is fine again and I am also. Lois's letter took one month to come. Louise's and Allie's, air mail, five days. Thanks for all correspondence. We know you are well thereby. Maybe there will be further word from home in Uruguay.

Lovingly,<br>Mother.

---

## BUENOS AIRES, ARGENTINA

**Monday, February 23, 1948**

**Daily Summary**
*Meeting with Argentine Mission presidency and letter to the First Presidency*

### ELDER HOWARD J. MARSH, ARGENTINE MISSION HISTORICAL REPORT[83]

<u>Feb. 23, 1948.</u> Elder Richards and President Young spent the morning in consultation with Elder L. Pierce Brady, and the afternoon in consultation with the newly formed presidency of the mission[84]—President Young, Elder Brady, and Elder E. Stott. Remained overnight in the home of Elder Brady.

### W. ERNEST YOUNG LETTER[85]

Mr. Henry A. Smith,<br>Editor, Church News Section,<br>The Deseret news Publishing Company,<br>Salt Lake City, Utah.

Dear Brother Smith:

Thank you for your letter advising of the new "mission section: of the Church News Section of the Deseret News. We are sure that news from the missions will be of great interest not only to ex-missionaries, but also to all readers of the News. We are happy to hear of the development of this important section.

Following is a brief biographical sketch of the members of the new presidency of this mission. Please feel free to alter it as you see fit.

"During the visit of Elder Stephen L. Richards, the organization of the Presidency of the Argentine Mission was completed.

"President W. Ernest Young has been presiding over this mission since September, 1944. He is a veteran missionary, having served in the Mexican Mission from 1910 to 1913. After serving as Bishop of the Juarez Ward, Juarez Stake from 1922 to 1933 and a teacher in the Juarez Stake Academy from 1919, President Young attended the Brigham Young University from 1933 to 1935 when he received a degree in Education. He was then called to serve as President of the Argentine Mission from 1935 to 1938 after which he returned to his teaching post in Juarez until called upon his present mission. Many years of experience and faithful service in various callings in the Church and his excellent knowledge of Latin American culture and customs especially qualify him for the responsibility he now holds. He is accompanied and efficiently aided by Mrs. Young.

"President L. Peirce Brady was set apart as First Counselor in the mission presidency in October, 1947 by President George F. Richards in Salt Lake City. Elder Brady was a missionary in the Argentine Mission from 1936 to 1939. He is a graduate of the Georgetown University, Washington, D.C., having studied Economics and International Trade. He served for several years as economic adviser in the American Embassy in Brazil and is at present Managing Director of the Iromac Commerical Corporation and Vice President of the Pan America Trade Development Corporation. He is residing with his wife and two daughters in Buenos Aires.

President E. Keith Stott was set apart as Second Counselor in February, 1948 by Elder Stephen L. Richards in Buenos Aires. Elder Stott studied Business Administration two years at Brigham Young University and one year at George Washington University before being called to Army service from 1942 to 1946. During this period he served as an Administrative Assistant in the Office of the Chief of Staff in the War Department and accompanied General George C. Marshall on trips abroad upon several occasions as personal secretary. He received the Legion of Merit for his Army services. He was called on a mission from the Arlington Ward, Arlington, Virginia in January, 1946 and was joined by Mrs. Stott and son in March 1947."

Enclosed is a photograph of the Argentine Mission Presidency.

We will try to comply with your request for mission news and hope to be able to forward to you from time to time items of interest.

Please accept our best wishes for continued success.

Very sincerely, your brethren<br>
Argentine Mission Presidency,<br>
by _____<br>
W. Ernest Young, President.<br>
Encl. photo

## STEPHEN L RICHARDS LETTER[86]

February 23, 1948<br>
The First Presidency<br>
47 E. South Temple St.<br>
Salt Lake City, Utah

Dear Brother:

We were happy to receive your letter of February 13th after you had received our cable. We have just finished a long and rather strenuous journey through the branches of the mission. We shall not attempt at this time to describe our experiences or the conditions we found. Suffice it to say that we believe the work is progressing in spite of handicaps.

We found all missionaries, with two or three exceptions, to be in good health, and steps are being taken to improve the conditions of those who are not well. We have extended your love and blessings to all the Saints and your greetings to many friends. Our reception has been most cordial wherever we have been. Our speaking through an interpreter, of course, has not been too satisfactory, but we have done what we could to help convey the message of the Church to those who have listened to us. We shall have much of a detailed nature to report to you on return.

During a part of the time we were away, Brother Brady, ~~Chief~~ Counselor in the Mission Presidency, has endeavored to make a study of housing, and the next few days here will be given over in a large measure to the continuation of that study. Nothing very concrete has yet developed.

You were kind enough in your letter to sound a caution about health. I am pleased to report that I have been th[r]ough the ordeal of travel and meetings and come out in pretty good shape. We think that the most strenuous time is over now. With the exception of a slight illness, Irene went through exceptionally well.

Our reservations are now almost complete for the following schedule: We leave Buenos Aires on February 27th for Montevideo. We leave Montevideo for the Brazilian mission on the Moore-McCormack boat, SS URUGUAY, March the 5th. We arrive at Santos, Brazil, March 8th and spend until March the 22nd in the Brazilian mission. On March 22nd, we sail on the SS ARGENTINA for New York, reaching there April the 5th. Unfortunately, this schedule will not get us home in time for Conference, but it is the best we can do on the transportation available to us. We have felt to follow the doctor's advice and not fly. We made arrangements so that we could have gone from Mendoza in the western part of Argentina to Santiago, Chile, but discovered that by railroad or auto, we would have to ascend elevations above 12,000 feet or fly up to 22,000 feet without pressurized cabin planes, so we decided it would be unwise to undertake the trip. We do have, however, reports from a number of men whom we have met who have had experience in Chile.

We hope this will find you all in good health. With our kindest regards to yourselves and the brethren, we are

Affectionately yours,
[Stephen L Richards]

## BUENOS AIRES, ARGENTINA

**Tuesday, February 24, 1948**

**Daily Summary**
*Irene reflects on events in Buenos Aires and Elder Richards prepares final instructions*

# IRENE M. RICHARDS LETTER[87]

Buenos Aires, Argentina
Feb. 24, 1948

Dear Georgia:[88]

Since we received your letter here we have traveled over Argentina to Rosaria in the south, where the roads ended up in dirt, and to Mendosa, to the west, where we saw the Andes....

At every city is a Palace, or Plaza Hotel. We have had the best and they are beautiful in Spanish style, but not American by any means. We are doing fine though and hope to live until spring. We can't realize that it is cold at Toledo, when we are melting and eating fruit and seeing flowers in profusion. The moon even seems different. We really see it on another side, don't we? There is no dipper, we see instead the southern cross. The sky and stars are very wonderful and clear.

There are no screens on houses and they must keep shutters closed to keep out insects and heat. So houses are dark but cool, and the mosquitoes do their dirty work at night. You wouldn't know your own mother now, but no one else knows how she should look so it doesn't seem so bad. This hired girl at the mission says she thinks Mrs. Richards is the sweetest person she has met; no doubt the mosquitoes thought the same thing last night. So I am doing O.K. It got around the mission that it was our 48th and we have received flowers and cakes, and a sweater hdkf [handkerchief], and scarf, and at least 6 telegrams. These people are killing us with kindness.... We met some college students from Peru who are sons of rich land owners, studying at La Platta University.[89] One of our missionary boys from San Leandro[90] is teaching them English. They were very interested in U.S. and knew something of some Californian names of cities, but they were eating up the Book of Mormon. Our boys make many friends at the universities with their chorus and basket ball team. The young people are the ones most interested in our church. The 3rd largest cathedral[91] in the world is here, a very magnificent interior, tall white marble pillars, gothic ceiling and marble floors (polished like glass) and stained glass windows. We also saw the museum of prehistoric animals. I think Noah was unable to get them into the ark, they were so huge and fierce, that's why they are extinct now. Papa says he's not worrying about that phase of creation, but it's wonderfully interesting.

Next week we start touring Uruguay. . . .

We hope you are well, and we thank you for your letters. . . .

Lovingly,<br>Mother.

### W. ERNEST YOUNG, ARGENTINE MISSION PRESIDENT[92]

**Final Instructions of Apostle Richards**

February 24, 25, and 26 Elder Stephen L. Richards spent most of the time on these dates at the mission home making his summary of his visit to the mission. He prepared his recommendations and counsel for the mission, offering suggestions that would help the proselyting work, also concerning costs of rentals, and the part to be paid by the elders.

### BUENOS AIRES, ARGENTINA

**Thursday, February 26, 1948**

**Daily Summary**
*Reviewed reports and attended baby blessing*

### ELDER HOWARD J. MARSH, ARGENTINE MISSION HISTORICAL REPORT[93]

**Feb. 26, 1948.** Spent the morning reviewing missionary reports. Lunched at the home of Pedro Sanchez (member from the Rama

*Baby Diana with her parents, Dale M. and Jean Christensen, in Palermo Park. Courtesy of Diana Christensen.*

*Blessing certificate of Diana Christensen. Courtesy of Diana Christensen.*

of Liniers). Spent the afternoon and evening in reviewing the mission situation with President Young. At night, as invited guests of President Young, dined with Brother and Sister Dale Christensen. Brother Christensen is a former Argentine missionary now connected with the embassy. A father's blessing was given to their baby, who was given the name of Diana Maria Christensen. Elder Stephen L. Richards acted as mouthpiece. He was joined in the circle by the father, President W. Ernest Young, and Elder J. S. Brammer.

## BUENOS AIRES, ARGENTINA

### Friday, February 27, 1948

### Daily Summary

*Meeting with Argentine and Uruguayan Mission presidents, departure by ship to Uruguay, observations of and recommendations for the mission, summary of Argentine tour, and letter from Elder Richards to the Argentine Saints*

### W. ERNEST YOUNG, ARGENTINE MISSION PRESIDENT[94]

February 27 a mission presidency's meeting was held at the mission home, with President Frederick S. Williams attending from Uruguay. Elder Richards conducted, and gave his final impressions and instructions for the two missions regarding the possible cooperation with literature and other Church facilities. In the evening Apostle and Sister Richards left on the riverboat for Montevideo, Uruguay. This is the first time that I had seen one of the General Authorities in the mission in my ten years in three foreign missions. Times have changed with faster and better travel and communications. This has been a great privilege to travel with an apostle and listen to his inspirational counsel.

### IRENE M. RICHARDS JOURNAL[95]

Bro. Brady [first counselor in the mission presidency] made a talk at the farewell meeting for us at Buenos Aires. He said "He had been in consultation with Government Officials in the U.S. and also with big business men of the countries, and after sitting in session with Bro Richards for several hours, talking about mission affairs, he had concluded that he had never met a man with such clear, good judgment and reasoning, and directive power as Bro Richards. He said if these said executives could have the acumen that Bro Richards had, what a great good could be accomplished." And Brady is the head of a few million dollar corporation. maybe he knows.

### MISSION PRESIDENCY MEETING[96]

Extracts of discussion held in Mission Presidency Meeting in Buenos Aires, 27 Feb 1948 directed by Elder Stephen L. Richards and attended by President W. Ernest Young with his two councilors (1) Elder Peirce L. Brady and (2) E. Keith Stott, and by President Frederick S. Williams.

## Locales

Brother Richards said that the system of locales used in the Argentine and Uruguayan missions was something new to him in missionary work; that they have apparently served a good purpose in times past and perhaps are the best available means at present. There are 23 locales in Argentina at present for which rent is paid. Query: Is the locale system better for the missionaries than "pensiones" (boarding houses)?

Bro. Williams said that a better method would be to build chapels with missionary quarters which is, of course, out of the question at present. Further stated that the system of pensiones was employed at one time with very poor results. At no time was the system successful. The food was different from that <to> which the elders were accustomed and was very bad. The natives prepare very greasy food including much pastry, etc. Very little advancement was made in missionary work under this system; missionaries had no place to which they could invite investigators for meetings. It is better to rent a place and invite friends to it. It is true that "friends" were made in the pensiones, but no members. Bro. Williams mentioned the case of some ex-Brazilian missionaries who were in their mission many months without the opportunity of offering a prayer in public or holding meetings, blessing sacrament, etc. for lack of a place in which to meet. There are at present seven (7) locales in Uruguay which are generally better than those in the Argentine Mission; a higher rental is paid, the average being around $55.00 per month. They were fortunate in renting new homes just about in the locations desired.

Bro. Richards pointed out several differences in the situation in the U.S.: Halls can there be rented or borrowed; schools can be utilized to hold meetings in, etc. Good boarding houses are available to the missionaries. He observed that locale rentals in the Argentine Mission are rather modest, the highest being at present $62.50 per month and the lowest around $16.00. Query: Could we hope to get better places by paying more rental? Could we consistently ask the missionaries to increase their contribution to the payment of rent?

Bro. Young stressed the difficulty in finding locales to rent; owners would rather sell at present than rent. Even after months of trying—using banks, newspaper adds and walking the streets—we have not been successful in obtaining locales to meet our needs.

Bro. Richards felt that asking higher rent from the elders would be justified. Although he had <heard> that missionaries could possibly get board and room here for about $25.00 a month, this policy is not acceptable. Inadequacy of the board in the pensiones was stressed by all present as being detrimental to the health of the elders over a period of time. The average contribution of missionaries per month toward paying rent of locales is $3.75 per individual. Missionaries in Uruguay are paying $5.50 each (in better locales).

Missionaries spend on an average of about $21.00 for food and room under the locale system although their total expenses run to an average of $50-52 per month. Some investment items, however, are included in this figure in cases, such as clothing, bicycles, etc. Food is generally much cheaper here than in U.S. Milk, 8 cents a litre; bread, 10 cents a heavy loaf; meat, 20 cents a pound for choice cuts; eggs, 45 cents a dozen (which is temporarily high price). Fresh vegetables cost about the same or in some items a little more than in the U.S. Canned foods used very little; prices exorbitant.

Bro. Richards pointed out that the Church makes an investment of about $1,000 in each missionary in the mission (transportation, etc.). Perhaps they should not get preference in expenses. Average rental of $3.75 does not seem quite fair in the Church and is below average in other missions. Seventy-nine (79) missionaries in the mission are paying a total of about $288.00 of a total rent paid of $646.00—about 45%. If increased to $5.00, the total paid by the missionaries would be $395.00, or about 60% of total rental. The Church is now paying as its share of the rental about $15.00 per month per local (average). This would not seem high at first glance, but upon considering the membership, it is a rather high per-capita rental.

Unanimously agreed that the regular weekly reporting system would be put into practice at once.

### *Study*

Bro. Richards emphasized that missionaries should not get into debates among themselves. Established principles and methods of approach, etc., should be stressed in study. Study must be supervised. Tracting methods should be studied and the "know-how" acquired by missionaries.

Reports should be studied carefully to determine, for example, if a missionary is spending too much time visiting saints and too little tracting and other proselyting.

Mission president should teach elders how to hold cottage meetings. Steps toward acquiring meetings might be: (1) get into the home; (2) use available slides, etc. (3) have prayer and songs; and (4) introduce lessons on the Gospel.

### Games and Musicales

Pres. Young said that the group of "Traveling Elders" (including 12 men composing a chorus and basketball team) had trained to render this service for a period of about two months. It is felt that they have made a great contribution in introducing the Church. The efforts of former organizations of this nature have attracted people to the Church who later became good members. Tracting and preaching when possible are included in the activities of the group.

Bro. Richards remarked that the great spiritual message should be kept foremost in the minds of the elders devoted to this work and every effort made to capitalize on their efforts. Work should be well supervised. When a missionary goes home, he should feel he has been on a mission and delivered his message.

### Club

Bro. Richards opined that, since recreation has an important place in our program, the club could stand improvement and made more attractive.

### Recreation Hall

Agreed by all that a recreation hall would be a very desirable thing. It should be built in such a location that it could be put to good use among the branches. In any building program, it would be among the first items. Would not have to be of expensive construction. It was felt that a basketball court should be included. Tile or cement floor could be used and would be cheaper than wood in this country. A plain finish would be adequate for recreation and for district and bi-annual mission conferences. A tentative project for the presidency of the mission would be to look for a lot and secure an estimate of costs of construction of a recreation hall.

### Mission Home
Bro. Richards favors the Belgrano section of Buenos Aires because it is more accessible to the center of town, where many transactions of the office force take place; it gives better impression as it is in a far better section of town than Liniers; it offers good school facilities to children of mission presidents. There are many large homes in the area, one of which could probably be purchased much more cheaply than a comparable building could be erected. <u>Recommended that the mission presidency be authorized to make a search with a view to obtaining a suitable mission home in Belgrano</u>. <u>Sustained by all present</u>.

### Chapels
It was <u>agreed</u> that the following steps be taken: (1) improve locales to the extent feasible; (2) as soon as possible get land and an estimate of costs and build a suitable hall for recreation and to take care of conferences; (3) find and buy a suitable mission home when the opportunity presents itself.

The present church-owned club could be sold to apply on the recreation hall. Space could possibly be acquired to include later on an adjoining chapel. Bro. Richards ventured a rough estimate that a hall would probably not cost less than 35–40 thousand dollars. The site of present club not considered appropriate.

The building of one or more chapels would depend on the progress of the work after the above projects have been completed. When the <u>need develops</u>, it would be a desirable thing to have a chapel in Buenos Aires. It would seem better in the beginning to have one big, creditable chapel (80–100 thousand dollars) than to build first small chapels in the area. Chapels in the interior cities must depend on needs.

### Branch Administration
Brother Richards suggested working toward local (native) administration as soon as possible. Clear the missionaries for proselyting work. The matter was left for study, having in mind (1) opening the way for more service outside the branch organization by missionaries (2) developing individual responsibility of branch members.

### Hospital and Clinic Service

Mission has been donating 500 pesos per year to the British Hospital and receiving free medical attention for the missionaries. Services received to date far exceed this nominal amount. We should have an understanding with the officials of the hospital as to the adequacy of our donation in view of increased number of missionaries. Bro. Richards felt it would be advisable to give all missionaries an examination each year to insure their health.

### Literature

Bro. Richards remarked that these missions should share in the new, attractive literature which the Church is putting out. U.S. tracts could be copied or adapted and printed in the mission. Is convinced that more books should be obtained. Spanish translation work is going forward. Bro. [Eduardo] Balderas needs a larger staff. Bro. Gordon Hinkley manager of the Church Literature Committee, will push the work.

Bro. Richards will recommend that the book by Bro. Hinkley ("What of the Mormons") be printed in Spanish. It would seem that the people need a non-controversial history of the church. Bro. Richards will suggest: (1) that steps be taken to get out immediately the translations already prepared; (2) that Bro. Balderas be provided with additional help; (3) that lessons be provided promptly; (4) that a search be made for materials to be adapted to our needs.

Argentine saints available to aid in translations are: Sister Euridece Turano, now attending the "Y"; Brother Fermín C. Barjollo, Córdoba, Argentina; and Sister Amalia Taffuri, who intends to leave Argentina for Provo in April, 1948 to attend the "Y" this fall.

### Missionary Training

Missionaries are here kept in the office three or four days upon arrival for orientation purposes, taking care of documents in Embassy, etc. Short classes and discussions give the president an opportunity to observe and properly assign missionaries.

Special language training in U.S. of missionaries for 3 months before departure would not seem advisable. Practical training in the mission seems to get the best results in the given time.

*Government Relations*
The Catholic clergy, which has a strong influence in immigration policy of the government, would oppose us as much as possible in anything we tried. It is felt advisable by all to avoid the raising of questions with the Argentine government. Missionaries should not be sent to the mission in groups of more than 5 or 6 in order not to alarm the clergy. It was suggested that we get names of missionaries from Salt Lake in sufficient time and procure landing permits as prescribed by the law of the country. The word "<u>missionary</u>" should <u>not</u> be used in application for passports in the U.S. "<u>Representative</u>" should be substituted. We should, of course, aim to make as many influential business friends as possible.

*Communications with Headquarters*
Any light mail of importance should be sent by air. Equipment such as projectors, etc., could be brought into the country through the missionaries as part of their standard equipment. Films might possibly be sent by air if necessary without import difficulties, but best to send by missionaries.

*Budget*
Bro. Richards suggested making an amended budget in view of organization of the mission presidency and other items recommended, including improving locales, higher rents, purchasing of bedding, etc.

*Packages from Home*
Parents should not send packages to missionaries because of the money and time needed in getting them out of the "aduana" (customs). In some instances the duty exceeds the value of the gifts. Perhaps the "Church News" could be utilized in securing the cooperation of relatives and friends. Missionaries should advise their own people.

*Office Organization*
Bro. Richards believes that the missionary staff in the office can be readily persuaded that efficient business methods are as helpful to them as to everyone else and to comply with a schedule and organization that is exacting. A well-defined plan is necessary. The matter should be studied thoroughly. Charts depicting positions and line of authority is always

helpful. When each one knows his duty, all enjoy their work more. Although the conveniences are bad in present home, they need not stand in the way of a well-defined organization. Get into a routine, allowing for exceptions.

### Mission Presidency

Suggested that Bro. Stott study offices activities, diagram the situation, and make recommendations to the presidency with the opportunity of carrying them out if approved. Bro. Brady could do the same in branch organization. Proper care of the missionaries is dependent to a very large degree upon the office organization. Time spent in the various activities of the office staff could well be studied with a view to greater efficiency.

Bro. Richards suggested that the doors of the office be kept locked and that no one enter unnecessarily. People could knock and call the person with whom they wish to speak into the hall to converse; entire office force should not be disturbed by the conversation of two individuals. Missionaries should <u>not</u> come to the office for mail. Those in the district should have little more reason to come to headquarters than those in the interior. It involves much wasted time.

### Mate[97]

Bro. Brady will send samples of mate by mail to Bro. Richard's office. A competent, impartial analysis will be made before final decision is handed down on the harmfulness of the drink. Mate is not a problem in the Uruguayan Mission.

### Mission Magazine ("El Mensajero")[98]

Serves the two missions.[99] Provides translated articles and talks by the general authorities from the *Era, Church News, Relief Society Magazine, The Instructor*, church books and other literature otherwise not available to this people. Includes local news for both missions and articles and editorials by both presidents.

Bro. Richards requested that when a study has been made of office organization, the magazine for the two missions, etc. a report be sent <u>directly to him</u> giving an outline of organization, assignments, etc.

*Return Travel*
Some missionaries want to go home by round-about routes. It is felt that permission of parents should be secured and that parents be advised that additional costs and risks are involved if such is the case.

At present there are only two passenger agencies to the States: Moore-McCormack to New York (1st class about $600 and 2nd about $425) and Delta to New Orleans (only one class, about $600). Passage by cargo boat is from $375 up to $500.

**Visiting Missions**
Visiting between missions on semi-annual conferences is objectionable. Mission presidents should not leave missions. If an exception is made, the First Presidency should be consulted.

**Conferences**
Conferences of church held in Buenos Aires twice a year. All missionaries have been attending. These conferences give the members a chance to visit and gives them and friends some concept of the magnitude of the organization and work. Five to six hundred people attend the variety programs, and the Liniers chapel is overflowing during the three religious sessions on Sunday. Meetings of mission auxiliaries held on Saturday. Youth convention held in conjunction with one conference and the Gold and Green Ball in connection with the other offer young people the opportunity to mix.

Bro. Richards does not intend to represent these people as having all the characteristics of an honest people with the integrity necessary for a great advancement in the work of the gospel. Expenditure of missionary efforts and funds should proceed with precaution. He is not favorable to going all-out in making big investments unless more advancement is made than demonstrated up to now.

Dear Elder Richards:

I have included in these notes some detail which may be of no value, with a view to reminding you in a small degree of the trend of discussion.

Let me again express my keen appreciation for your visit and your helpful guidance.

> Very sincerely,
> /s/ Elder E. Keith Stott
> E. Keith Stott

## ELDER HOWARD J. MARSH, ARGENTINE MISSION HISTORICAL REPORT[100]

<u>Feb. 27, 1948.</u> President and Sister F[rederick] Williams of the Uruguayan Mission arrived in the morning. The day was spent in consultation with the Presidency of the Argentine Mission and President Williams. At night a farewell party was held in the Liniers chapel. (6 p.m. to 7 p.m.). 120 were present. Departed from Argentina on the river-boat bound for Montivideo, Uruguay, in the company of President and Sister Williams, at 10 p.m.

> BON VOYAGE/
> s/s H.J. Marsh

## NEWS ARTICLE: *CHURCH NEWS*[101]

**An Apostle Tours Argentina**

> By Elder H. J. Marsh
> (Special To The Church News)

Buenos Aires, Argentina—Millions of Argentinians were informed of the visit here during the past month of Elder Stephen L Richards of the Council of the Twelve through the great newspapers of this country.

But to the people of the interior among whom are many of the members of the Church in this land the visit of the Apostle was heralded by the sight of a blue Ford car bouncing along back-woods roads still bearing the license plates which proclaim Utah as "This is the Place."

The meaning of this phrase was explained to the delight of the crowds, large or small, which gathered around the car at each country stop....

Traveling exclusively by automobile, Elder Richards completed a 2,600 mile trip that took him to every district of the Argentine Mission. This extensive tour gave every member and every missionary in this vast country an opportunity to meet the Church leader. For most all of the members it was a first chance to see and talk with one of the general authorities of the Church. This is the first South American visit of a general authority since Elder Melvin J. Ballard created the mission in 1925.

The tour of Argentina began officially with a report and testimony meeting of the missionaries of the Buenos Aires district on February 7....

On Sunday, February 8, Elder Richards visited four of the local branches in Buenos Aires. At night a special district conference was held with 338 in attendance and a translation of Elder Richard's address to the congregation was made by Mission President W. Ernest Young.

Monday was spent in travel to Tres Arroyos, 500 kilometers to the south. Another missionary meeting was held for elders in the Tres Arroyos, Tandil, and Bahia Blanca branches, comprising the district.

A highlight of the stop here was the baptism service the following day in which eight persons, seven of one family, were baptized and confirmed members of the Church, the father being confirmed by Elder Richards.

That night a special conference was held in Tres Arroyos and to an audience of 78 people the visiting Apostle spoke on the theme, "Brotherly love through the eyes of a Latter-day Saint."

This concluded the first part of the mission tour. The next day was spent in returning to Buenos Aires and preparation for the westward swing of 2,000 miles for a visit to the more remote parts of the mission.

In brief this western trip consisted of a stop at Pergamino, where a chapel recently acquired by the Church was dedicated; inspection of the chapel at San Nicolas; a three-day conference at Rosario and a one day stop-over and conference in Cordoba, Rio Cuarto, and Mendoza.

In Rosario the paths of Elder Richards and the "traveling missionaries" crossed. The latter is a group of elders having special musical and athletic talents, who are touring the republic giving concerts, and playing basketball against the best teams of the country. Both the programs and games are meeting with great success and the Argentine people are coming to know the Church because of the favorable publicity given to the team of "Los Mormones."

The Church leader's last official visit was made in La Plata. There a two-day reception and conference was held during which Elder and Mrs. Richards were especially honored on their 48th wedding anniversary.

The people of the Argentina Mission are deeply grateful for this opportunity of meeting Elder Richards; they now feel more a part of the great Church organization; their testimonies have been strengthened and they look forward with zeal to the future of the Church in their land.

Their constant thoughts and prayers are with the men who have been called to guide them. They wish to be remembered to the former missionaries, and send their "Saludos" to their brethren in "Los Estados Unidos de Norte America."

### STEPHEN L RICHARDS LETTER[102]

#### Suggestive Message for Mission Paper

*Latter-day Saints in Argentina*

It has been a rare privilege as we have traveled through the mission to greet our brothers and sisters in the several branches. Although the meetings have been held in humble places, we have received a royal welcome. The warm handclasps, the smiling and happy faces and other expressions of good will, although some were in language we could not understand, have breathed a cordiality in true brotherhood that has touched our hearts. We give our thanks to all.

It has been gratifying to observe your interest and activity in the work of the Lord. Our commendation goes out to all who have given support to the organizations of the church in good lives and faithful labors. Our Father will abundantly bless those who are true to Him.

We hope that <our> brethren and sisters will ever be aware of the ~~great~~ high contribution they may make to the great country in which they live. It is a rich land with abundant resources, and equable climate and unusual beauty. It sorely needs the principals and the way of life which have come to men through the restored gospel of our Lord Jesus Christ to further its economic, cultural and spiritual development. If its' people could come to understand <and accept> this divinely given way of life its they would be happy, and the high destiny of the nation would be assured. Every righteous Latter Day Saint can make a contribution to that end.

If our visit shall in any measure serve to remind our members that we of the Church belong to one great true brotherhood, we shall be very grateful indeed.

Let it always be remembered that while there may be differences in language, customs and environment, there is one common purpose,— To establish the Kingdom of God in earth, which shall bring to all who embrace it peace and joy in this life, and exaltation in the presence of the Father and the Son in the life to come. As we depart from the mission, we leave with the members of the church and their friends, who have so graciously greeted us our love and blessing and favor from the first Presidency of the Church, whose humble representatives we are. We have made observations concerning the needs of the people in the various establishments of the Church which we will in due course report to our brethren at headquarters. We have been impressed with the devoted services of the missionaries with President Young at their head, and we earnestly plead with all, members and friends alike, to give heed to their message and support to their unselfish labor of love.

Gratefully and faithfully yours,

Brother and Sister Stephen L. Richards

## NOTES

1. Howard J. Marsh, "Historical Report of Stephen L Richards's Visit to the Argentine Mission," February 3–27, 1948, Stephen L Richards Papers, 1921–59, CHL. Marsh recorded this report while serving as the mission secretary in the Argentine Mission
2. The name of the newspaper translates into English as "The Reason."
3. The name of the newspaper translates into English as "Criticism."
4. The name of the newspaper translates into English as "The Graphic News."
5. *La Crítica* (Buenos Aires), February 3, 1948, 5, Argentine Mission Manuscript History and Historical Reports, CHL.

6. The reference is to branches of the Church, not missions.
7. Mahatma Gandhi, a worldwide pacifist and Hindu leader in India, was assassinated on January 30, 1948, a few days before the Richardses arrived in Argentina.
8. Irene Richards, *Dear Children*, February 4, 1948, Richards Family Papers, 1879–2004, CHL.
9. Philip Longstroth Richards was the Richardses' eighth child.
10. Irene received letters from three of her children: Alice Leila Richards, Richard M. Richards, and Irene "Louise" Richards.
11. Richards, *Dear Children*, February 4, 1948.
12. Alice "Allie" Leila Richards was the Richardses' fourth child.
13. Jesse Knight Allen was Alice's husband.
14. Marsh, "Historical Report."
15. Welcome meeting.
16. "Mormon Apostle, Who Has Just Arrived in Buenos Aires, Admires Gandhi," *La Crítica*, February 4, 1948, Stephen L Richards Papers. This article appears here as translated into English by Elder Howard J. Marsh, with original spelling and punctuation preserved. The dashes signal quoted matter.
17. See note 7 above.
18. Elder Richards made brief stopovers in Brazil and Uruguay as his boat made its way to Argentina. His actual mission tour would start in Argentina, continue to Uruguay, and conclude with Brazil.
19. This apparently unpublished article was attached to the English translation of the *La Crítica* article "Mormon Apostle, Who Has Just Arrived in Buenos Aires, Admires Gandhi." It is filed in the Stephen L Richards Papers.
20. Marsh, "Historical Report."
21. *Rama* is the Spanish word for a branch or unit of the Church.
22. Richards, *Dear Children*, February 6, 1948.
23. Lois and Louise were the Richardses' third and second of nine children.
24. A famous opera written by Giacomo Puccini and first performed in 1904.
25. Stephen L Richards to the First Presidency, February 6, 1948, Stephen L Richards Papers.
26. Elder Richards's signature appeared here.
27. Walter Ernest Young, *The Diary of W. Ernest Young* (Salt Lake City: n.p., 1973), 449.

28. W. Ernest Young to Henry A. Smith, May 20, 1948, Argentine Mission President's Records, 1946–56, CHL. Smith was editor of the *Church News*, and President Young sent this information about Brother Brady: "President L. Pierce Brady was set apart as First Counselor in the mission presidency in October, 1947 by President George F. Richards in Salt Lake City. Elder Brady was a missionary in the Argentine Mission from 1936 to 1939. He is a graduate of the Georgetown University, Washington, D.C., having studied Economics and International Trade. He served for several years as economic adviser in the American Embassy in Brazil and is at present Managing Director of the Iromac Commercial Corporation and Vice President of the Pan American Trade Development Corporation. He is residing with his wife and two daughters in Buenos Aires."
29. Marsh, "Historical Report."
30. See Ramos Mejía Branch Manuscript History and Historical Reports, 1935–53, CHL. Ramos Mejía is a small city in the greater Buenos Aires area. A branch started there in 1935.
31. See Haedo Branch Manuscript History and Historical Reports, 1935–54, CHL. Haedo is a city located a few miles west of the Federal District of Buenos Aires in the province of Buenos Aires. A branch was started there in 1935.
32. See Ciudadela Branch Manuscript History and Historical Reports, 1936–52, CHL. Ciudadela is a city in Buenos Aires and is west of the Liniers area. A branch started there in 1936.
33. Young, *Diary*, 450.
34. See Tres Arroyos Branch Manuscript History and Historical Reports, 1941–83, CHL. *Tres Arroyos* literally means "three streams." Tres Arroyos is a city 289 miles south of Buenos Aires and inland from the Atlantic coast.
35. Branches began in these cities in the following years: Tres Arroyos (1941), Bahía Blanca (1938), Tandil (1941), and Coronel Suárez (1939). Many branches were closed or curtailed during the Second World War. The branches were starting to grow again by the time of the Richardses' visit in 1948. See Tres Arroyos Branch Manuscript History and Historical Reports; Bahía Blanca Branch Manuscript History and Historical Reports, 1938–83, CHL; Tandil Branch Manuscript History and Historical Reports, 1941–83, CHL; Coronel Suárez Branch Manuscript History and Historical Reports, 1939–77, CHL.
36. Edwin Richardson to Ray Richardson, February 11, 1948, Edwin J. Richardson Papers, CHL.

37. Edwin Richardson to Ray Richardson, February 11, 1948.
38. Irene Richards to Ellen and Lloyd Bolton, February 11, 1948, Ernest L. Carroll Jr. Mission History, 31, in private possession.
39. Ernest L. Carroll. Ernest Leroi Carroll Jr. served a mission in Argentina from 1946 to 1948. His aunt and uncle Lloyd William Bolton and Ellen Maxwell Bolton lived in Salt Lake City and were friends of the Richardses.
40. Richards, *Dear Children*, February 11, 1948.
41. Lynn Stephen Richards was the Richardses' eldest child.
42. She means the name *Tres Arroyos*.
43. Lee Richards was the Richardses' nephew. He was serving as a missionary in Argentina at the time.
44. Georgia Gill Richards was the Richardses' sixth child.
45. Young, *Diary*, 450.
46. See Pergamino Branch Manuscript History and Historical Reports, 1936–83, CHL. Pergamino is a city about 125 miles northwest of Buenos Aires in the Buenos Aires province. Missionary work started there in 1936.
47. First Presidency to Stephen L Richards, February 13, 1948, Stephen L Richards Papers.
48. "There Will Arrive Today to This City a Mormon Apostle," *Tribuna* (Rosário, Argentina), February 13, 1948, 3, Stephen L Richards Papers.
49. The term *local* refers to a branch meetinghouse.
50. "The Mormon Leader E. L. Richards in Our City Today," *La Capital* (Rosário, Argentina), February 13, 1948, 7, Stephen L Richards Papers.
51. Progressive Center.
52. Exchange Club.
53. Marsh, "Historical Report."
54. See Pergamino Branch Manuscript History and Historical Reports. President Young notes that the meetinghouse was originally a "Protestant purchased chapel." Young, *Diary*, February 13, 1948.
55. Stephen L Richards, "Pergamino Argentina Chapel Dedicatory Prayer," February 13, 1948, Stephen L Richards Papers.
56. Richards, *Dear Children*, February 14, 1948.
57. Georgia Gill Richards was the Richardses' sixth child.
58. Lee Gill Richards was the Richardses' nephew.

59. See Mendoza Branch Manuscript History and Historical Reports, 1940–83, CHL. Mendoza borders Chile and lies at the foothills of the Andes. Missionary work and a branch started there in 1940.
60. Hebgen Lake is in southwest Montana and is a popular outdoor vacation place.
61. Marsh, "Historical Report."
62. Marsh, "Historical Report."
63. See Sorrento Branch General Minutes, 1940–48, CHL. Missionary work began in Sorrento in 1938, and the branch was organized on February 17, 1940.
64. Lee Richards was the Richardses' nephew.
65. Córdoba Branch General Minutes, 1937–77, CHL. See also Córdoba Branch Manuscript History and Historical Reports, 1936–84, CHL. Missionaries began working there in 1936.
66. Young, *Diary*, 451.
67. See Río Cuarto Branch Manuscript History and Historical Reports, 1941–43, CHL. Missionary work began there in 1941.
68. Marsh, "Historical Report."
69. Approximately 684 miles.
70. Young, *Diary*, 451–52.
71. Young, *Diary*, 452.
72. See La Plata Branch Manuscript History and Historical Reports, 1936–86, CHL. La Plata is the capital of the Buenos Aires province. Missionaries arrived in the city in December 1936 and organized a branch on January 1, 1937.
73. The name of the newspaper translates into English as "The Day." "The Mormon Church Will Speak Today in the La Plata Mission," *El Dia* (La Plata, Argentina), February 22, 1948, 2, Stephen L Richards Papers.
74. Post-Flood.
75. Marsh, "Historical Report."
76. Henry C. Gorton, Missionary Journal, 54–56, CHL.
77. Another part of Gorton's journal entry discusses a member in the branch causing problems and aspiring to become a leader in the branch. See Gorton, Journal, 54.
78. Richards, *Dear Children*, February 22, 1948.
79. Lynn Stephen Richards was the Richardses' eldest child.
80. Juan Perón was president of Argentina from 1946 to 1955 and again from 1973 to 1974.

81. Apparently, missionaries incorrectly shortened *locales* to *locale* instead of using the proper singular, *el local*.
82. La Plata is the provincial capital of Buenos Aires and means "the silver" in Spanish.
83. Marsh, "Historical Report."
84. The Stephen L Richards Papers contain the minutes of the General Authorities' annual meeting with mission presidents held in the Salt Lake Temple on April 2, 1947. In the meeting mission presidents were authorized to call two counselors and form a mission presidency. An option was also given for the counselors to be missionaries or local members.
85. W. Ernest Young to Henry A. Smith, May 20, 1948, Stephen L Richards Papers.
86. Stephen L Richards to First Presidency, February 23, 1948, Stephen L Richards Papers.
87. Richards, *Dear Children*, February 24, 1948.
88. Georgia Gill Richards was the Richardses' sixth child.
89. A reference to the Universidad Nacional de la Plata, an Argentine national university in La Plata, Buenos Aires.
90. San Leandro, California.
91. The Cathedral of La Plata is one of the largest in South America.
92. Young, *Diary*, 452.
93. Marsh, "Historical Report."
94. Young, *Diary*, 452.
95. At this point in the trip Sister Richards either bought or was gifted an address book that she used as a journal for the rest of her journey. Irene M. Richards, Journal, February 27, 1948, Lynn Stephen and Annette Richards Family Papers.
96. "Mission Presidency Meeting Minutes," February 27, 1948, Stephen L Richards Papers.
97. Yerba mate is an herbal tea that is very popular in Argentina and parts of South America. It contains caffeine. The chemicals in it are less harsh than those in coffee, tea, and green tea.
98. *The Messenger*.
99. The Argentine and Uruguayan Missions were the only Spanish-speaking missions in South America at the time.
100. Marsh, "Historical Report."
101. Howard J. Marsh, "An Apostle Tours Argentina," *Church News*, March 6, 1948.
102. Stephen L Richards, "Suggestive Message for Mission Paper," Stephen L Richards Papers.

CHAPTER THREE

# URUGUAY

### HISTORICAL BACKGROUND

After a tiring expedition throughout Argentina, Elder and Sister Richards found welcome respite in Uruguay from February 27 to March 5, 1948, where they were kindly hosted by Frederick S. Williams, president of the newly created Uruguayan Mission, and his wife, Corraine. President Williams had presided over the Argentine Mission in the late 1930s. As noted in the prologue, in 1941 he asked the First Presidency to consider sending a Church leader to tour South America as a blessing to the Saints and a stimulus for the work there. A few years later, while stationed in Montevideo, Uruguay, on business, he requested permission from Church headquarters to establish a branch there. The Uruguayan Mission was formed not long after.

President Williams relished the opportunity to introduce the Richardses to the new mission, the third one in South America. The mission had been organized less than a year before the Richardses' visit. Twenty missionaries worked to share the restored gospel with investigators and invite them to attend newly created Sunday Schools and branches, though there were no conversions to the faith yet in the country.

## THE DOCUMENTS

In this chapter Sister Richards continues her letters back home. However, the predominant writer of events in Uruguay is President Frederick S. Williams, who described the visit of Elder Richards in one chapter of his landmark book *From Acorn to Oak Tree*, cowritten with his son Frederick G. Williams.

---

## ON BOARD SS *GENERAL ALVEAR*, FROM BUENOS AIRES TO MONTEVIDEO

**Friday, February 27, 1948**

**Daily Summary**
*Travel by ship to Montevideo, Uruguay*

### FREDERICK S. WILLIAMS BOOK[1]

On February 26, 1948, pursuant to a telephone invitation from him [Elder Stephen L Richards], Corraine and I traveled to Buenos Aires to return with him and Sister Richards on the boat.

[February 27, 1948] Elder Richards held a conference with President Young and me, and later that evening the three couples attended a farewell in Brother and Sister Richards' honor before they boarded the S.S. *General Alvear,* one of the night boats that crossed between Argentina and Uruguay. The ships sailed each evening at ten and arrived at seven the following morning.

That night before going to bed, Brother Richards expressed his concern about clearing customs. I told him there would be no problems and no delays getting into Uruguay. He told me, however, that they had arrived in Buenos Aires from Montevideo at seven in the morning and it was two o'clock in the afternoon before they had cleared customs, and the ordeal had exhausted him even before his tour of the mission started. As I recall, President Richards was still recovering from a recent heart attack and wasn't feeling very strong. In fact, in his initial letter to us he indicated as much:

*The Richardses arrive in Montevideo with Frederick S. and Corraine Williams of the Uruguayan Mission. Courtesy of CHL.*

> *We do not wish to incur excessive expense and yet the brethren desire us to have lodging and service which will be adequate to the needs of people of our age. Neither of us is in the most robust health and we have to be a little careful.* [Stephen L Richards to Frederick S. Williams, December 10, 1947]

Visiting the far-flung branches of the Argentine Mission by car had also taken its toll. Thus, it was with a great deal of trepidation that he anticipated our arrival in Uruguay; he feared a repeat of the delays going through customs. I assured him that there would be no problems.

---

## MONTEVIDEO, URUGUAY

### Saturday, February 28, 1948

**Daily Summary**
*Arrival in Montevideo and news articles about the Richardses' arrival*

## FREDERICK S. WILLIAMS BOOK[2]

The next morning [February 28, 1948], to add to his concern, we learned that another ship had arrived a few minutes before ours; we had to dock quite a distance from the customs house itself. As we were leaving the ship, Harold Brown,[3] who was working for the American Embassy in Montevideo, met us with his camera to take pictures of Elder and Sister Richards and Sister Williams and me. In fact, all the missionaries were at the dock to welcome our party. The photo session delayed us even more, and Brother Richards urged us on with the statements like: "Look, let's go, let's get through customs." I again reassured him, and told him that in all likelihood our bags were already in the car. "Oh," he said, "it can't be." We walked up to customs and, sure enough, his bags had already been cleared and were out in the mission car, awaiting our arrival. He couldn't believe it. Once again, my friends in the inspection department had allowed our baggage to go through without delay. Elder Richards was very relieved and grateful.

## IRENE M. RICHARDS JOURNAL[4]

We arrived in Montevideo at 7. The missionaries and friends were there at the docks to meat us. A Mrs Brown[5] gave me a corsage and we had our pictures taken. Pres Williams seems to know how to get them to pass our bagage without inspection at the customs. We just walked through. Quite different [illegible] <from> Argentina. Sister Larson[6] and mother[7] are here from Rio. The day is beautiful. We rested and then rode to the top of a hill where there is an old fort, from which eminance we saw the whole panarama of Montevideo. The river is red and the ocean blue as they gradually mix. Then we went to a steak house. It was a real entertainment. The waiters were shouting to each other over our heads in spanish and when the customers added their babble to the maze it was really fun. There were 8 of us. We had fillet and teabone an inch or more thick. Nothing else only salad. It was quite an experience and once will suffice. Thats' how Uruguay acts they say. Col Scouson[8] took Mrs Larson home to Rio on a plane.

*Page from the journal of Irene Richards. Courtesy of CHL.*

This morning we went to S.S.⁹ We met the bank Pres. <named Deaver>¹⁰ on the hill Sunday School. Four locals, new, clean and noisy. They have a higher plane than Argentina, and at the night meeting in Y.M.C.A. there were 70 investigators, and 40 saints, missionaries and those attached visitors etc. There are no saints who are new members. This branch¹¹ has started in a new place and for about five mo[nths]. Their audiance was a higher class than Argentina. I hope they soon make some converts, but it should take a while to be sure they understand.

### NEWS ARTICLE: *LA MAÑANA*¹²

**One of the Twelve Apostles of the Mormon Church Will Arrive Today in Our City.—Mr. Steven L. Richards, Attorney and Banker**

*The President of the Uruguayan Mission makes some interesting statements*

Today, Dr. Steven L. Richards, one of the twelve people who exercises the calling of the Twelve Apostles of the Mormon Religion, arrives on board the s/s "General Alvear." To be able to give to our readers some information about his personality and about the object of his trip, we interviewed Mr. Frederick Williams, President of the Uruguayan Mission of the Church of Jesus Christ of Latter-Day Saints,—more commonly known by the name of Mormon Church.

Mr. Williams courteously answered our questions and made, among others, the following statements.

*Who Are the Mormons?*

... Quite a number of Senators and Representatives in Washington have been members of the Church. At the present time there are two Mormon Senators and five representatives. The first Councilor to the President of the Church was Ambassador of the United States to Mexico.¹³ He came to Montevideo as one of the delegates sent by Roosevelt to the Foreign Ministers' Conference held in the year of 1932.¹⁴ His name is J. Reuben Clark Jr.

February 28 – Dichoso Dia! The first apostle to visit Uruguay officially, Stephen L. Richards arrived with his wife, and a number of new missionaries.

*The Richardses with those serving in the Uruguayan Mission. Courtesy of CHL.*

A President elected by the Twelve Apostles presides over the Church. He chooses two Councilors. These 15 men are the principal authorities at the head of the Church.

### *The Personality of Steven L. Richards.*
Steven L. Richards, attorney and bank director, exercises the calling of one of the Twelve Apostles. He is traveling to visit the Missions of our Church in South America. He has been in Argentina for nearly one month, where the Church established a Mission in the year 1925. That Mission now has 93 missionaries and about one thousand members.

He will be in Uruguay for one week before going to Brasil, where he expects to remain for two weeks. The Brasilian Mission has many members.

The Uruguayan Mission was established September 1, 1947, although a number of Mormons lived in Uruguay before that time.

Mr. Williams was the Business Manager of the Interamerican Cooperative Public Health Service when it was established. There were other members here in the course of their Military Service working in the Naval Attachee's office of our Government.

### *The Church in Uruguay.*

At the present time, there are 38 missionaries in Uruguay. Nearly all of them have been in the armed service of our country. We do not like war, but when it comes, we support our Governments all that we can. The headquarters of our Mission is on Brito del Pino street. The Mission Home was recently purchased by the Church. There are four branches[15] in Montevideo and one in Treinta y Tres, Mercedes and Paysandú.[16] Upon the arrival of other missionaries, we will open branches in other departments (states).

We believe in a healthful life and we enjoy sports. We hope to soon organize a basketball and baseball team.

The missionaries pay their own expenses while in the mission field. The length of their mission is two and half years, after which they return to their homes in North America, to be replaced by others. There are nearly five thousand throughout the world. The missionaries do their own cooking and housekeeping. They are nearly all young men between 20 and 30 years of age.

### *They Are Not Polygamists.*

The practice of polygamy ended in the year of 1890. Since that date, any member that advocated this practice has been excommunicated by the Church. We believe that we must obey the laws of the country in which we live. When the Supreme Court of the United States sustained the law making polygamy illegal (May 1890), the Church ended this practice.

This belief was accepted before that date (since 1843) as a commandment of God. Only three percent of all the members of the Church ever practiced polygamy.

---

## MONTEVIDEO, URUGUAY

**Sunday, February 29, 1948**

**Daily Summary**
*Church meetings in Montevideo area*

## FREDERICK S. WILLIAMS INVITATION[17]

The Uruguayan Mission of the Church of Jesus Christ of Latter-day Saints is happy to invite you and your family to attend a religious and cultural meeting that will be held in honor of the visit of Elder Steven [L] Richards, a member of the Council of the Twelve Apostles, to our Mission.

In this meeting, Elder Richards will give an important message of interest to all.

The meeting will be held in the Assembly Hall of the Young Men's Christian Association which has been graciously conceded to us free of charge.

Colonia street, corner of Agraciada Avenue

Sunday February 29th, at 7:30 P.M.

<blockquote>
Frederick S. Williams<br>
Mission President
</blockquote>

## FREDERICK S. WILLIAMS BOOK[18]

On Sunday, February 29, 1948, Brother and Sister Richards visited the Sunday Schools of the Malvín, Arroyo Seco and La Comercial branches.[19] He spoke in each one, giving advice and bearing his testimony. That evening, instead of Sacrament meeting (with no members to take the sacrament they were really preaching meetings anyway), we held a combined branch meeting of the Capital District at the YMCA auditorium. Investigators as well as some especially invited guests came from all over Montevideo. The Mission History records:

*Missionaries standing in front of the Malvín Branch meetingplace: William N. Jones, Melvin Brady, Terry C. Smith, Kay W. Young, Cecil Millett, and Gerald Nielsen. Courtesy of CHL.*

> A mixed chorus furnished special music and Oscar Nieves played two piano solos. Apostle Richards spoke at some length explaining the practical aspects of Mormonism.
>
> His words were well received by the people in attendance, amounting to 145 investigators. The concluding speaker was President Williams, who also acted as interpreter for Brother Richards throughout the day. At the close of the meeting almost all of the investigators and friends came and shook hands with Brother Richards, expressing their great pleasure in meeting him and for his splendid message. They requested that he return soon to visit them again.
>
> The public meeting was a great success. We appreciate the courtesy of the Y.M.C.A. in permitting us the use of their hall free of charge. [Uruguayan Mission History, 6]

After Sunday School Elder Richards asked how the people lived. "What do they do on Sunday?" I said, "If you want to see the people, then we'll have to go to the beach; that's where they are." He said "Then we'll go to the beach." And we drove along the *rambla* or ocean front. I think as far as Carrasco. Uruguay's beautiful beaches are jam-packed on Sundays.

### IRENE M. RICHARDS JOURNAL[20]

I tried to list all the boys who were from home so I could telephone their mothers.[21]

### CORRAINE S. WILLIAMS'S MEMORIES OF IRENE RICHARDS[22]

She [Sister Richards] didn't have any voice; she never did speak all the time that we were in the mission; she never spoke at any of the meetings. And I was really surprised at this because I felt like it could have been a help to the women if she had. But I think she had surgery or something, but anyway she spoke very softly.

In the Argentine Mission and in the Uruguayan Mission I was used to sitting on the stand with my husband. But she never would; she'd sit in the congregation, so I sat with her in the congregation, once when they were there. I thought about it and wondered, "Do I do wrong?" Because I don't hold the Priesthood; but on the other hand I was a leader[23] in that mission. I'm sure that that was the right way.

## MONTEVIDEO AND TREINTA Y TRES, URUGUAY

**Monday, March 1, 1948**

**Daily Summary**
*Missionary meetings held in Capital District and Treinta y Tres*

### FREDERICK S. WILLIAMS BOOK[24]

On Monday, March 1, we held a meeting with all the Capital District and Treinta y Tres missionaries. The highlight of the all-day meeting was Brother Richards' testimony and instructions. First, each missionary bore his testimony and expressed his feelings concerning the Lord's work. The majority were military veterans and expressed joy in the service of the Lord, which brings life, rather than in the military, which had so recently brought death. One quite, new elder stood up to say "I don't know if I have a testimony or not, but I've come on this mission to see if I can get one." When Brother Richards rose to speak, he rather severely castigated the elder, saying he should not be on a mission if he didn't have a testimony. I remember seeing my son Fred[25]—who was quite young at the time—looking pained at the way Elder Richards dealt with this young missionary, a particular friend of Fred's. At the close of his remarks, however, Brother Richards apologized to the elder, explaining that he had admonished him to make a point.

Because of his exhaustion after his visit in Argentina, Elder Richards had asked that we not schedule any event without first checking with him. His only really strenuous day had been the day of the elders' meeting, so he felt rested well enough to travel a little. I recommended that we visit Mercedes and stay overnight; it wasn't too far from Montevideo and the roads were almost all paved. He agreed.

# IRENE M. RICHARDS LETTER[26]

Montevideo, Uruguay
March 1, 1948

Dear Folks:

After our strenuous touring of Argentina, we were glad to come to Uruguay. This seems a freer country, more air, more freedom. The walls are not so tall and defaced with placards "Vive Perone" etc. This mission is new, there are no members as yet, but they expect to have one baptized soon.[27] There are about 40 missionaries commencing work in different parts of this country. They are located in locals, much the same as our wards, where two boys live and teach Eng. classes, hold meetings, Primaries, and Mutuals and invite visitors for conversations. These locals are new, fresh and inviting, much nicer than the old ones in Argentina. The boys are enthusiastic and ready to go. There was held a report meeting in the house yesterday in which all were heard from and then Papa gave some clear cut and understandable advice and instruction on how to proceed.[28] I think it should have been recorded for future use, it seemed to me to be unusually good. Anyway, all seemed thrilled and inspirited. Sister Williams served a fine lunch. I have never seen so many hamburgers

Playa Pocitos in Montevideo. Courtesy of CHL.

before and the good things that were eaten with them satisfied the bunch. This is a nice new house, in a fine district, and it seems to be a very portentious beginning for a new mission. Sunday eve we held a meeting in the Y.M.C.A. at which 70 investigators were present. The people seem to be a higher, more intelligent class, superior to those in Argentina. It is said that this is a freer country and not so bound down with tradition and custom. I asked one lady where she learned to speak English. She said, I don't speak English, just "Mormon". These elders are surely attractive, as they are in other missions. People like them.

This morning President Williams took us to have our pictures taken for the Desert [Deseret] News. We stood in front of a statue of pioneers, a wonderful work in bronze, placed along the slope of a hill in a park. I hope we have some pictures of the art here, really, it comes from Italy I guess but is very expressive and real. It seems that that has been the most time wasting thing of our mission. So many pictures. But these people will grow up finally.

Papa has gone to Rotary and he meets men of note. He enjoys it and I am glad. He is invited to see a man whom we met on the boat, who has a nice home here in Montevideo. They took us for a long ride to the beaches on Sun., when they were crowded. It was a sight, colorful and crowded. There are some fine homes along the shore also. More English, Dutch, and American people live here than in Argentina. They don't like "Perone" much. Tomorrow Papa is invited to speak at the "American" Club. Some business men. He is glad that he doesn't need an interpreter. It's really difficult to be interrupted with some babble that doesn't mean anything to you every few words you utter. And when we arrive in Brazil it will be Portuguese. When we get too tired of chatter we go into our room and talk about the Hebgen.[29] In this way I am sure we will be able to live for another month, when we land in N.Y. on the 5th of April.

Love to all. We are well and hope you are.

Mother and Father.

## IRENE M. RICHARDS LETTER[30]

Montevideo, Uruguay
March 1, 1948

Dear Lois:[31]

Your letter was just one month getting to me, and they said sometimes it takes longer. I guess the officials just deliver the letters they think are important. We went at such a pace in Argentina to finish up there, that we were rather in a maze when we were dumped into Uruguay among 40 new missionaries. This place is just being opened up and there are no local members as yet. Everyone is enthusiastic and planning their organization. I am glad they are starting on a much higher plane than in Argentina. The mission home is new and more modern, in a new district, near a park. The houses are more open and the walls not so high and confining, more gardens visible, so it gives one a freer outlook and happier feeling. The locals, or homes of the missionaries, are new and up in the sunshine instead of walled in as in Argentina. They held a meeting Sunday in the Y.M.C.A. hall, and had 70 investigators and 40 of our own people, so the room was fairly well filled. Two boys, or four, live at each local, like our wards at home, and they hold meetings, teach Eng., and do their own cooking. They prefer that so they can have meat without bay leaves, salad without oil and garlic, and they don't need to eat raw ham as an appetizer with melon. 200 boys in South American are teaching a lot of English. Most of these people are ready for the gospel. They are tired of religion and are looking for a simple, happy solution. The class of investigators are much higher than those in Argentina. It seems to be becoming more modern and self expressive in Uruguay. In fact, quite a number do not even know what the Bible is and don't seem to care about it. One doesn't see the smoking here as in North America and the people dress modestly. No doubt we at home go to extremes. I have yet to see "the new look" anywhere. I have inquired several times for a long black skirt. "No." I think there is an ultra class somewhere that reads Vogue, but no one on the street knows about it yet, and they wear short dresses. I have been pointed at, and talked about on account of my longer skirts, by two ladies that I noticed. And no one wears a hat, unless at night if she is a married woman. I suppose I have broken many laws and disregarded niceties, but I didn't understand, so "excusio".

Yesterday we held meeting in the morning and then had dinner. I never saw so many hamburgers in all U.S. as these 40 missionaries put away. And all the trimmings were like ones at home, only the buns were very thin and flat. President Williams tried to explain to the baker how he wanted them. They were heavy like lead. No bread here is light, all soggy and dark in color. After dinner we held another session and by 6 o'clock Papa had heard from every missionary and had given them his instructions, which were definite and impressive and should truly start them out on a mighty conquest for the church in this new field. I wish his remarks could have been preserved for all missionaries who are released from Salt Lake. If anyone can observe, and figure out the best methods to use here, Papa can.

Our present plan is to not visit every out of the way hamlet in Brazil, but have the boys come to some central point to meet Papa instead. They are young and can take it. The roads and conditions are no good. He has seen the likes in Argentina. President Rex will be disappointed, but it may save Papa's life.

He has gone to Rotary. He has enjoyed it all thru our trip. We really should stay for May Rotary meet at Rio. Then we would have the "Mormons" double quartette sing and enjoy that beautiful resort, or really gambling house, "Quitendenah"[32] at Potropolis.[33] But we will leave here at the end of the week and be two days on the boat, then two weeks in Brazil and be home in N.Y. on the 5$^{th}$. Perchance you are there, O.K. If not, we will spend a day with Georgia[34] and continue on. . . . The weather is hot, and cool at night. It's so noisy no rest until after twelve, but a fine "siesta" from 12 to 3 in the afternoon.

Lovingly,
Mother and Father.

## MERCEDES, URUGUAY

**Tuesday, March 2, 1948**

**Daily Summary**
*Travel to Mercedes in rainstorm*

### FREDERICK S. WILLIAMS BOOK[35]

On Tuesday, March 2, 1948, after attending a luncheon as guests of the Montevideo Rotary Club, Elder Richards and I and our wives as well as Elder Keith Dexter, began our trip to Mercedes in the mission car. Near the end of the paved road we were overtaken by tremendous wind and rain, a typical Uruguayan storm. The rain was so dense it was impossible to see any distance and we slowly felt our way along. I noticed a poor rain-drenched woman standing by the side of the road, trying to get a ride. I stopped and invited her into the front seat with me and my wife. It was a mistake; that she was soaking wet was bad enough, but she had evidently been cooking in small, unventilated quarters and smelled of burnt meat and smoke; it was not very pleasant. Then Brother Richards remarked: "The Brethren advise us not to pick up anyone." I was embarrassed and more than a little uncomfortable until we dropped her off.

*First convert baptism in Uruguay, fall 1948. Left to right: President Williams, Brother and Sister Rodriguez, Sister Diber Preciozi, and Elder Preston J. Bushman. Courtesy of CHL.*

We finally arrived in Mercedes, on the beautiful Río Hun [Hum],[36] and went directly to the Brisas del Hun Hotel, where comfortable quarters had been reserved. After resting and eating, we began an elders meeting at 10:00 p.m. with the four missionaries assigned to Mercedes[37] and the four assigned to Paysandú[38] at the Mercedes *local*. Work had just begun in Mercedes; as yet no Sunday School or other meetings had been held.

Elder Richards' instruction was most edifying, as were the sweet testimonies borne at that meeting as the spirit of the Lord poured out upon all present.

### IRENE M. RICHARDS LETTER[39]

Montevideo, Uruguay
March 3, 1948

Dear Georgia:[40]

Yesterday [March 2], after Rotary, we started by auto to go to Mercedes. We traveled about four hours through green rolling country and reached our town in the evening. At our hotel "River Breeze" (Only in Spanish) was a troupe of players (ballet) quite amusing at dinner. They were not good looking but thin. In the center of every town is a park and a church. The bells pealed and the paved walks thru the park made an attractive design from our window. Here we met the remaining eight missionaries in this branch. This is a new project only 6 months old. They are starting out with a new house, beautiful and big, and four "locals" where the elders live and teach English, hold Primaries, Mutuals and cottage meetings for investigators. These "locals" are of about four rooms and most attractive. The elders do their own cooking, which pleases them, because the customs and food in these countries are strange and different and don't agree with Americans. Even I get on the blink about once a week. We left Argentina last week-end, and will leave Uruguay this week-end for Brazil. I have a long list of names to call mothers up when I get home. The missionaries are such fine boys and I will be glad to report them as such.

I have not had any orchids but many gardenias. Brazil is where they grow most. It rained heavily but I have not used my raincoat, or rubbers or umbrella yet. Montevideo is a lovely town, mostly a summer resort for the surrounding country in the heat. The beaches stretch for miles and are thronged. There are more nationalities here than in Argentina and the elders had 70 investigators at a meeting in the Y.M.C.A. where Papa preached. They were quite enthusiastic and interested. The people are kind, as have all others been. We are beginning to feel that we are heading for home. Just two weeks in Brazil and then on the boat for New

York. We don't know what your plans are but we will soon see you there or in Toledo soon.

Yesterday [March 2] the farmers were plowing in the fields with oxen, three span. They surely need machinery here. I think it will come in the next hundred years if not sooner. . . . [Papa] is surely doing a good job here. I would like to have recorded his talk to the missionaries at the conclusion of the report meeting. It was clean-cut, definite and inspiring.

Tomorrow [March 4] he has been invited to address the "American Business Mens Club". He is glad he can speak without needing interpretation.

Love to you three,<br>Mother and Father.

---

## MONTEVIDEO, URUGUAY

**Wednesday, March 3, 1948**

**Daily Summary**
*Evening at the mission home in Montevideo*

### FREDERICK S. WILLIAMS BOOK[41]

We said good-bye to the missionaries . . . and returned to Montevideo. We lunched in Colonia Suiza at the exquisite Nirvana Hotel, a beautiful resort show place. Corraine and I had spent a weekend there some years before. The Richards enjoyed it very much. In fact, the whole trip was most pleasant, and we especially delighted in the beautiful rolling hills of the Uruguayan countryside known as "*la tierra purpúrea*," or the purple land, because of the purple sheen of the spring flowers.

That evening at the mission home, Brother and Sister Richards related some of their experiences, especially those associated with the dedication of various temples. She would encourage him: "Stephen, tell the one about . . ." and he would tell another experience. Then he would say: "Irene, now you tell them about," and she'd begin a story. Some were serious, others instructive or spiritual; still others were humorous, and we had many good laughs. We especially enjoyed their anecdotes about the lives of the General Authorities. I had always thought Brother Richards possessed one of the most orderly and serious minds among the Brethren. After a week with them, I also saw what warm and genuine people they were; each possessed a keen sense of humor and enjoyed life and all its beauties. In every respect they were wonderful human beings as well as committed servants of the Lord.

## MONTEVIDEO, URUGUAY

**Thursday, March 4, 1948**

**Daily Summary**
*Sightseeing and shopping in Montevideo*

### IRENE M. RICHARDS JOURNAL[42]

Thur. 4th 1948. March.

We met the lady missionary[43] then Pres Williams took us to see the Congressional Building of Uruguay. The guide was very fine and explained things to us. It stands on an eminance and is excessively ornate with statues and embellishments. Inside is all kinds of marble, floors pillars and part of the walls; the rest in Mosaic and inlay and gold leaf. It was brought over from Italy and assembled. The woods are also beautiful and polished. The halls and benches of marble are more intricate and ornate than anything yet. The senate chamber made our Washington cheap.

The outside walls of the inner court were carved and chiselled in Roman scenes and characters. I suppose I have not seen any of the finery in Europe. I

*Sister missionaries Edie (Eduarda) Argualt and Juana Gianfelice from Argentina. Courtesy of CHL.*

guess there never will be any more buildings like it because modern people do not worship a diety like they once did, and there will be no more slave poor labor. I hope.

The sun was setting as we came out showing the river and city.~~upon~~ When we returned the missionaries came in to the home and presented us with an album of our visit in pictures. It is very fine. Sister Williams gave us two doilies made by the native indians of Paraguay.—doing which fine work they go blind at about 20 which is not so happy a thought. If they had a little education and magnifying glasses, it probably would save the sight.

### FREDERICK S. WILLIAMS BOOK[44]

On Thursday, March 4, we shopped downtown. I purchased a very beautiful pigskin wallet for Brother Richards which he thought was the finest he had ever seen....[45]

Later, we took Brother and Sister Richards to dinner at a famous restaurant named Moroni's [Morini's].[46] I asked Brother Richards whether he liked steak, and he said he did, so we ordered a chateaubriand for him. We knew it would really impress him. When the steak was brought in on a large platter and placed in front of him he said "I can't believe it. There is no such thing!" The meat hung over the sides of the platter and each serving was as large as a Sunday roast. It was very delicious, and he ate every bite of it.

That evening most of the missionaries from the Capital District visited with the Richardses at the mission home. The missionaries sat on the floor and listened to his counsel and to the very interesting stories both he and Sister Richards told.

I had asked Brother Richards whether he would be willing to speak before the American Association of Montevideo and he replied he would enjoy doing so, so I called the program chairman and arrangements were made for Brother Richards to address the Association. The meeting was scheduled for noon, Friday, March 5, at the Nogaro Hotel.

# MONTEVIDEO, URUGUAY, AND ON BOARD THE SS *URUGUAY*

**Friday, March 5, 1948**

**Daily Summary**
*Address at the American Association of Montevideo and departure by ship to Brazil*

### FREDERICK S. WILLIAMS BOOK[47]

His [Elder Richards's] address [at the American Association of Montevideo] was entitled "Knowledge is power, not wisdom"; it was a beautiful talk and was very well received:

> *Those in attendance at the luncheon expressed many complimentary remarks about Elder Richards' address, "Knowledge is power, not Wisdom". They commented upon the practicability of the Mormon theology and Brother Richards' speaking ability. President Williams, Elder Farnsworth and Harold Brown were also in attendance at the luncheon.* [Uruguayan Mission History, 7]

Friday evening the Richards, Williams and Browns attended a reception at the American Embassy hosted by Ambassador Briggs. Before leaving the mission home Brother Harold Brown, who worked at the Embassy, alerted Elder Richards that "Probably the only thing they will be serving tonight besides scotch and bourbon will be Coca-Cola." He then asked: "Would you be averse to drinking Coca-Cola?" Elder Richards answered: "No, I would not." Harold asked: "Has the Church ever taken a stand against Coca-Cola?" and Elder Richards answered: "No, it has not." And sure enough, that night only hard liquor and Coca-Cola were served. When the waiter offered a tray of drinks, Brother Richards served glasses of Coke to Corraine, Leonore Brown, Sister Richards, me, Harold Brown, and finally to himself, and we all drank them. We met many people that night, officials of the U.S. Government as well as members of the American community, some of whom had heard Elder Richards speak at luncheon. It was a most enjoyable evening. . . .

After the reception with the Ambassador, we returned to the mission home where the Richardses made final preparations for their departure later that night. A large group of both members and investigators escorted them aboard the S.S. *Uruguay* which was to take them to Santos, Brazil.

### IRENE M. RICHARDS JOURNAL[48]

We were not far from Williams home and left a little early to catch the boat. Then we waited a long while for the customs office to open up the gates. We were told they would take us out to the Uruguay by smaller boats, but they finally decided not and the big ship came to dock. It was after midnight before we could say goodbye to the friends who had come to help us off. The boat sailed at 2 and it was long after that before we slept, although it had cooled off. The Uruguay is a much nicer boat than <the> Argentina furnished better, but the waxed floors are dangerous. especially on stairs[.]

### IRENE M. RICHARDS LETTER[49]

Hotel Sao Paulo
Sao Paulo
March 11, 1948

Dear Louise:[50]

No one is so thoughtful and kind to write as often as you have done. We do appreciate knowing what has transpired at home etc. since our leaving. . . . When we finish this mission we surely will be either among the quick or the dead.

The folks at Uruguay pampered us as much as in Argentina. We rode on the *Uruguay*, which is a nicer ship than the one we came down on, and we just rested and relaxed for two days. We needed it, because Papa gave a talk at the American Club at noon. We were accorded a chicken dinner farewell at the Mission Home at 6, where they gave us some lovely remembrances and made us feel entirely foolish. Papa was used to the splurge because of meeting the men at his luncheon. Then we went to a reception given by Ambassador Briggs from Maine, at his home, which was a magnificent mansion in very good taste and appointments. The spacious garden, formal, thru the high gates onto the long front porch with tall pillars, all white. Then into the entrance and marble hall. The receiving line stood in front of a marble staircase, which divided nearer the top to certain bedrooms. Briggs proved to be a fine gentlemen and friend. He also had been to the American Club and heard Papa speak. So it turned out that he, Papa, was quite a popular figure. There were several there from home and one girl from the 18th ward who had been to Whitney Hall and had some acquaintances there. She had married some government officer, I think. The parlor, sun room and library were attractive and rich, and the dining room, always the biggest one in the houses in South America was filled with guests surrounding an immense table of foods and drinks, fine china and flowers. Oh, such a babble and such sociability, when one really gets inside their high walls. But Uruguay is a freer, forward looking country than Argentina.

---

### Saturday, March 6, 1948

**Daily Summary**
Church News *and President Williams report about the Richardses' visit to Uruguay*

### NEWS ARTICLE: *CHURCH NEWS*[51]

**Elder Richards Spends Week on Tour of New Uruguayan Mission**

By Elder E. Keith Dexter<br>(Special to the Church News)

Montevideo, Uruguay—The long awaited visit to this country by one of the General Authorities was realized on Saturday, February 28, with the arrival here at about 7 a.m. of Elder Stephen L Richards of the Council of the Twelve and Mrs. Richards.

They were accompanied in their visit here by President and Mrs. Frederick S. Williams of the newly created Uruguayan Mission, who had attended a conference of mission presidents held by Elder Richards at Buenos Aires.

The Church leader was met at the "Aduana"[52] by a group of Uruguayan missionaries, and spent the day visiting points of interest about Montevideo including the "Cerro," the mount from which Montevideo acquired its name and upon which a famous old fort is built.

Sunday was spent, first in visiting the various Sunday Schools in the Montevideo area, where Elder Richards left his blessings and greetings to members[53] and investigators alike, and then in addressing a general session of the membership of all branches in the evening. Many investigators were present and Elder Richards' remarks were translated by President Williams.

The visit of Elder Richards, his graciousness and the import of his timely messages have done much to further the established work of the Church in this section.

Elder Richards spent Monday giving advice and counsel to the missionaries in the testimony and report meeting. It began at 10 a.m. and continued to 7 p.m. with but a noon luncheon recess.

On Tuesday both Elder Richards and President Williams were guests at the Montevideo Rotary Club and in the afternoon they left with their wives for Mercedes, an outlying branch, for a meeting with the missionaries and members. Elders also came her from Paysandu, a neighboring branch.

The beauties of the interior country were unfolded to the visitors on Wednesday as they returned to Montevideo. A luncheon was enjoyed at one of the attractive resort hotels.

The evening was spent in the Mission Home where Elder Richards and Mrs. Richards relate some of the traveling experiences. Elder Richards told of attending all of the dedications of temple of the Church since the Salt Lake Temple was dedicated in 1893.

Further counsel and advice, and the relating of faith promoting experiences was the fare for most of the elders of the capital district who visited with Elder and Mrs. Richards at the Mission Home on Thursday evening.

On Friday the visiting Church leader addressed the luncheon of the American Association in Montevideo. This was perhaps a highlight of Elder Richards' stay in Uruguay. Those in attendance at the luncheon expressed many complimentary remarks about Elder Richards and his address, during which he gave a word picture of the practicability of Mormonism.

A final reception in their honor was given Elder and Mrs. Richards on Friday evening in the official residence of the American Ambassador to Uruguay. The cordiality and friendliness extended the visitors exemplified the warmhearted appreciation and respect for them on the visit to this land. After the reception they returned to the Mission Home where final preparations were made for their departure.

Later that night they were escorted by missionaries aboard the S.S. Uruguay for their next stop—Brazil.

### FREDERICK S. WILLIAMS LETTER[54]

March 6th, 1948
President W. Ernest Young
San Eduardo 4499
Buenos Aires

Dear President and Sister Young and all:

Brother and Sister Richards left last night after spending one week with us and we very much enjoyed their visit. We did not plan too much for them because they were rather tired. I believe they were more rested when they left and I believe they enjoyed their stay in Uruguay.

He gave the impression that he was well pleased with what he saw in Argentine, and appreciated your many kindnesses to them.

We talked about additional books being needed for the Spanish Missions and I believe we can make a small start toward supplying them. He agreed on the securing a translation of the new book "What of the Mormons?".

He said that they would try and secure a translation of the book and that they would send the manuscript to Montevideo for printing. Knowing how long it takes to get a translation done in the States, I suggested that Brother Barjollo[55] be requested to make one, to which he agreed. As he had given away all of his copies of the book and as this mission has not yet received a copy, Brother Richards requested that I write you and ask if you would be kind enough to loan Brother Barjollo the copy that he gave you so that he can begin as soon as possible on the translation.

He said he would give us a chance to see what we could do on the publishing of books in the south lands. So I hope we can do a creditable job on this first book. This would help a good deal in the decentralization of the Spanish publishing for the Church.

I am writing Brother Barjollo about this to see if he would be kind enough to undertake the translation as soon as possible.

I believe that this would be a start toward in the right direction and perhaps may develop into something in the future. When the mannscript is finally approved, we can ask for bids in both Buenos Aires and Montevideo to see where it would be more advantageous to publish.

I am sorry to know the ruling with regards to leaving our Mission. I feel that that interchange would perhaps be beneficial to both of us. However I feel sure that on special occasions, the First Presidency would authorize these visits. I feel sure it would be too soon for us to request permission to go to the Conference this month but six months from now, I intend to request permission to go to Buenos Aires.

Things are progressing very nicely and we have great hopes for the future. I believe Brother Richards was impressed with our prospects which is about all we had to show him.

Thanks very much for your kindness to us during our last visit and for all the other favors that you have shown us. Please give our regards to everyone.

Sincerely,<br>[Frederick S. Williams]

---

### NOTES

1. Frederick S. Williams and Frederick G. Williams, *From Acorn to Oak Tree: A Personal History of the Establishment and First Quarter Century Development of the South American Missions* (Fullerton, CA: Et Cetera, Et Cetera Graphics, 1987), 239.
2. Williams and Williams, *From Acorn to Oak Tree*, 239.

3. Harold Brown served as a missionary in Argentina (1937–40), as Argentine Mission president (1949–52), and as the first stake president in Mexico City (1961–72). He also became the first president of the Mexico City Mexico Temple when it opened in 1983.
4. Irene M. Richards, Journal, February 27, 1948, Lynn Stephen and Annette Richards Family Papers, CHL.
5. Leonor, wife of Harold Brown.
6. Jeanne Joyce Larson. Her husband, Rolf Larson, was employed by the US government in Rio de Janeiro and was a former Argentine missionary. See Williams and Williams, *From Acorn to Oak Tree*, 242.
7. Amelia Waterstreet Joyce, the mother of Jeanne Larson. Amelia was visiting her daughter.
8. Williams stated that after the war, "three former Argentine missionaries, Samuel J. Skousen, Rolf L. Larson and L. Pierce Brady, all were working in Rio for different agencies of the United States Government. By 1948 Skousen was working in Paraguay and began the Church there." Williams and Williams, *From Acorn to Oak Tree*, 282.
9. Sunday School. In the original text, Irene Richards abbreviates it *S.S.*, makes the sentence about seeing the bank president, and continues on her line of thought by spelling out *Sunday School*.
10. The words "named Deaver" appear on the next line after the words *Sunday School*, but Irene Richards has drawn a line connecting "bank Pres" to the words "named Deaver."
11. See Williams and Williams, *From Acorn to Oak Tree*, 219. A branch had been organized on June 25, 1944, with Williams as branch president in Montevideo when he worked for the US government. Members at that time were all from the United States. The branch had a new beginning with the organization of the mission in 1947 and then the arrival of missionaries in 1948.
12. "One of the Twelve Apostles of the Mormon Church Will Arrive Today in Our City.—Mr. Steven L. Richards, Attorney and Banker," *La Mañana* (Montevideo), February 28, 1948, Stephen L Richards Papers, 1921–59, CHL.
13. J. Reuben Clark served as US ambassador to Mexico from 1930 to 1933.
14. See South American Mission Manuscript History, CHL. In December 1933 President J. Reuben Clark of the First Presidency returned to Montevideo as a US government representative at the Pan-American Conference. He also had brief stopovers in Argentina and Brazil. On January 2, 1934, he addressed

Church members in the Liniers chapel of Buenos Aires. President Clark then returned to the United States.

15. See Williams and Williams, *From Acorn to Oak Tree*, 231–32, 242. Meetings throughout Uruguay were only with investigators at the time of the Richardses' visit; there were no members in these branches.
16. Branches in Treinta y Tres, Mercedes, and Paysandú were organized January 22, February 16, and February 18, 1948, respectively. See Williams and Williams, *From Acorn to Oak Tree*, 250–51.
17. Frederick S. Williams' Invitation to Meeting, February 29, 1948, Stephen L Richards Papers. The invitation was given to the general members of the Church.
18. Williams and Williams, *From Acorn to Oak Tree*, 242.
19. See Williams and Williams, *From Acorn to Oak Tree*, 250–51. In 1948 fourteen branches existed throughout Uruguay.
20. Richards, Journal, February 29, 1948.
21. In her journal, Irene made lists of the home addresses and phone numbers of the missionaries she met in her travels so that she could call and talk to their mothers after returning to Utah.
22. Sister Corraine Williams reflected about the Richardses' visit years later. She commented about Sister Richards's role and involvement during the mission tour when attending Church meetings. Corraine S. Williams Oral History, interviewed by Frederick G. Williams, 1975–76, 22–23, CHL.
23. See Williams Oral History, 10. As wife of the mission president, Sister Williams was the president of all three women's auxiliaries in the mission and was in charge of starting these organizations in Uruguay.
24. Williams and Williams, *From Acorn to Oak Tree*, 242–43.
25. See Williams and Williams, *From Acorn to Oak Tree*, 252. Frederick and Corraine Williamses' son, Fred G., was about eight years old and was the first Latter-day Saint baptism in Uruguay, performed a month after the Richardses' visit, on April 3, 1948.
26. Irene Richards, *Dear Children*, March 1, 1948, Richards Family Papers., 1879–2004, CHL
27. See Williams and Williams, *From Acorn to Oak Tree*, 253. A steady stream of conversions began almost eight months later when the first three Uruguayans were baptized on November 4 and five more joined two days later.

28. See Richards, Journal, March 1, 1948. Irene Richards mentioned one subject of Elder Richards's talk that day. She stated, "There was quite a controversy about 'if' and Stephen gave them a very clear straight message about being definate."
29. Hebgen Lake, in southwest Montana, is a popular fishing and camping area.
30. Richards, *Dear Children*, March 1, 1948.
31. Lois Bathsheba Richards Hinckley was the Richardses' third child.
32. Palácio Quitandinha was a casino and resort built in the 1940s in Rio de Janeiro.
33. Petrópolis is the capital of the state of Rio de Janeiro.
34. Georgia Gill Richards Olson was the Richardses' sixth child.
35. Williams and Williams, *From Acorn to Oak Tree*, 243.
36. The Río Hum is the indigenous name for the Río Negro.
37. Mercedes is in western Uruguay along the banks of the Río Negro.
38. Paysandú is in western Uruguay. The city is on the banks of the Uruguay River, which forms the border with Argentina.
39. Richards, *Dear Children*, March 3, 1948. Though written on March 3, much of the letter describes events of March 2.
40. Georgia Gill Richards Olson was the Richardses' sixth child.
41. Williams and Williams, *From Acorn to Oak Tree*, 243.
42. Richards, Journal, March 4, 1948.
43. According to Williams and Williams, *From Acorn to Oak Tree*, 249, the first sister missionary in Uruguay was Sister Eduarda Arguault, who began her mission on January 7, 1948. She was joined by Elza J. Vogler from Río Cuarto, Argentina. Williams states, "Sister Vogler had been set apart in Buenos Aires by Elder Richards, and arrived in Uruguay March 4, 1948." The "lady missionary" reference by Irene Richards is to Sister Vogler.
44. Williams and Williams, *From Acorn to Oak Tree*, 243–44.
45. Continuing, Williams said, "After my release as mission president three-and-a-half years later, I bought another wallet for him and gave it to him personally when I returned to Salt Lake City. As I presented it, he pulled out his old one and said, 'This is the finest wallet I ever had. It's kind of worn now, so I sure do appreciate getting this new one. I suppose he used it until his death.'" Williams and Williams, *From Acorn to Oak Tree*, 243–44.

46. Ristorante Morini opened in 1854 and closed in 2000. It was the longest-running restaurant in Montevideo. "Un Clásico Menos en Uruguay," El Tiempo, November 23, 2000, http://www.eltiempo.com/.
47. Williams and Williams, *From Acorn to Oak Tree*, 244.
48. Richards, Journal, March 4, 1948. From the context of the entry it is clear this is really March 5.
49. Richards, *Dear Children*, March 11, 1948.
50. Irene Louise Richards Covey was the Richardses' second child.
51. E. Keith Dexter, "Elder Richards Spends Week on Tour of New Uruguayan Mission," *Church News*, March 27, 1948.
52. Customhouse.
53. With no Uruguayan converts, this must either be an error or a reference to the missionaries or members like Harold Brown who were Latter-day Saints working in Uruguay and attending the meetings.
54. Frederick S. Williams to W. Ernest Young, March 6, 1948, Frederick S. Williams Papers, CHL.
55. Fermin Claudio Barjollo, an Argentine, translated for the Church.

CHAPTER FOUR

# BRAZIL

### HISTORICAL BACKGROUND

Elder Richards became the first Apostle to set foot on Brazilian sand and soil. Missionaries first came to the country in 1927, and the Brazilian Mission was organized in 1935. For unknown reasons, President George Albert Smith did not direct that either Uruguay or Brazil be dedicated for the preaching of the gospel by Elder Richards. Perhaps the Apostles viewed Elder Melvin J. Ballard's dedication for all of South America in 1925 as sufficient.

Reinvigorated from their calmer experience in Uruguay, the Richardses traveled by ship to Santos, Brazil, and from there by car to São Paulo. They stayed in the country from March 8 to March 23, 1948. As in Argentina, Elder and Sister Richards spent considerable time journeying to the branches by car and associating with the approximately four hundred members. Elder Richards's heart problems and resulting fatigue increased in Brazil. Exhaustion in Curitiba led to an opportunity for Elder and Sister Richards to take an airplane ride to São Paulo. This was their first experience flying on an airplane.

Travel in the three South American missions helped Elder Richards appreciate more fully the needs of missionaries and mission presidents in such large countries. This increased awareness would help the work in South America after Elder Richards returned to Church headquarters and related his observations.

## THE DOCUMENTS

One difficulty Irene Richards faced on the trip was access to stationery for correspondence. By the time she arrived in Brazil, she had obtained a new journal that would supplement the record of her experiences at the end of the trip. Some Brazilian entries are more difficult to decipher in the journal, so documentary editing marks and footnotes have been added to aid the reader.

*Harold and Diania Rex with children Yara, Jeff, and John (standing). Courtesy of CHL.*

In this chapter there is very limited information from Brazilian Mission president Harold Rex because of a dearth of records by him. Many insights into the Brazilian tour come from correspondences of President Rex's missionary counselor Elder Wayne Beck and entries from missionaries, mission records, and newspaper articles.

---

## ON BOARD SS *URUGUAY*, OFF THE COAST OF BRAZIL

**Sunday, March 7, 1948**

**Daily Summary**
*Sunday service on the ship*

## IRENE M. RICHARDS LETTER[1]

Dear Louise:[2]

... Mrs. Britton, who was in charge of publicity, and whom we had met on the Argentina, asked Papa to speak at a service on Sunday. So he did, but he had to pray and preach and nearly sing. But we found a young lady who sang "Nearer My God to Thee", and the congregation joined in "Onward Christian Soldiers". It went off well and introduced us to the world for good or worse. We missed the missionaries who were on the *Argentina* coming down, who sang and prayed at our other meetings.

---

## SANTOS AND SÃO PAULO, BRAZIL

**Monday, March 8, 1948**

**Daily Summary**

*Itinerary, arrival in Brazil, view from hotel room, and travel to São Paulo*

## ELDER AND SISTER RICHARDS ITINERARY IN BRAZIL[3]

ITINERARY

| | |
|---|---|
| March 8–9–10 | In São Paulo |
| March 11 | Travel to Campinas, visit city and coffie ranch, 110 kilometers. |
| March 12 | Travel to Riracicaba [Piracicaba] and Ribeirão Preto, conference in Ribeirão Preto, 290 kilometers. |
| March 13 | Return to Campinas before noon. Attend baptism in afternoon and conference in evening. |
| March 14 | Return to São Paulo before noon. Conference in afternoon; German meeting at 1:30; Portuguese meeting at 3:30 P.M. |
| March 15 | Depart at 6:30 A.M. for Curitiba, 500 kilometers. ~~Conference~~ [cannot read the rest] |
| March 16 | Travel to Joinville, 143 kilometers. Conference in evening. |
| March 17 | Return to Curitiba. Visit city, conference in evening. |
| March 18 | Conference with Missionaries. |

| | |
|---|---|
| March 19 | Return to São Paulo. |
| March 20 | Depart for Rio, if by automobile at 1 P.M, overnight at Club 200, arrive in Rio before noon on Sunday 21ˢᵗ. Train leaves São Paulo 10 P.M. arrives in Rio 9 A.M. |

## IRENE M. RICHARDS JOURNAL[4]

Entering Brazilian Mission
Mar 8, 1948 Santos [Brazil]

Monday and we passed the inspector, left the *Uruguay*. Bro DeJonge[5] was waiting for us at the bottom of the ladder. We chatted about an hour before some elders showed up. Then Pres Rex just in time for customs. Then we came to Sao Paulo. Our rooms are lovely and nearly stunned us they are so big. The view from the window is: Parking, then a foot bridge where hundreds are passing—another bridge in the distance and then town and mountains and clouds and sky. The people speak Portug[ue]se here. We are riding to see some new homes for the mission.

We saw two beauties—A reporter or two came to chat with Stephen and take his picture for the paper. A Brazilian and a negro. The negro seemed the most intelligent and educated. Sister Rex came with the Pres. and we enjoyed a visit in our lovely hotel suite.

*Sister Rex standing in front of the Brazilian mission home in São Paulo. Courtesy of CHL.*

### IRENE M. RICHARDS LETTER[6]

Hotel Sao Paulo
Sao Paulo
March 11, 1848

Dear Louise:[7]

... President [Harold M.] Rex took us to this lovely hotel, because he is crowded at home and has a small family. We have a suite of two rooms, two halls and a bath, all furnished nicely. It tickles Papa's pride to be sitting at a table in beautiful chairs, eating a nice light breakfast in his dressing robe. At first we tried to tell the waiter what to bring us, and after gesticulating vociferously we finally fell back on our pillows exhausted and wondered if he would show up with, cigars to put in our mouths, or a pot of "mate" which they suck thru a straw, but after an hour here came the waiter with a nice meal. It has been the same every morning, nothing we ordered but a uniform breakfast the hotel serves for everyone, and we can pick out plenty for us. Out from the corner window, we look over the center of town.

We will leave for the interior today and may be able to tell more about roads and conditions later. . . .

Lovingly,
Mother and Father.

### IRENE M. RICHARDS LETTER[8]

Sao Paulo, Brazil
March 10, 1948

Dear Allie:[9]

... From Santos we traveled 40 miles up through the hills, very scenic and a new road, to Sao Paulo, about 2800 feet and much nicer climate. We have a hotel room and it's the nicest setup we have had. Really a suite, well furnished and comfortable. From a corner window on

*Elder Pinegar, President Harold Rex, and Elmo Turner standing in front of the mission jeep. Courtesy of CHL.*

the 9th floor we see a mile or two in the distance, where buildings and trees finally fade out and the hills and sky come into view. There is a low avenue with four separate lanes parked and shrubbed up the bank to another level where a bridge arches the park. This bridge is crowded with people going back and forth on higher streets, and it's on this level that many palms and trees make it interesting. We see up another avenue, steps leading to the other level also. Really there are ten streets meeting at this point, and when the autos begin to go home it's more than the little man in the elevated box under an umbrella can do to control the traffic. There is a constant horn blowing for two hours, while autos jam and unwind and mix again until finally evening is here and the streets are clear again. We see many tall new modern buildings, some not finished yet, with shades and modern equipment, and many old ornamented ones with balconies where people, parrots, potted plants and what not spend the cool evenings, after the lights go on. We have seen many lovely homes here. But really a modern trend is going on and finally there will be a new place in this big land. People here don't even know what the Bible is. They don't care about anything much but to live, so it will be encouraging for the elders to search out the "honest in heart". Several have said they have been looking for something like our gospel for a long time. It will surely help them to be somebody in the future. We have met some of the missionaries and heard their why's and wherefores and testimonies, and Papa has given them advice and counsel as he can do and they seem thrilled. Tomorrow we will travel a little and in two weeks we will know more about Brazil. . . .

Lovingly,
Mother and Father.

## SÃO PAULO, BRAZIL

**Tuesday, March 9, 1948**

**Daily Summary**
*News article about the Church, and missionary meeting in São Paulo*

*The Richardses arrrive in São Paulo and are greeted by the Rexes. Their new automobile is shown behind them. Courtesy of CHL.*

### NEWS ARTICLE: UNIDENTIFIED NEWSPAPER[10]

#### Mormon Preacher

*Caption: Mr. Stephen Richards and wife with Mr. Alius and Mr. Rex*

Mr. Stephen L. Richards, preacher of the Church of Jesus Christ of Latter-day Saints, is in São Paulo, accompanied by his wife Mrs. Irene Richards. Mr. Richards has come to our State to hold some conferences. He received the newspaper men in company of the missionaries Johannes Alius and Harold M. Rex. Mr. Richards said that the American sect, the Church of Jesus Christ of Latter-day Saints also called "Mormons," was founded in 1830 in the United States by Joseph Smith, with the publication of his biblical book the "Book of Mormon." Joseph Smith's principal activity consisted of propagating the doctrine and constructing new temples....

"We were in Uruguay having been received at the American Club of Montevideo. In Brazil, I am very much impressed. I intend to visit several

*News clipping of the Richardses and President Rex visiting with a reporter. Courtesy of CHL.*

states, holding conferences and propagating the doctrine. Tomorrow I intend to go to Campinas, where I shall hold a conference and on the 14th return to this city, holding a conference that day at 3:30 p.m. at 165 Rua Seminario 1st floor. Afterwards I will continue to Argentina.[11]

### SÃO PAULO DISTRICT MINUTES[12]

**Missionary Meeting São Paulo District[13]**

March 9, 1948

Song—The Spirit of God
Prayer—Elder Bynon D. Thomas

Brother Stephen L Richards outlined the meeting and gave a small piece of paper to each missionary requesting him to talk on those items, or, explain in a few words what he thought of these items. . . .

Brother Richards gave instructions to the missionaries cautioning them in the use of their time. He bore his testimony which was faith promoting to hear.

Song—We Thank Thee O God for a Prophet. (in Portuguese)
Prayer—Elder Orson Tew.

---

## SÃO PAULO AND CAMPINAS, BRAZIL

### Wednesday, March 10, 1948

**Daily Summary**
*Brazilian Mission presidency meeting, ride to Campinas, and update by President Young from Argentina*

### BRAZILIAN MISSION PRESIDENCY MEETING[14]

**Minutes of Mission Presidency Meeting**

March 10, 1948 at 2:30 p.m.
Presided over by Elder Stephen L Richards
Prayer: President Harold M. Rex

A Short discussion on prayer was given by Elder Richards. It was pointed out that no set condition for prayer was necessary, i.e. in a circle, all standing, or, all sitting. Particular mention was made that any form of prayer imitating prayer circles was wrong and should not be permitted.

Missionary System. The arrival of the missionaries in the mission field, the meeting and the interviews made by the mission president. Instructions to

*The Brazilian Mission presidency. Courtesy of CHL.*

all new missionaries on conditions here, the best methods used in the promulgation of the gospel and taking care of one's health. The departure for their field of labor.

Skeleton outline:
| | |
|---|---|
| 6:30 a.m. or earlier | Get up |
| 6:30–7:30 | Toilet and Breakfast |
| 7:30–8:30 | Study period |
| 8:30–11:00 or 12:00 | Tracting |
| 11:00 or 12:00–1:00 | Study and Lunch |
| 1:00–1:30 | Rest |
| 1:30–2:30 | Study |
| 2:30–5 or 6 p.m. | Tracting, Cottage Meetings, Visiting Investigators or Members |
| 5 or 6–7:00 | Supper |
| 7:00–10:30 | English classes, mutual, visit investigators or members cottage meetings |
| 10:30 | Retire |

*Missionaries in Brazil, with the mission presidency and their wives seated in the front row. Courtesy of CHL.*

Missionary Activity Report Forms and Uses: Visiting Investigators is included in tracting time provided no special trip has been made to visit the investigator. Missionaries should not do unnecessary things which take up the time that should be used in the spreading of the gospel.

Projection Machines: Should know their condition and whereabouts. They can be used very effectively in getting cottage meetings started.

What the Missionary Does in His Day Off: Generally a missionary meeting in the morning followed by athletics or other things as, cleaning up quarters, clothes, shoes. Afternoon—Such things as, laundry, a show, visit friends, or study.

Delivery of Mail: Do Missionaries receive their mail regularly? Is there a waste of time by them going to the post office to receive it. Arrange system whereby no time is lost in receiving mail. Recommended that missionaries do not receive packages from the states through the post office because of the time wasted and the duties paid.

Notes:
Make better use of time. Time is precious.
Missionaries need direction.
Mission President to be relieved of some duties by counselors in order that he may work more closely with the missionaries.

Closing Prayer: Elder Stephen L. Richards

### IRENE M. RICHARDS LETTER[15]

Hotel Sao Paulo
Sao Paulo, Brazil
March 10, 1948

Dear Georgia:[16]

Your letters have been informing and lovely. I did not have orchids dripping from my shoulder, but I had gardenias. Everyone has been most gracious and overwhelmed us with flowers and gifts. . . .

I am glad you all write and take care of one another as you do. And you certainly have kept us posted. Sorry spring left so soon in Toledo.

The weather here is good. Ideal late summer and fall like. Pleasant days and cool evenings. . . . I like to read the signs and I find it more difficult to make them out than I did the Spanish ones in the other two countries.[17]

. . . The people have such poor roads they have jumped from ox teams to the airplane. We are going to travel a bit tomorrow and see just how rough the roads are. We have seen six oxen plowing and an airplane above. The prairie schooners have wheels about 8 or 10 feet high to negotiate the mud in rainy weather. Everyone lives in the city and has a new car. From our window all the cars have pointed hoods. If someone should set up a "hot shop" on these streets they would make a fortune. There are no drive-ins and ice cream or hot dog places.

*Vehicles used by the Brazilian Mission. Courtesy of CHL.*

### IRENE M. RICHARDS JOURNAL[18]

Mar. 10—1948. We rode to Campinus,[19] a beautiful place. We are in a nice hotel.

Campinus.—Alfrado [Vaz] rode with us to the conference.[20] The country side is up and down, green and flowery. The road is red mud. We made it over every hill. Our Hotel is extra fine. A new building in the midst of tile roofs which have grown brown with dead moss. It rained in the night. We rushed to close the windows. The dinning room is modern and lovely. The green and gold ball was held here in a grand room. There are many nationalities about. We ate with Bro and Sister Rex.

## UPDATE FROM ARGENTINA: W. ERNEST YOUNG TO STEPHEN L RICHARDS[21]

March 10, 1948.
Elder Stephen L. Richards
Sao Paulo, Brasil.

Dear Brother and Sister Richards:

We have taken the liberty to take out your letter and re-mail it, since it came by slow mail and in a rather heavy envelope. May we say, also, that we just received a nice letter from your nephew, Lee Richards, from Rosario. He states that he is following, strictly, the advice of the Doctor, and that he is feeling much better. With the reassigning of Elders at our general conference, we shall do our best to give him a new place to labor.

Many Elders and saints send their appreciation and gratitude for your visit with us. We, also, thank you for your wise and kindly help for our betterment in our labors. Our weekly reports have returned to us filled out as per your instructions.

[not clear, ink stained]◊◊◊◊◊◊◊◊◊◊◊er B◊◊◊◊◊r ◊nd [and] I ◊◊◊◊◊◊◊◊◊◊ng the papers, and have agencies looking for a home in the Belgrano district of the city, but to date we have not been successful.

Wishing you every success and a happy visit in Brazil, we remain,

Respectfully,
THE MISSION PRESIDENCY
/s/ W. Ernest Young
Per W. Ernest Young

P.S. Please give our best wishes to President and Sister Rex.

---

## PIRACICABA AND RIBEIRÃO PRETO, BRAZIL

**Friday, March 12, 1948**

**Daily Summary**
*Visit to Piracicaba and conference and missionary meeting in Ribeirão Preto*

## IRENE M. RICHARDS JOURNAL[22]

Mar. 12

Piracicaba—We met two elders in a nice local. This [is] a beautiful place, tropical. Crossed river Campenis, red with silt, but the banks are green.

Zubu cow from India. There are many in the fields white and colored. The jungle is thick and orchids are growing among the trees. We could see the plants but its' not in season or else they grow thicker back in the jungle. Beautiful flowering trees, pink, yellow and purple abound. Poinsettias are all along and oleanders and many bright bushes grow among the mass.

At an intersection in the <road was a>[23] drinking fountain made in Rock, to accommodate travelers. The roads are built by digging down below the bumps and that makes a smooth surface with banks on each side, there by digging a drain ditch it makes those everlasting Lanes with rows of lemon grass growing. (planted there on about 2 feet-high soil on either side. Uniform all the way). No shoes are worn by most people, so they can wash the mud off before entering houses. Many carry bundles of sticks or reads for firewood or other uses. I guess the early priests, before roads were as good as now built brick and tile shelters so often for travelers to rest in. For miles one can see sugar cane plantations. When they reap it is like in Louisiana by cutting a wide swath straight through the field first oxen 4 span with wood or any kind of a load. The oxen are mostly white and are called Yabu [Zebu] oxen from India. Bamboo is grown all along which is cut for use and piled in rows. Some to build huts, some smaller pieces for stakes.

Mar 12—1948. Fri

We held a public meeting at a Gomez (famous musician) hall. Alfrado [Vaz] interpreted for Stephen very well. After we held a meeting for the missionaries

## ELDER GRANT C. TUCKER JOURNAL[24]

At 6: P.M. Apostle Richards and President Rex and wives with Alfredo [Vaz] arrived and then at 7:30 we held our Conferance and it was a fair turn out to the Conferance we had between 60 and 70 persons attend the meeting. Afterwards we held a missionary meeting which was very ~~inspiriancial~~ inspirational. the Ones who spoke in the Conferance were Alfredo, myself, President Rex and Elder Stephen L. Richards. We got to bed at 12 or after.

---

## CAMPINAS, BRAZIL

**Saturday, March 13, 1948**

**Daily Summary**
*Baptismal service held outside Campinas and missionary and member conference*

### ELDER FREDERICK H. DELLENBACH MISSIONARY JOURNAL[25]

Dull, gloomy, clouds look like rain. Thats the outlook we had when we woke up. . . . Ate and went home to get ready for the baptism. We met at the church and took onibuses to Sousa St was a ride of about ½ hour over dirt roads that had been turned into mud. It was sprinkling as we held a meeting in the open p[r]ior to the baptism. We sang a song had prayer and then Apostle Richards dedicated some remarks to the candidates for baptism. He said that they were taking the first step toward gaining glory in the Celestial Kingdom and returning to the presence of their Father. He also stated that he hoped that the families of these young people could see the happiness that they knew and join with them. The river water was moving fast because of the rain. The baptisms came off without an

*Alfredo Vaz with Clarisse Marotta at her baptism, July 1947. They later married. Courtesy of CHL.*

*Jessie McMulley baptism, 1947. Alfredo Vaz was the witness. Courtesy of CHL.*

accident. Maria Augusta cried with joy after she came out of the water. Her father met her, and embraced her. That service must have left a deep impression on his mind. We sang going back on the bus. The missionaries sang some American numbers that the brazilians liked.

[Entry from March 15, 1948, about the baptism]
    In writing on Saturday's baptism I forgot an important thing that happened. After the baptisms were over it stopped raining and the clouds parted in a hole directly above us. This was a manifestation to us that the ordinance found favor with God.

### ELDER FREDERICK H. DELLENBACH
### MISSIONARY JOURNAL[26]

We went home changed clothes and hurried to the conference. It was held in the Terminus Hotel which is one of the most modern buildings in Campinas. It has a beautiful hall and they there were 120 people there. Elder Alfredo [Vaz] spoke and Elder Beck and an Elder Maxwell from Hollywood sang solos and a duet "The Morning breaks." Apostle Richards address the audience and told them he came as another missionary in their midst. He spoke on education and how it frees us from fear because of ignorance. I cannot write what he said but the audience enjoyed it. After the meeting the elders sang "Come, Come ye Saints" as the girls of the branch presented Sister Richards with flowers and a huge spray of 22 orchids.

### IRENE M. RICHARDS JOURNAL[27]

Mar 13th 1948 Saturday.

We stopped to investigate the coffee plants. Green bushes, about 12 to 20 feet high. Small green leaves, and branches covered with green berries, which later turn red, brown and black. It looks like (Pyracanthus) and is dried, shelled and browned, bagged, ground, etc. "There's an awful lot of coffee in Brazil."

Bro Beck worked for Charles is here on a second mission. He is a councellor to Pres Rex. His wife is a girl from Malad, a lively girl. They are tending the Rex baby while we are on this trip together.[28] They say to Call Charles. They hope to be home in September

Stephen attended Rotary and met some more men of note. He took Pres. Rex this time.

We attended meeting in the hotel dinning room. There were 171 present. Bro Maxwell sang. also Bro Beck sang, and Stephen spoke well. Afraido [Alfredo Vaz] interpreted and the branch, relief and Mutual and elders, presented me with 2 dozen orchids, in one bunch. Never before was any gift so beautiful. Then there were roses, asters and chrysanthums. Really we were overwhelmed. And tired enough to sleep in a nice room.

. . . Yesterday we witnessed 7 baptisms at the banks of a red river. It rained and still there were about 50 present. Quite a thrilling sight. The father and mother were not members but they were willing their daughter should be baptized. ~~After~~ At Rotary the father told Stephen he was going home early to spend a few hours with his family, because it was being

**ORCHIDS IN BRAZIL** — Elder and Mrs. Stephen L. Richards are seen here at Campinas, Parana, with a bouquet of orchids she received there as a token of love from the Saints.

*The Richardses receive orchids in Campinas from members. Courtesy of CHL.*

broken up, their daughter was joining the Mormons. After the service he came to Stephen and said he was sincerely happy. So I guess he will be O.K. now.

### NEWS ARTICLE: UNIDENTIFIED NEWSPAPER[29]

**Campinas Is Host to One of the Most Eminent Figures of the Contemporary Religious World**

Apostle Stephen L. Richards will speak at a Conference Tomorrow in the Hotel Terminus.

Campinas is host, since yesterday, of one of the greatest figures of the present religious world.

Coming from the United States, Apostle Stephen L. Richards, together with his esteemed wife, has already traveled through several countries of our continent, leaving where ever he has been an impression that will never be forgotten, for such is the beauty and spiritual power of his words. In Argentina, where his church has a large number of members, the newspapers did not spare the eulogies, and there was one that called him "True minister from Heaven." Apostle Stephen L. Richards is one of the twelve apostles of the Church of Jesus Christ of Latter-day Saints, (Mormon) besides being a practicing lawyer of long standing. He is visiting Brazil now to come in contact with the Brazilians and officially visit the Mission of his church in our country, one of its newest fields of labor.

Campinas is one of the very few cities of the interior where he will speak, thus, tomorrow at 8 P.M. the Salon of Hotel Terminus will be opened to the public which certainly will flow there to hear this, his first and only conference in our city. We invite the general public and especially those who are interested and know how to appreciate the beautiful things of the world to come to the above mentioned address to hear the profound and authoritative word of this illustrious visitor.

### NEWS ARTICLE: UNIDENTIFIED NEWSPAPER[30]

**A Representative of The Church of Latter-day Saints in Campinas**

Apostle Stephen Harold [L.] Richards spoke in the Hotel Terminus Yesterday.

Under the direction of Mr. Harold Rex, President of the Brazilian Mission of The Church of Jesus Christ of Latter-day Saints, a solemn service of that church was held yesterday in the Salon of the Hotel Terminus, to pay homage to Apostle Stephen—Richards who is visiting Campinas. Mr. Richards, who resides in Salt Lake City, Utah is traveling throughout all of South America with the object of coming into direct contact with the Mormon communities of the continent.

The meeting, which was very well attended, began with the song "The Battle Hymn of the Republic" followed by a prayer of thanks by Mr. Remo Roselli, Counselor of the Campinas Branch. Following, a homage was paid to Mrs. Richards which consisted of a rich bouquet of orchids delivered by Miss Maria Augusta de Almeida.

M. Alfredo Lima Vaz, President of the Campinas Branch gave a welcoming speech to the visiting Apostle, making a dissertation of the Church. Following were musical and vocal numbers given my Messers Maxwell and Wayne Beck, respectively from the Piracicaba and Campinas Branches.

As the principal part of the meeting program, Mr. Richards gave a discourse in English, of high religious and social sentiment. His words, upon immediate translation by Mr. Alfredo Lima Vaz caused a profound impression upon the audience.

At the end of the meeting all of the organizations associated with the Campinas Branch paid homage to the Richards by giving various bouquets of natural flowers.

The meeting ended with the singing of the hymn "God be With You Till We Meet Again" after which all the missionaries sang the traditional hymn of the Mormons.

## SISTER EVELYN BECK LETTER[31]

Campinas, S.P.<br>March 15, 1948

Dear Mother, Dad and All:

... Apostle and Sister Richards have been out here. They came Thursday afternoon [March 11] and stayed here in the hotel that night. Then

*Sister Diania Rex and her children. Courtesy of CHL.*

Friday morning [March 12] early they left for Ribeirao Preto with President and Sister Rex in the new Studebaker. They had a conference there that night and returned here Saturday [March 13] before noon in time for Brother Richards to attend the Rotary Luncheon. At 4:00 P.M. we all went to Souzas where the baptisms took place. It started to rain Thursday—no Wednesday and hasn't stopped yet. Well we thought the baptisms would be postponed, but when Wayne and President went up to the Church about three o'clock, seventy people were waiting for the two chartered busses that they had arranged for earlier in the week. So Wayne went on the bus and the kids and I went with President and Sister Rex and Apostle and Sister Richards. There were five candi-

*Baptism in Campinas, São Paulo, Brazil. Courtesy of CHL.*

*Gold and Green Ball held in Campinas, August 27, 1948. Courtesy of CHL.*

dates. Elder Lewis baptized two, Wayne two and Elder Walker one. These people go through with their plans here in Campinas rain or shine.³² I've never seen their equal. Brother Richards was very impressed with the baptisms. They held a short service before on the river bank and he talked a few moments while someone held an umbrella over his head. That evening he invited Wayne and me to have dinner with them and the Rex's at the Hotel. We did and thoroughly enjoyed it as the food was delicious. That's the first time we've done that since we've been in Campinas. So it was quite a treat. At 8:00 our conference started. It was beautiful. Wayne sang a solo and a duet with another fellow and Alfredo, Elder Claudio, President Rex and Brother Richards spoke. Alfredo translated for Brother Richards. There were 170 people there. By the way, it was held in the Terminus Hotel, the same hotel and room where we had our Gold and Green Ball. The Branch gave Sister Richards a bouquet of two dozen orchids. The arrangement was more like a lei that went around her neck and down to the floor. She was so thrilled. She said she had only had two orchids in her life and one was when she left to come down here. They wanted to have her picture taken with them. Besides the orchids, the Relief Society gave a bouquet, Priesthood, Mutual and Sunday School. So she received five bouquets of flowers out here. She is Charles Merrill's sister, Wayne's boss. Brother Richards said he'd never visited a Branch here in South America with a better spirit than we have here. He acted so pleased with everything. Then Sunday morning [March 14] at 7:00 we had a missionary meeting. It also was beautiful and of course we all cried. Brother Richards told Wayne after the meeting, "Elder Beck, you're doing a marvelous job. I congratulate you." They left for Sao Paulo at 9:30 that morning and had conference there that afternoon. This morning [Monday, March 15] they left for Curitiba and Joinville and will go to Rio to catch the boat which leaves March 24th. Every one of the members was happy to see him and he was so kind to all of them. They won't be able to tour the entire mission here in Brazil which is bad because all the members have looked forward to his visit for so long.

## CAMPINAS AND SÃO PAULO, BRAZIL

### Sunday, March 14, 1948

**Daily Summary**

*Meetings in Campinas and São Paulo, summary of trip to Brazil so far, and brief general history of the Church in Brazil*

### ELDER FREDERICK H. DELLENBACH MISSIONARY JOURNAL[33]

Were up at 500. Went back to sleep. Wake up ½ hr. before we were supposed to be in meeting. We held a missionary report meeting at 7:00 AM with Apostle Richards. We all arose, gave our names, wards and from what stake and then told of our work, our problems, our ideas for improvement and then bore our testimonies. We felt the Spirit of God in our midst and my voice cracked and there were tears in my eyes as I bore my testimony. It [is] a wonderful experience to fell [feel] that Spirit and humbleness which I felt then. Elder Beck and his wife broke down too. Apostle Richards commended the work in Campinas and promised us

*São Paulo Branch picnic, 1946. Courtesy of CHL.*

many blessings if we would look unto the Lord. Apostle Richards left with President Rex for São Paulo to attend the conference there.

### IRENE M. RICHARDS JOURNAL[34]

We returned about noon and attended a German meeting. They didn't seem too happy. They are refugees who came to Brazil their transportation paid if they would work out in the fields for a certain many years, then they'd be free. By now they are more Portuguise than German and their children are growing up to be real Brazilians. Some old ones speak German yet. Some underwent many embarrassing things but their lives were saved and their children will have a home. One lady gave me a bunch of zinnias.

Then we held a Portuguesi meeting. The elders sang. . . . Stephen spoke well interpreted. ◊◊◊◊oth. The saints presented us with orchids and a beautiful tray. One with butteries[35]—"ɛZarboleta" in blue and yellow and brown. I was so hoarse when we finished our thank you's that I just fell into bed.

NEWS ARTICLE: *CHURCH NEWS*[36]

### Elder Richards Ends Trip with Tour of Brazilian Mission

By Elder John A. Alius

SAO PAULO—Leaving behind them a wake of inspiration and friendship, Elder Stephen L Richards of the Council of the Twelve, and Mrs. Richards have completed about half of their tour of the Brazilian Mission.

As the first apostle to visit this mission since its organization as such in May of 1935, Elder Richards' stay in Brazil is attracting much attention and in each of the branches visited so far, halls were filled to capacity. Considerable press attention was also accorded his advent here.

Apostle Richards and his wife are in Brazil on the last lap of their review of the South American Missions of the Church. Before arriving here, they had visited the Argentine and Uruguayan missions.

In their travels around the mission Elder and Mrs. Richards were accompanied by President Harold M. Rex and his wife, Diania Rex.

So far, Elder Richards is favorably impressed with this country, especially with its progressive young people, and the beautiful architecture and landscaping of the larger cities.

The tenor of his speeches in the branches visited so far has been one voiced by the general authorities in all nations: The need for faith and repentance, and of living close to God.

He told some hundred people who attended the conference held in Sao Paulo under the most adverse weather conditions, that God will be our best friend if we will but become His friend and this we accomplish by accepting and living His teachings, and going to Him in prayer.

One of the outstanding meetings held to date was in the industrial city of Campinas, a model town of the state of Sao Paulo. There, more than 170 persons attended, although the Church membership numbers only 50. At Campinas, Elder and Mrs. Richards witnessed also the baptism of five persons on the banks of a beautiful little river a few miles from the city.

In another town in the same state, Riberao Preto, where four missionaries have been laboring for only a few months, and where there are no members of the Church, whatever, 65 persons came to hear the inspired words of Elder Richards.

While Elder Richards is here to present a message of encouragement and hope to the people of Brazil, his main reason for visiting this country is to review existing conditions as applied to missionary labors present and future. His report will be presented to the First Presidency and Council of the Twelve upon his return to Salt Lake City.

While his review of conditions here is the first visit of one of the Twelve in the Brazilian Mission, Apostle Melvin Ballard had been to this country in 1925, when the east coast of South America was dedicated as a field of missionary labor. At that time, the South American Mission was established, with Brazil figuring only as a district. Missionaries started their labors, with headquarters in Jolnville [Joinville], Santa Catarina, in 1927.[37]

In 1935 the Brazilian district became a mission in its own right, with Elder Rulon S. Howells as first president.

At that time, as in the years since the work was first started here, and until 1939, the teachings of the Lord were preached here in the German language exclusively, on the theory that people of northern and central European extraction were more receptive to the Gospel.

In the first years of World War II, however, the Brazilian government passed a law prohibiting the use of language other than Portuguese, and the mission suffered a set-back from which it is only now recovering.

Evidence of the knotty matter was the necessity, in some branches, of Elder Richards' speeches being translated into two tongues: Portuguese for those persons converted since 1939: German—it now being permitted again on a limited scale—for those who had accepted the Gospel in the time when the work was carried on in that language.

Many German members and investigators in this country, having gone through their lives associating with people who were almost without exception, of their own race, have never learned the tongue of this country.

The complete withdrawal of the missionaries for almost three years during the war, leaving the ◊[m]ission with a lack of qualified leadership in the priesthood as well as other phases of the work, struck another hard blow, which is only now being healed, with the coming of more and more missionaries.

There are, at the moment, 56 missionaries laboring in this mission. All of them, as well as the mission's 450 members—little less than half of whom are now of non-German extraction—feel that the visit of Elder and Sister Richards, and their observations and suggestions made here, and to the authorities at home, will see the work of the Lord progressing in this nation at an unprecedented tempo.

---

## TRAVEL TO CURITIBA, BRAZIL

**Monday, March 15, 1948**

**Daily Summary**
*Traveled 300 miles to Curitiba*

### IRENE M. RICHARDS JOURNAL[38]

March 15th ~~16~~- 1948—~~Tuesday~~ Monday

It's wonderful how one can get up the next morning.

We started early, without breakfast which was wrong for Steve. He must yet learn that he can't start out a trip before 8 and still be served breakfast in S..A. Well, we traveled in the rain and red mud for 500 K.M. which is about 300 miles I guess, through a hand made highway, cut thru hills with picks and made with donkeys and carts, by Brazilians, I imagine very many years ago. There are some 100 feet cuts and it winds continually up and reaches about 300 K.L. in altitude. Then we wound down in the same way until we reached a pretty valley and came to where 6 elders were housed in a new local. "Coritiva" is in the States of Paraná◊[39] in Brazil. The road is wide—enough for passing, and the nativis keep it up beautifully. They rake it and keep the gutters in repair. When we pass them they turn their umbrellas to keep the splash from their clothes. We saw one woman washing in a wheelbarrow by a trickle of a stream. The idea is to soap the clothes and spread them

Curitiva, State of Paranae[40]

out in the sun, which does the work, they rinse them after and dry them again which makes them white. which is impossible because of the red water they use. All along are huts where dirty unfed children sit or peer out, and I never saw so much human pack animals ever. The women carry babies, and bundles, and sticks. The donkeys carry baskets of stuff tied on each side and every man has a burden of some sort. We saw one gurrnie [guinea] hen, then we saw a man with a rifle, so it won't be there long. The roads are so bumpy that no auto attempts them. The only other one we saw was one we lent our jack to just before we arrived here. Many trucks and some jeepes. The rail road comes in a dusty way from a great way a sound distance taking two days, which is more sensible than an auto in one day. The plane doesn't land here, but comes to "point Elegro" [Porto Alegre] and "joinvilla" [Joinville] in about 3 hours from Sao Paulo. People here know that if you cannot use the plane you had better stay at home, because you can't travel if you don't. Business men do just that, but we are strangers and didn't know. So we are literally "all in." I am afraid Bro Rex new car won't have the resale value he hoped it would have after we are gone. I notice there are a few autos in town but they are not covered with red mud. The rich people use them around town.

There never was such a lovely canvice [◊◊◊◊◊◊◊] place. The mountains are covered with a jungle growth. Some fine trees and finally on the highest point were the "Paranáe" pines—a tall flat-topped spreading pine tree like an umbrella. We have seen these peculiar trees no where else. The profusion of pink, yellow, and purple blossoming trees are lovely among the very green other foliage. One fellow had caught a snake and it was squirming and striking but he seemed to enjoy its antics, and knew how to control it. We were exhausted and didn't want to dress for dinner, so they sent us up something we said light—like "bread butter milk fruit." When it came it was two heavy meals including wieners steak and fish, so we laughed at the idea of people too tired to eat. "Oh, for a clean kitchen and two eggs and some butter and toast and cold arden milk."

---

## JOINVILLE, BRAZIL

**Tuesday, March 16, 1948**

**Daily Summary**
*Heart problems in Curitiba, travel to Joinville, and conference in Joinville*

# IRENE M. RICHARDS JOURNAL[41]

This morning Steve's pulse was 41. We dosed him up and it came to 48. Then it went down again. At about 10 it seemed fair. But we decided to go on and have him ~~ride~~ sit in front [of the car]. So as the people say "With God willing" we trusted a lot.—

The ride was marvelous. Such scenery and such awful roads. I am sure the front seat was better and we are here and he is still 60–58. There is a German here and his hotel is clean. I think that makes Stephen feel better. The filth of some places kills him. The road thru a canyon wound as did the one yesterday but it was extra beautiful. Some waterfalls and streams and high hills, and distant views were marvelous. I am glad he felt better so we could all enjoy it. The missionaries are coming to dinner together before meeting. This German "Joinvilla" is refreshing and not Spanish. No high walls, no dark corners. We are ~~eating~~ dinning out under the trees in a garden. Bro Rex took us around the town in his auto. There are some people here who won't join our church because the elders got in bad a while

*Joinville Branch meetinghouse, 1930s. Courtesy of CHL.*

ago, and being Germans they can't forgive. This may have been the place where the S.A. mission began under a "Stohl" and started with a very poor class, and they can't raise the standard yet.⁴²

## NEWS ARTICLE: *A NOTICIA*⁴³

**Religious Movement**

**Two Missionaries of The Church of Jesus Christ of Latter-day Saints Visit "A Noticia"**

We had the pleasure yesterday of receiving two young men "Elders," Kent Tyler and Elmo Turner, missionaries of The Church of Jesus Christ of Latter-day Saints, who informed us of the arrival Saturday, the 16th of Mr. Stephen L. Richards, who is presented as one of the twelve apostles of that Church. The two missionaries explained to us that their church is based upon the organization of the primitive church the which, as their adepts believe, was lost until the year 1830, the year of the organization of their church. They further explained to us that they are two of nearly 5000 missionaries spreading the gospel to all parts of the world.

Mr. Richards is journeying here accompanied by his wife and also by Mr. Harold M. Rex, president of the Brazilian Mission and his wife. Mr. Richards will stay in Joinville only one day where he will deliver a discourse in the Church of Jesus Christ situated on Rua Frederico Hubner; the discourse will be translated into Portuguese and German.

Mr. Richards and his wife are making a journey of inspection of the South American Missions of the Church already having visited Argentina and Uruguay. Their plans include holding conferences in Joinville, Curitiba, Santos, São Paulo, Campinas, Priacicaba [Piracicaba], Sorocaba, Ribeirão Preto, Belo Horizonte, Juiz de Fora and Rio de Janeiro. Upon terminating this excursion, they will return to Salt Lake City in the state of Utah, USA which is the Center of the church. There in one of the General Conferences of the church Mr. Richards will make a report of his inspection describing the conditions and problems here encountered and offering counsel for their adequate solution in the interest of their church.

The young missionaries whose visit we appreciate invite the public to meet with them in their meeting Tuesday at 7:30, the entrance being free.

*Joinville Branch Primary activity, 1937. Courtesy of CHL.*

## BRAZILIAN MISSION RECORD[44]

Brother Stephen L. Richards, of the Council of Twelve, and his wife arrived in Joinville today about 2:30 P.M. with President Harold M. Rex and wife. They came in the mission's new Studebaker. Brother and Sister Richards rested in the afternoon at Hotel Trocadero. They are both elderly and have endured a very strenuous journey through Argentina, into Chile,[45] back through Uruguay, and now Brazil, and as a result are tired and worn. However, the rest did them much good and they seemed to recuperate marvelously. The missionaries ate dinner with them and President and Sister Rex. Then at 7:30 P.M., the Joinvile District Conference commenced with Brother Richards presiding and Elder C. Elmo Turner conducting. The conference has been well announced both through the newspaper and on the radio and there were 127 present, 85 of whom were friends, and filled the church to capacity, leaving some standing in the back.

President Rex was the first speaker and then Brother Richards spoke. He was inspired to say many beautiful and enlightening things about the gospel and bore a strong testimony to the divinity of Jesus Christ and the restoration of His church in these latter days through the Prophet Joseph Smith. The main theme of his talk was on brotherly love and kindness. He was inspired to stress especially the need of being a true friend and refusing to believe tales about anyone until such things are proven. There is a great deal of "Quatch", or underhand stories circulating about the different members and this talk was exactly the thing needed.

It was a beautiful conference with many, many beautiful flowers about the rostrum and new, heavy dark red curtains lending a certain dignity that was noticeable. Elder Turner translated the talk into Portuguese. Pres. Rex translated Brother Richard's greeting to the members in German.

## IRENE M. RICHARDS LETTER[46]

We have traveled about 100 miles west and south, since I began writing. At one town the saints presented me with 2 dozen orchids. So Georgia, I was dripping with them from my shoulder down to the floor. I was so taken off my feet and thrilled. So now I have had all that's coming to me. Everyone is disappointed because I don't speak but they would be more so if I did. We have traveled thru the most primitive country possible. Thru a mountain pass, cut by hand. . . . It was too rough, but we made it, and it was too much for Papa. He is O.K. now. We won't come back the same way. No one travels in Brasil by auto or train, just by airplane. The roads are impassable; we found that out. The scenery was magnificent. The falls, mountains, streams, jungle and distant views. I am glad we saw it, but we will try anything once. I have no other definite word about our coming home as yet. We came back by air. It was fun. Now I will want to do all my traveling by plane. There is no word other than that I wrote. So we will either see you in N.Y. or at Toledo. You decide which. We are fine and will spend three days in Rio and embark on the Argentina on the 24$^{th}$, see N.Y. on the 5$^{th}$ of April.

Lovingly,
Mother.

---

## CURITIBA, BRAZIL

**Wednesday, March 17, 1948**

**Daily Summary**
*Travel back to Curitiba and meeting and conference in Curitiba*

### IRENE M. RICHARDS JOURNAL[47]

We rode back from Joinvilla a German town, to Corativa [Curitiba].[48]
    Last night the meeting was a full one but peculiarly cool. The people don't feel so well toward Americans for fighting Germany, and it is shone in their faces and demenior. There was some good music, but the elders said two men left because the girl sang in German instead of Portuguise, which shows they are a problem.
    It had rained which made the roads more passable. Stephen rode in front and I am sure he stood it better. The waterfalls and distant scenery are beautiful, and no one saw a more true discription of a jumgle [jungle]. The boys came in the jeep and followed us in.

We have rested, aten [eaten] and are now ready for the meeting with the elders at one. It is Allies and Phils' birthday and I have been thinking of them among the South American cenery◊ [scenery] There are 20 men here. . . .

At the meeting in a public hall the table was strewn with gardenias. Stephen kept us for an hour after the elders were finished and gave the usual good advice. All the boys were pleased. This is the last meeting of elders. Tomorrow we are taking the plane maybe.

## BRAZILIAN MISSION RECORD[49]

About 6:30 A. M. Elders Turner, Tyler, Wilson and Stringham left for Curitiba in the jeep. They were met on the road by Brother Richards, Pres. Rex, and their wives in the Studebaker and the jeep followed it to Curitiba, arriving there at 10:00. Twenty missionaries from the Ipomeia, Curitiba, Joinville, and Porto Alegre[50] Districts met there and attended an inspirational meeting from 1 to 6 P.M. in the Curitiba branch hall. Brother Richards gave us all some very good advice and we all reported to him our activities and our needs, etc. giving him a better over-all picture so that he may return and report more completely the conditions and needs of this mission when he returns to Salt Lake City. At 8:00 P.M. in a rented hall, the Curitiba District Conference was convened and again Brother Richards gave a forceful discourse that thrilled all listeners. Elder Turner again translated the talk into Portuguese. The missionaries stayed at a hotel and the following morning, March 18, they departed to their various fields of labor. The four brethren, Elders Turner, Tyler, Wilson and Stringham returned to Joinville the same day, having made a safe, enjoyable and very worthwhile trip.

## ELDER MILTON R. BLOOMQUIST MISSIONARY LETTER[51]

Saturday afternoon 3 pm, 27 March 1948

Dearest Folks,

. . . Well, there isn't too much news from down here, but there have been a few things. As for one, our supposed conference with Apostle Stephan L. Richards here in Novo Hamburgo. We didn't have it! Elder

Richards is 70 years old,[52] and after he and his wife had made their visits through Argentina, Paraguay, Chile,[53] and Ury◊guia [Uruguay], they were very, very weary; but at ~~that~~ that they visited all but 4 branches here in Brazil! As you can perhaps picture though, we were pretty disappointed down here when we received news to cancel our conferences and just the missionaries go up to Curitiba to hold a missionary conference. The saints took it very hard and could hard[l]y be reconciled.

All 6 of us Pôrto Alegre district missionaries left here 13 March a Friday morning at 6 a.m. [T]wo of us, Elders Bowles and Sellers (my companion), had to take all their bagage and believe me, that train ride would have been pretty rough on them alone if there hadn't been four others of us to help them carry their stuff and change from one train to another you know, the trains down here are a lot different from those in the U.S.A., however, these here must resemble the 1860 models nearly 100 years ago there! It is like every thing else down here—Atraz da lua—or as translated means 'behind the moon'. We are still in the cart and oxen era down here—in fact we seem to be just coming into that! I will have to show you some pictures I have been taking after I get back.

We had a nice trip up to Curitiba and back. It took us 3 days <and two nights> going up and 3 days and 2 nights coming back to Pôrto Alegre also. It was a trip that afforded us some excellent scenery to view—more than on[e] ordinarily sees from a train. It gave me an oppertunity to see some of Brazil's thick interior and the odd hillbillyish people who live there.

Apostle Richards gave us a fine address, advising us of all the darkness of the political world at this time and our need of having the branches as self supporting as possible with as many local brethren presiding in branch affairs as possible should we missionaries have to leave for causes of war or any such thing. He also explained to us the shortness of our missions and the big job which rests upon us as ambassadors for the church here in Brazil, then he impressed us with the need of organization and diligence to make the most of our time. No one knows any better than do I just how fast this mission time can fly by. 9 months have passed since I left Salt Lake City in June, it seems impossible to me—how does it seem to you?

We had only one day of conference in Curitiba and it wasn't a full day. From 1 PM to 6 PM Wednesday, 17 March we 20 South Brazilian missionaries met in our meeting with Brother Richards & wife and also President

& Sister Rex. Then at 8 PM until 9:30 PM we missionaries attended the Curitiba branch conference and after that we held a business meeting at the missionaries apartment home for an hour discussing mission problems and receiving and giving helps and advise one from another. The day ended at 11:30 PM, and at 7:30 AM Thursday we were aboard the train to begin our long, s[l]ow, dirty ride back home.

## CURITIBA TO SÃO PAULO, BRAZIL, VIA AIRPLANE

**Thursday, March 18, 1948**

**Daily Summary**
*Returned to São Paulo by airplane*

### IRENE M. RICHARDS JOURNAL[54]

The Rexes have just driven away, for Sao Paulo. We are going to miss their company and the beautiful drive thru the hills but we will try the plane. Stephen will try anything once. Bro Jenson came and took us for a taxi ride about 25 K.M. from the city to the airport. He brought us a beautiful tray from the elders and saints of Parana. It's beautif<ul> with wood inlay, and is a fine rembrance of the country. They are very generous I'm sure.

The air trip was <u>glorious</u>—no trouble and very smooth. The view over fields and villages hills and jungles was interesting and the clouds were so light and snowy. I am surely

*The Rex family standing in front of a DC-3 airplane. The Richardses' first flight was on a DC-3 airplane in Brazil. Courtesy of CHL.*

grateful for such an opertunity. We flew it in 1 and ½ hours. Our ears ached while coming down. We landed well and felt fine From Curitiba to Sao Paulo. The taxi brought us back to Hotel Sao Paulo, and we feel at home. From our window we see the same scene we saw at [room numbers] 907 and also 1507 and now we are 807. They are nice suites of rooms. I have entirely worn out my pen and am using Stephens, which doesn't seem so good either. We walked a little for which I suffered cramps in my feet.

## SÃO PAULO, BRAZIL

**Friday, March 19, 1948**

**Daily Summary**
*Mission presidency meeting*

### IRENE M. RICHARDS JOURNAL[55]

Pres Rex, Elders Beck and the other <Bro Neilson> [Nielsen] are coming here for a meeting this morning. I am going to write some letters.

I wrote to Lynn[,] Allie, Georgia, Philip and Richard, Ellen and Sister Young.

After dinner the elders resumed their discussions here. Pres Rex brought us some pictures of orchids and oxen and baptisms and "Yara."[56] Instead of taking the train we are going to "Fly down to Rio"[57] sunday a.m. ◊

### BRAZILIAN MISSION PRESIDENCY MEETING[58]

Minutes of Mission Presidency Meeting
March 19, 1948
Presided over by Elder Stephen L. Richards

Prayer Elder Wayne M. Beck

Chief among the factors that Brother Richards believed was necessary for the improvement of this mission was the adoption of a plan which would give greater stimulation to the missionaries. The best supervision is in their progress. We must live with them, stay with them, help them and show them.

Second to this factor was that we get a new start in Sao Paulo. We can get the lower class to come up to the higher level, but we cannot get the higher class to go down to the lower level. We must work for self-sustaining groups of Latter-Day Saints.

Following the above two factors the housing conditions and factors involved were to be considered next.

In view of these factors Brother Richards recommended the following three measures be taken here:

I. Arrangement of a program which would create a more effective system of stimulation of the Missionaries and their work.
II. Establishment of a program which would give a more promising outlook in Sao Paulo.
III. Housing, factors and conditions.

I. Brother Richards suggested:

a. A division of the mission in so far as supervising of the missionaries is concerned. Elder Wayne M. Beck to move to Curitiba and supervise, under the direction of President Harold M. Rex, the activities of the missionaries. He should work, tract, assist in Cottage meetings and show them how to do and also to improve their methods on teaching of the Gospel. In general stimulating them onward to a better performance.

b. President Rex would assume nearly the same role in respect to the missionaries of the northern half of the mission. Working with them more closely and stimulating the missionaries and their efforts. In addition a division of this type would reduce the travel time normally taken by the Mission President and therefore allow more time for him to devote to the supervision of the mission as a whole.

c. Elder Thayle Nielsen[59] would remain in Sao Paulo and supervise the operation of the mission office and other duties as suggested by the Mission President.

How much time should be given by missionaries to out of the way places deserves our careful consideration. Likewise, work that does not contribute directly to the proclamation of the gospel. A study should be made of the problem of cutting down time on housekeeping duties and allow more time to the teaching of the gospel. This is an administrative problem and would require close and frequent supervision.

It is wrong to lead missionaries to believe that they may become District Presidents. Policy of the Church is to visit missionaries oftener than every 6 months. We must be careful not to scatter the missionaries out too thin. Missionaries should show a breakdown of other expenses in their weekly reports.

IV. Establishment of a program which would give a more promising outlook in Sao Paulo.

It would be well if we had a new beginning here in Sao Paulo. The higher class people are reluctant to visit meeting places in a lower class district. It was recommended that we obtain a place of meeting in a higher class district and begin to tract and do other missionary work in that area. Other missionaries would continue to carry on in the old sections.

V. Housing, factors and conditions.

The first objective in the selection of a mission home is to obtain a suitable place for the executive offices of the Church. Second is locating in a good residential district. Third—a good living place for the Mission President and his family.

Much discussion was given to the selection of a mission home in an excellent residential district. Brother Richards visited some fine homes in excellent districts here.

It was urged that we investigate carefully and thoroughly all zoning restrictions before we recommend a purchase. Matters such as costs and upkeep, tax exemption, and transportation facilities would require our very careful consideration.

Other Subjects Discussed.

Branch in Ipomeia,[60] State of Santa Catarina. We must work to the end of making that branch self-sustaining. The amount of time spent there by missionaries is to be carefully considered.

Basketball Team and Chorus. A great deal of consideration was given to the many factors involved. Have we the necessary talent, musically and athletically? Is the time used in this manner going to give better results than a more direct means of proclamation of the gospel?

Visas. Letter given to Brother Richards prior to his departure.

Closing Prayer—Elder Stephen L. Richards

## SÃO PAULO, BRAZIL

**Saturday, March 20, 1948**

**Daily Summary**
*Sister Richards remembers traveling conditions and discusses various ventures in São Paulo*

### IRENE M. RICHARDS LETTER[61]

Hotel Sao Paulo<br>Sao Paulo, Brazil<br>March 20, 1948

Dear Allie:[62]

On your birthday[63] we were riding through a dense jungle on a narrow road cut by the hand of man with only rude implements and with the help of a donkey and cart, and mostly not even a donkey. . . . This single lane is cut for about 350 miles, then there is a big town. Then we traveled 150 more to another big town. People seem content to live in these, and they don't travel. Those who are rich go by airplane, and trucks carry food thru the road, which no auto can use and last long. We only met a few autos and we were willing to take the judgment of the Brazilian business men, who say they all do their traveling by plane, after we tried it once and so we returned on a big plane to Sao Paulo and enjoyed an hour and a little more of smooth, beautiful sailing above the clouds and were glad we were not bumping up and down on that one road cut thru hills and jungles, which we got glimpses of now and then. There were as many as six planes that landed and took off during the short time we were at the airport. So everyone who can't afford to fly, just stays home. There is a railroad, mostly freight, which takes about two days to make the grades. So interior Brazil has a long way to go to become modern and very popular with outsiders.[64] They don't care, they are happy.

I just spend my time writing while Papa does the work. It would have been fine for you to have heard some of his admonition, advice and informing talks to the Presidents, elders and saints. Those interpreting have done a good job, they say. I wouldn't know. We have visited Spanish, German, and Portuguese for the most part. Question: Should one be intelligent to join the church, or should the church bring intelligence to people? I guess both, Some are illiterate and superstitious and need brightening up. Some have said they were disappointed that I didn't speak. I think they would have been more so had I spoken. I think it's hard enough to listen to a man talk, let alone a woman. We are finishing our last lap of our journey this week-end and will be on our way home again.

. . . Papa is holding a meeting while I write.

He finished his appointment and we rode out to see some locations for a new mission home. There are some beautiful mansions and some very lowly homes. I hope they choose a new upcoming district.

We have come across a waiter who speaks English and have succeeded in getting some pretty good things to eat so tonight we had a fillet split in half and done through and rice. Then a fruit salad for dessert. I guess they hate to see us come in the dining room, we are so hard to please and dumb to them.

We won't be home until the middle of April just about, so as soon as school will let you, come over. We will have two months to be around before summer, and we could do a lot of visiting in two months. . . .

President Rex says the pullman train to Rio is not good, so we are going to fly. Then we can see the lay of the land and the water. "Flying down to Rio"[65] in technicolor, on Sunday morning. Then we have meeting and stay at the—I've forgotten the hotel's name, but it's a nice one, and then we play around Monday. Maybe Papa will have a cruise or something and we leave Tues. eve for home. I just can't wait, although I have had such a fine trip.

Hope you are all well as we are.

Lovingly,<br>Mother and Father.

---

## RIO DE JANEIRO, BRAZIL

**Sunday, March 21, 1948**

**Daily Summary**
*Flight to Rio de Janeiro*

### IRENE M. RICHARDS JOURNAL[66]

We took the D.C. 3 at 7:30 a.m. We were the first ones to enter, and had our choice of seats. As we sailed over Sao Paulo we could see the town and then we got above the clouds, which lay like a white sheet over the earth, Once in a while could we see down through them onto the green fields and rolling hills. Sometimes roads would wind and end in some small town. Then we came over the ocean where beaches spread in and out and maybe some few inhabited spots, but mostly jungle. We did not ride high. My ears only popped once or twice. It was more smooth than car, or boat, and the steward was especially kind to show us maps, and explain things. Thank goodness he could speak a little Eng. He had been to Texas and Florida. All the personel are trained in the U.S. they say. We loosened our belts after we rose off the ground. Later we were served sandwiches, cracker and a drink. Brazilian coffee is a little cup of coffee, black, poured over sugar. So its like syrup of coffee. I took lemonade. Our plane skirted the land until we reached Rio, then circled the bay, and then over the apartment houses (which I am glad are not mowed down) then onto the airfield on the edge of the bay. We turned on 2 runways before we came to a stop. It was an unforgetable sight to see the Bay, below us was "Coconevade"[67] or the peak with the Christ on. The sugar loaf where the cable <car> takes one for a view, and the entire city, beaches and whole picture in our grand panarama. This seems to be the crowning peak in all of South Am. travels, a thrills to be remembered all our lives. We suffered no discomforture, the landing was so easy. Sister Larson[68] was at the airport to meet us. I am afraid it was an imposition for her. We were only a few blocks from the Hotel Serrador, a new, beautiful round front building facing the park and beach.

From our 20th story window we can see over the town, hills beach and park. As we lay on our beds resting we can view, out of two immense windows, the scene. Surely there could be no prettier place in this world or the next. I must send my other five boys a card from our air trip.

---

### RIO DE JANEIRO, BRAZIL

**Monday, March 22, 1948**

**Daily Summary**

*Missionary meeting and visit to embassy; last night in South America*

#### IRENE M. RICHARDS JOURNAL[69]

Last night after the Rex's came we had a quick supper and went to a Brother Blazurs for a meeting. There were about 20 present. Sanders, Bird, people from home who are working here. There was a "camelian" <chameleon> on the wall, and when I looked again it was gone. I hope every one looked in their pockets because it hid someplace. We were tired and had a good room to rest in on the 20 floor but the big clock was lit up all night. [A drawing of a clock appears here in the actual journal entry.]

The elders are coming for a meeting and then we will have seen them all one [once], who is in the Mission. (Rex ~~Fra◊◊◊~~ goes with address written below it.)

~~Mar.~~ We stayed in the auto while Stephen called on the Enbasy [Embassy] until late. Then we went to dinner at Blazurs, the place we were at for meeting last night. We enjoyed an american meal and conversation.

They are fine people. He was on a mission with Henry Richards in Germany.

The drive was thru two beach parks and at night they are also beautiful. Our last night in South America.

---

## RIO DE JANEIRO, BRAZIL

**Tuesday, March 23, 1948**

**Daily Summary**
*Toured and shopped in Rio and boarded the SS* Argentina *bound for New York in the evening*

### IRENE M. RICHARDS JOURNAL[70]

We are free to day and we hope we can go to the beach and have a cruise on the Bay. but there were no clubs for us. So we contented ourselves with just looking. There were many lovely boats. and there was to be a luncheon ◊◊◊◊ [soon]. We rode about and saw the gorgeous parks and places for the last time in Rio. We had a pear and an apple for lunch and rested. Then we walked thru on[e] of those autoless streets which was crowded with shoppers. The displays are fine but the goods are not so. There is nothing here of any merit much everything imported, lovely things from Eng[land] and Europe and some cheap things from America. We inquired for a Ballorena skirt and we had drove in Buenos Aires and Montevedeo and one place had one just from U.S. but it was not big enough for me. The women are so tiny. Their shoes are so cute also. Around one window was a crowd of ladies, trying to see the "new look." It was near to a riot. I stepped back to save myself from being run over. The skirts are extra shirt [short] here yet. We ate dinner at the "Serrador" and the Larsons were with us. The man who played the music was an American and played beautifully. I enjoyed it all, and we visitid and said our goodbye's. We rode to the docks with Larsons and the Rexes and they came on deck where we visited until midnight. Larsons had placed a big basket of roses on our dresser. Mrs. Rex gave me a journal and Sanders had left a couple of cocoanuts for us.

When we arrived at Rio, Rex and Larson were with us first and so we parted with our oldest friends in South America We enjoyed them much.

---

## SS *ARGENTINA*, ATLANTIC OCEAN

**Wednesday, March 24, to Monday, March 29, 1948**

**Daily Summary**
SS Argentina *leaves Brazil, the Richardses relax, and Elder Richards gives the Easter sermon; later in general conference Elder Richards shares a story about a minister he met on the boat*

### IRENE M. RICHARDS JOURNAL[71]

[Thursday, March 25, 1948]
We are upon deck where it is cooler. The sea is calm and blue. Last night the moon rose where the sun had just set, full and <u>big</u>. I think it was a perfect evening in a tropical country, as far as I know. The guests preferred to dance on the deck and a very heavy man and woman took the prize in the Rumba or sumba or Tango, or whatever their nationality was. It was quite a demonstration. Billy says the Rhumba is Cuban but america has perfected it. The Tango is Rio or Brazilian, and the Somba is Uruguayan.

[Friday, March 26, 1948]
The wind blows constantly thank goodness, because it is so warm. We will soon cross the equator. The meals are excellent and the reading good. . . .

We came upon deck early and Stephen is playing shuffle board with a man named Richards. He has a son named Richard like we have. Mr. <u>Hartnet</u> is the manager who arranges for the service on Sunday. Stephen is to be the speaker. Easter services. We are waiting for the moon. We thought it was a ship on fire last night as it came out of the sea with a bang.

[Sunday, March 28, 1948]
Stephen gave the easter sermon, very big audiance, and several appreciations from people who had been to Salt Lake. "One lady I heard say. "I

*Elder Richards preached the sermon at the Easter Sunday service on the SS* Argentina. *Courtesy of CHL.*

have never heard a mormon preach". The music was good and some fine man prayed. We went down stairs to rest. Stephen got kind of excited and it made his heart miss. So we missed the easter parade on deck. They say there were about a dozen hatted ladies and one man with a baloon for a hat. It changes our lives when everyone knows you are a mormon. It makes one feel apart. I wonder what the children are doing at home. Who is rolling eggs on our lawn? etc. We did not wait for the moon tonight. We have crossed the equator some time today. We find many are complimentory about Stephens speech.

## STEPHEN L RICHARDS CONFERENCE ADDRESS[72]

I am going to tell you of an incident which occurred on a ship while I was returning from a visit to South America a number of years ago. On this voyage, which included two Sundays, I was asked by those representing the captain of the vessel to conduct what were called "divine services." There was no one on board of our own faith to whom I might appeal for assistance. I had made the acquaintance of a rather elderly man who was a retired minister of another church, so I asked him if he would participate and offer prayer. He gave a very beautiful prayer at one of the services. After the prayer I engaged him in conversation, and among other things we spoke of the care of youth and family responsibility. He recited an impressive incident in his own experience. He said that while he was an active minister there was among his parishioners a very lovely family. They had a promising son who married. He established a home and began to have his own family. Most unfortunately, however, he took up the habit of drinking, and within a comparatively short time reached the stage where he might be classed as an alcoholic. His wife and his family were, of course, greatly distressed. They pleaded with him, and so did this minister, to abandon his wayward course, but seemingly to no avail.

One day my friend, the minister, met this young man coming down the street. He recognized him some little distance before they met. The young man offered his hand in greeting, but the minister rejected the offer, and he said, in substance, to the young man: "John, I rebuke you, and in the authority of my ministry I command you to cease the terrible practices which are ruining your home and bringing such sorrow to your loved ones." With these words the minister left the young man, confused and shocked, standing on the sidewalk. My friend told me that after he had gone a short distance he was tempted to go back and apologize. He said that he had never done such a thing before, and he could not understand how he had come to speak such seemingly cruel words to one of his friends for whom he felt such responsibility.

When he had finished telling me of the incident, I picked up a volume which I had with me, and I read to him these words:

"No power or influence can or ought to be maintained by virtue of the priesthood, only be persuasion, by longsuffering, by gentleness and meekness, and by love unfeigned;

"By kindness, and pure knowledge, which shall greatly enlarge the soul without hypocrisy, and without guile—

"Reproving betimes with sharpness, when moved upon by the Holy Ghost; and then showing forth afterwards an increase of love toward him whom thou hast reproved, lest he esteem thee to be his enemy;

"That he may know that thy faithfulness is stronger than the cords of death." (D & C 121:41–44.)

"That's it, that's it!" the old minister said to me excitedly. "Where did you find that?" I told him that it was part of a revelation concerning the nature of the Holy Priesthood, given to the Prophet Joseph Smith more

*Stephen L Richards at the Salt Lake Tabernacle during the April 1958 general conference. Courtesy of CHL.*

than a hundred years before this conversation took place. The minister then told me that after he had given the rebuke to the young man, a few weeks passed, and the man came to him and thanked him, and said to him, "All the pleading of my family and friends made me sorrowful but did not bring to me the courage to act. That rebuke which you gave to me that day on the street has given me a strength that I could not acquire before. I have never taken a drink since, and I have the resolution and the faith to believe that I never will again."

It is a kindness to reprove in the spirit of love. It is an unkindness to mitigate the gravity of offenses in those for whose guidance and direction we have responsibility.

### IRENE M. RICHARDS LETTER[73]

S. S. Argentina<br>March 29, 1948

Dear Louise:[74]

Won't it be nice to see Lois? I wonder what kind of a hat she will wear. It's really after Easter. The wind has blown constantly so my hats are about spoiled. People don't wear them here. I suppose you have three or four new ones since I left? What did you do for Easter and who rolled what eggs on which lawn? There were about a dozen hatted ladies who paraded here on deck and one man with a balloon for fun. Papa gave the Easter speech and it was delightful. Others said so and many have expressed themselves to us this morning. There was quite an audience. Some young man sang and led the songs: he rendered "The Lord's Prayer" beautifully.

We crossed the equator and it was hot. We are glad for the breeze. Some flying fish are about. Such tiny silver things. Some big black propoise [porpoise] were playing yesterday. There are white caps most of the time. The clouds change continually. We don't have much sunshine and the moon is not visible much. I think as we get away from shore it's so. The sunsets are not as they were near shore either. The astronomer is going to tell us about the stars, if the weather permits tonight. The moon has another face as we now see it.

I suppose we never will see the time again when we haven't a thing to do but watch the sea, sky, people playing deck games, and sunning themselves and filling the pool, and parading the deck, playing cards, eating, drinking, etc., as we see this last week of our cruise. I am satisfied it's a waste of time. How some people can do nothing much all their lives and do any good to themselves or others I can't judge, I guess. . . .

Anyway the meals are still elegant after the abominable cooking of South America. We do enjoy this boat. The worst of it I eat too much good bread and butter. The milk is still canned or powdered. So when we see a good cold Arden bottle of milk we will be happy. I wish you and Steve could finish out this last week for us. I can't read, it makes me sick, but I can write, and will get all my letters ready to mail, so they will beat me home. Stephen is playing shuffleboard and rather excels. It's intensely interesting to observe the variety of characters about us, and some darling children who are just their sweet selves. We trust spring will be just around the corner and that you are all well and happy. We hope it will be cooler from now on.

Lovingly,<br>
Mother and Father.

# NOTES

1. Irene Richards, *Dear Children*, March 11, 1948, Richards Family Papers, 1879–2004, CHL.
2. Irene Louise Richards Covey was the Richardses' second child.
3. Trip itinerary, March 10, 1948, Stephen L Richards Papers, CHL. Some adjustments were made to this itinerary since the Richardses ended up flying in an airplane.
4. Irene M. Richards, Journal, March 8, 1948, Richards Family Papers, 1879–2004, CHL.
5. Gerrit de Jong Jr. spent the academic year of 1947–48 serving the US government as director of a cultural center in Santos, Brazil. He was a professor of languages and music at Brigham Young University and became the first dean of the College of Fine Arts. "Gerrit de Jong, Jr.," BYU College of Fine Arts and Communications, last modified July 22, 2015, https://cfacwiki.byu.edu/index.php/Gerrit_de_Jong,_Jr.
6. Richards, *Dear Children*, March 11, 1948. The excerpt was written at a later date but describes this time period.
7. Irene Louise Richards Covey was the Richardses' second child.
8. Richards, *Dear Children*, March 10, 1948.
9. Alice "Allie" Leila Richards was the Richardses' fourth child.
10. *Mormon Preacher* is an unidentified São Paulo newspaper, 1948, Stephen L Richards Papers, 1921–59.
11. Perhaps a misunderstanding of the reporter since Elder Richards had already traveled to Argentina.
12. São Paulo District Minutes, March 9, 1948, Stephen L Richards Papers.
13. The Church in Brazil first started in São Paulo on May 19, 1935, when mission president Rulon S. Howells held a meeting with three Church members. See South American Mission Manuscript History and Historical Reports, CHL.
14. Minutes of Mission Presidency Meeting, March 10, 1948, Stephen L Richards Papers.
15. Richards, *Dear Children*, March 10, 1948.
16. Georgia Gill Richards was the Richardses' sixth child.
17. For more cultural information about Brazil, see the seminal work *Nicolás Sánchez-Albornoz, The Population of Latin America: A History*, trans. W. A. R. Richardson (Berkeley: University of California Press, 1974).

18. Richards, Journal, March 10, 1948.
19. Campinas is located about 55 miles (88 km) from São Paulo.
20. See "Like a Dream," *Church News*, October 18, 1997, 16. The first members of the Campinas Branch were baptized on June 4, 1942, and included Rute Mendes, Alfredo Lima Vaz, Remo Roselli, Walter Carmona, and Flavia Garcia Erbolato. Alfredo Vaz was Campinas Branch president and local missionary at the time of the Richardses' visit.
21. W. Ernest Young to S. L. Richards, March 10, 1948, Stephen L Richards Papers.
22. Richards, Journal, March 12, 1948.
23. The phrase "road was a" was inserted above the word *drinking*.
24. Grant C. Tucker, Journal, March 12, 1948, CHL.
25. Frederick H. Dellenbach, Journal, March 14, 1948, Frederick H. Dellenbach Papers, CHL.
26. Dellenbach, Journal, March 14, 1948.
27. Richards, Journal, March 13, 1948.
28. Evelyn Beck recalled, "I remember President Rex called and asked if I'd take care of their baby while they toured up into Piracicaba and Americana, wasn't it? Remember how we polished that house? We had to use that hand buffer, and we polished those ten rooms with that red wax. We had everything just spotless. They were coming early the next morning. And it started to rain. Before we could get our shutters closed, our downstairs was just covered with water. We had to dip it out with buckets. He [Elder Richards] came the next morning. We had all of our things draped over chairs and barrels because it had just soaked everything." Wayne M. and Evelyn M. Beck Oral History, interviewed by Gordon Irving, January 17–31, 1974, 29, CHL.
29. "Campinas Is Host to One of the Most Eminent Figures of the Contemporary Religious World," [n.d.], 1948, Stephen L Richards Papers.
30. "A Representative of The Church of Latter-day Saints in Campinas," March 14, 1948, Stephen L Richards Papers.
31. Evelyn Beck letter, March 15, 1948, Wayne M. Beck Papers, in private possession. Evelyn and Wayne Beck served as missionaries with their young family in Brazil after the Second World War. Wayne Beck had already served a mission in Brazil and was the first counselor to President Harold Rex.
32. The Becks added this detail about the baptismal service in an oral history. Evelyn: "When we got there—didn't we go out on a bus out there?—and the sun came out. I'll never forget how impressive that was. And it impressed

Sister Richards too. She was with him and she just couldn't get over that." Wayne: "It rained all the way out and all the way back." Evelyn: "But during that time of the baptism the sun came out. It was just beautiful." Wayne M. and Evelyn M. Beck Oral History, 29.

33. Dellenbach, Journal, March 14, 1948.
34. Richards, Journal, March 14, 1948.
35. Possibly butterflies.
36. John A. Alius, "Elder Richards Ends Trip with Tour of Brazilian Mission," *Church News*, April 3, 1948.
37. For more on the history of the Church in Brazil, see "The Church in Brazil," *Ensign*, February 1975.
38. Richards, Journal, March 15, 1948.
39. Curitiba is in the state of Paraná. Missionary work began in the city in 1937. See Brazil São Paulo North Mission Manuscript History and Historical Records, CHL.
40. Written at the top of the journal page.
41. Richards, Journal, March 16, 1948.
42. Reinhold Stoof, South American Mission president from 1926 to 1935, visited Brazil in 1927 and gave a lecture in Joinville about the Church to German immigrants. He sent missionaries to southern Brazil in 1928. The first branch in Brazil was organized in Joinville on July 6, 1930, among German-speaking Saints. The first Church-owned meetinghouse in South America was dedicated on October 25, 1931, in Joinville. See South American Mission Manuscript History and Historical Reports.
43. "Religious Movement," *A Noticia* (Joinville, Brazil), March 16, 1948, Stephen L Richards Papers.
44. Brazil São Paulo North Mission Manuscript History and Historical Reports, March 16, 1948.
45. Chile was part of the original itinerary, but the Richardses did not visit there.
46. Richards, *Dear Children*, March 10, 1948. Letter to daughter Georgia. The letter was started on March 10 and then continued with events up to March 16.
47. Richards, Journal, March 17, 1948.
48. Missionaries held their first meetings in Curitiba in 1937. See São Paulo North Mission Manuscript History and Historical Reports.
49. Brazil São Paulo North Mission Manuscript History and Historical Reports, March 17, 1948.

50. Missionary work began in Porto Alegre in 1933. See South American Mission Manuscript History and Historical Reports.
51. Milton R. Bloomquist to Mr. and Mrs. Ira D. Gagon, March 27, 1948, Milton R. Bloomquist Papers, CHL.
52. Stephen L Richards was sixty-eight years old.
53. The Richardses did not visit Paraguay or Chile on their trip.
54. Richards, Journal, March 18, 1948.
55. Richards, Journal, March 19, 1948.
56. President Rex likely showed a photograph of his daughter named Yara.
57. Reference to the movie "Flying Down to Rio" that paired Fred Astaire and Ginger Rogers for the first time.
58. Minutes of Mission Presidency Meeting, March 19, 1948, Stephen L Richards Papers.
59. Thayle H. Nielsen served as second counselor in the Brazilian Mission presidency from 1948 to 1949.
60. Missionaries visited German members in Rio Preto and baptized the first converts in 1931. This later became the Rio Preto Branch and then the Ipomeia Branch. See South American Mission Manuscript History and Historical Reports; Ipomeia Branch Manuscript History and Historical Reports, 1935–83, CHL.
61. Richards, *Dear Children*, March 20, 1948.
62. Alice "Allie" Leila Richards Allen was the Richardses' fourth child.
63. She was born on March 17. The rest of the material in this paragraph pertains to that date.
64. For information about the challenges of opening up the Brazilian interior, see E. Bradford Burns, *A History of Brazil* (New York: Columbia University Press, 1993), 48–61.
65. Reference to the 1933 movie musical starring Fred Astaire and Ginger Rogers.
66. Richards, Journal, March 21, 1948.
67. The Corcovado is the hill with the statue of Christ overlooking Rio de Janeiro.
68. Jeanne Joyce Larson. Her husband, Rolf Larson, was employed by the US government in Rio de Janeiro and was a former Argentine missionary. See Frederick S. Williams and Frederick G. Williams, *From Acorn to Oak Tree: A Personal History of the Establishment and First Quarter Century Development of the South American Missions* (Fullerton, CA: Et Cetera, Et Cetera Graphics, 1987), 242.

69. Richards, Journal, March 22, 1948.
70. Richards, Journal, March 23, 1948.
71. Richards, Journal, March 25–28, 1948.
72. Stephen L Richards, in Conference Report, April 7, 1957, 96–97.
73. Richards, *Dear Children*, March 29, 1948.
74. Irene Louise Richards Covey was the Richardses' second child.

CHAPTER FIVE

# REPORTS AND CONFERENCE TALK

### HISTORICAL BACKGROUND

Stephen L and Irene Richards journeyed on the SS *Argentina* back to New York, arriving in early April 1948. They stayed in New York for a week and then headed back to Salt Lake City. They barely missed the April general conference. Elder Richards worked for the next couple weeks finalizing his report to the First Presidency. In the October 1948 general conference he described the lessons learned on his special mission to South America.

### THE DOCUMENTS

This chapter features an article from the *Church News* that contains a report of the tour with a direct interview with Elder Richards. Additionally, the observations and recommendations of Elder Richards are documented in his report to the First Presidency and his October 1948 general conference talk.

## Saturday, April 17, 1948

### NEWS ARTICLE: *CHURCH NEWS*[1]

### Missionary Work in South America Makes Definite Gain

Missionary work in the Argentine, Uruguay, and Brazil Missions is beginning to take definite steps forward now missionaries have returned since the end of the war, Elder Stephen L Richards of the Council of the Twelve noted upon his return to Salt Lake City early this week.

With Mrs. Richards, the Church leader spent three months touring the three South American missions. Elder Richards is the first General Authority to visit South American missions since they were opened and dedicated by Elder Melvin J. Ballard in 1925.

Prior to the war nearly all of the branches were presided over and conducted by missionaries, Elder Richards said.

"During the war, while there were no missionaries laboring in their countries, the local Saints carried on the activities of the Church. These Saints continued to be a devoted and faithful people, but because of their lack of experience in being administrative officers there was little growth in the size of the branches, and hardly no missionary work was accomplished.

"In our tour the South American Saints were most cordial to us in their reception," he said. "It was a delight to meet and travel among them."

Elder Richards visited and heard the reports of the nearly two hundred missionaries laboring in the three countries. With only two minor exceptions, he found them to be in excellent health. "These missionaries are faithful and devoted ambassadors; they are a credit to the Church, their parents, and themselves," he noted. "Some of the elders experi-

*Elder and Sister Richards and friends. Courtesy of CHL.*

ence difficulty in adjusting themselves to their living conditions and food. Most of them maintain their own apartments and prepare their own food, which helps to make their adjustment easier."

Perhaps the most appealing element of the gospel to the people of South America is the altruistic motives of the missionaries, who give their time without recompense and who sustain their own expenses. "This is so contrary to what the South Americans are accustomed to," Elder Richards said, "that they never stop marveling at our missionaries' unselfish devotion to the interest of others."

*The Richardses at the park with President W. Ernest Young. Courtesy of CHL.*

Generally the press was friendly and expressed good will toward the Church, the missionaries, and the tour of Elder Richards and his party. "Occasionally, however, we were grossly misrepresented," he said. "One paper printed, among other untruths, that I had fifteen wives.

"Missionary work is difficult to pursue. To reach the landed wealthy class is no small problem. Working among the lower classes presents many problems of proportions too; one among these many problems is the illiteracy of the masses, millions of whom are not even aware that there is such a book as the Bible. We noted that the concepts of liberty and democracy, as we understand them, are not generally understood. Only education of the masses can remove these many serious problems.

"There is great contrast in South America. The countries suffer greatly because of a complete lack of middle class; there just isn't any. The population is divided into two groups, the landed aristocracy who are fabulously wealthy, and the great masses of poor workers who are almost destitute. There appears little hope of improving the condition of the present generation of the great masses. Right now the poor worker is even worse off than usual for he is caught in a maelstrom of heavy inflation.

*The Richardses and Youngs with missionaries. Courtesy of CHL.*

"The great hope of these nations is in its youth, who are determined to better their conditions, both economically and socially; they seek education and learning. Everywhere we visited, we found them anxious and desirous of learning the English language and customs.

"The peoples of Brazil and Uruguay are generally friendly to the United States," Elder Richards said. "But it is common knowledge that the Argentines look with suspicion toward the United States feeling perhaps that we want to provide the leadership for South America, a position they covet.

"One of the great drawbacks to the development of their countries is their completely inadequate transportation systems. It is almost impossible to get from one place to another. Gasoline is rationed; automobiles are limited, and what few roads there are, are impassable except in jeeps. To meet with one branch, it was necessary for us to travel 50 miles in a jeep—but never again.

"In every city it is a common sight to see a queue of people more than a block long on many street corners trying to board a worn-out and dilapidated bus or street car. In Brazil practically the only means of transportation is by airplane.

"We missed almost completely a winter, the seasons being reversed in the southern hemisphere. Everywhere we went we were told that they were having an unusually mild and cool summer. But in Brazil the heat to us was most suffocating and unbearable—along with the 100 per cent humidity," Elder Richards said.

Elder and Mrs. Richards enjoyed unusually good health on their journey and reported the two ocean voyages were particularly restful.

---

**Monday, May 10, 1948**

### STEPHEN L RICHARDS FINAL REPORT[2]

May 10, 1948
The First Presidency Building

Dear Brethren:

I respectfully submit the following recommendations after my visit to the South American missions.

I. <u>ALL SOUTH AMERICAN MISSIONS</u>

1. That the numbers of missionaries be maintained at about their present levels, at least for a sufficient length of time to enable us to appraise the results of the work.
2. That a more careful screening of missionaries sent to these missions be brought about, especially with reference to health, maturity, capacity to acquire the languages, industry, assured moral character and firm testimonies of the Gospel. It might be

well to have extra physical examinations and specially assigned interviewers for these missionaries.
3. That no large groups of missionaries be sent to any mission at any time.
4. That careful study and investigation be made in an attempt to get permanent visas for missionaries during the terms of their missions to avoid the great amount of time and large expense incurred at present by missionaries and mission presidents in their effort to secure renewals of visas.
5. That in connection with the foregoing we undertake to secure contact men to make application to consulates for visas.
6. That an effort be made to secure less expensive transportation for missionaries to and from South American mission fields.
7. That missionaries on their long voyages be specially admonished with reference to their conduct and the profitable employment of their time.
8. That careful study be given by the General Authorities to the foreign-language preparation of these missionaries. I discovered that a very considerable portion of the time and efforts of senior missionary companions and the missionary himself was given to the acquisition of the language, thus greatly limiting the productive work of each.
9. Parents and friends of the missionaries should be discouraged from sending packages to missionaries at Christmas or any other time. A large amount of missionary time is given to getting such packages out of customs and the contents are often, substantially worthless when the packages are finally secured.
10. Some means should be adopted to curtail the time and expense wasted by the missionaries on photographic materials and picture taking.
11. Attention should be given to the matter of clothes, books, blankets and other accessories taken by these missionaries to their fields of labor. It is generally better to equip for the mission before leaving home because the buying of clothes is difficult in the South American countries, most of the men's suits being tailored. At present they are more expensive than in the United

States. Instructions regarding dignity in appearance and conduct of missionaries should be re-emphasized. The practice of taking blankets and sheets to South America is open to question but at the present time there is some justification for it on account of the excessive cost of these articles in the foreign countries. As a normal practice, however, I recommend that the Church completely furnish at admission [mission] expense, the locals in which the missionaries live and that the missionaries' contributions to the rental of these locals be standardized as nearly as possible and generally increased. I found the contributions to these rentals to vary from $3.50 per month to $7.50 per month per missionary.

It has been the practice for the missionary to furnish his own blankets and sheets and sometimes other items of furnishings. When the missionary leaves he usually sells the articles to missionaries succeeding him. This practice has brought about some irritation and in a few instances bad feelings which have been pos[i]tively harmful.

12. Remittances of money should be made in the methods which will bring the greatest realization in local currency to the missions and the missionaries. I satisfied myself that there is no justifiable criticism against using the public exchanges which are numerous and which I understand are licensed by the governments themselves. Certified checks, travelers checks and express money orders should be used wherever necessary to avoid the excessive charges of banks for the exchange service.

II. <u>ARGENTINE MISSION</u>

1. With the concurrence of the mission presidency and President Williams[3] of Uruguay whom I invited to participate in the discussion I recommend that a mission home be purchased in the Belgrano district of Buenos Aires to conserve the time of the mission office force, to be near the American schools and to give more dignity to our work in the hope of reaching some of the more educated people.

2. To encourage particularly the young people of the Church and their friends, I recommend that the mission presidency be authorized to submit for purchase in Buenos Aires in a respectable section of the city, a site for a recreation hall and a possible future chapel. The recreation hall would serve to accommodate all of the larger meetings of the mission and should greatly increase the capacity of the mission to interest and convert the youth. An outdoor recreational lot is at present owned by the Church. It is said that it can be sold at a profit and the proceeds could be applied to a new and better recreational establishment.
3. Two other properties are owned by the Church,—a meeting house in Liniers section of Buenos Aires and a small local Church in <u>Pergamino</u>. I do not recommend the acquisition of additional properties at this time when values are so inflated, with perhaps two exceptions. If any small church should come on the market such as we acquired in <u>Pergamino</u>, it could be considered and in LaPlata which is one of the thriving branches of the mission where the saints are taking steps to secure a lot it might be feasible to undertake some modest construction there.
4. For the elevation of the missionary work in Argentina, one of the most necessary things is the renting of better locals in better sections of the cities. This is a very difficult undertaking with an acute shortage of housing but I recommend that the mission president be encouraged to secure better housing even at considerably higher rental expense. Many of the present locals are positively discouraging to the missionaries in their endeavors to get respectable people interested.
5. I recommend that study be given to the continuation of mission-wide conferences of missionaries and saints at Buenos Aires as at present conducted in April and October of each year.
6. Additional Church literature is much needed. I recommend that Brother Balderas[4] be given additional help to produce more Spanish translations and for the revision of some Spanish literature now in use.
7. Film strips, transcription records and additional missionary facilities are in great demand. Some of the people approached

cannot read. Pictures and transcribed music can be used to great advantage. Productions in Spanish would be most acceptable. They would, of course, serve all Spanish-speaking missions. I recommend study and early action.

8. This mission for a long time has maintained basketball teams made up of missionaries for the advertisement of the Church and in making contacts particularly among the young. Some good results are reported, but missionaries who play on the team and give concerts have little or no time for regular proselyting work. Perhaps much depends on the way the mission president handles the situation and his ability to capitalize on these public appearances and the contacts made. I think we should call for frequent reports on such activities and try to appraise the results.

9. I was furnished by Brother L. Pierce Brady[5] a treatise on maté,[6] the drinking of which is more or less a national custom. Brother Brady is also sending to me some samples which, when they arrive can be chemically analyzed. I am informed that the drink is passed around and imbibed through a tube, a most unsanitary practice. I think there is not sufficient evidence available to warrant the conclusion that the drinking of maté is an infraction of the Word of Wisdom, but I think that President Young has done well to ask the missionaries not to partake of it. An effort is being made in the country to establish the drink as a competitor to coffee. When I get returns on the chemical analysis, I will report.

10. I made rather definite recommendations to the presidency of this mission with reference to the organization of the presidency largely in accordance with the terms of the circular letter sent out by the First Presidency with the objective of making self-sustaining branches, the prosecution of more vigorous and well directed missionary effort, the organization of the mission office staff and work, the securing and handling of weekly reports from the missionaries and various other items which should be more or less reflected in the monthly and annual reports received from the mission. I recommend that most careful attention be given to these reports.

III. URUGUAYAN MISSION

1. I recommend that immediate consideration be given to the purchase of land adjacent to the newly acquired mission home as per description of plat hereunto attached. This additional land would serve the immediate purpose of providing some recreational facilities at moderate cost and would likewise provide space for a permanent recreational hall and chapel if the success in this mission in the future should warrant the same. The land seems to be so much in demand, being in a rapidly growing section of the city that it is not likely that any loss would be entailed in a future disposition of it.
2. I recommend that gas be installed in the mission home to supplant kerosene as the fuel at a cost of approximately $500.00. The Church owns a gas stove and the sale of the kerosene equipment would realize approximately $150.00. The number of meals served in the mission home makes it highly desirable to have gas and it is estimated that the difference in the cost of kcroscnc and gas would pay for thc installation in about four years time.
3. I recommend that table silverware be purchased for the mission home for the service of 18 people. Stainless steel was sent when the home was furnished and will do for everyday use but is not compatible with the dignity of this fine home, especially in the entertainment of the kind of guests which come from President William's contacts. The silverware should be purchased in the United States and sent down, either with missionaries, or to Brother and Sister Harold Brown through the mailing facilities of the United States Embassy.
4. I attach hereto an express direction prepared by President Williams for the transmission of funds to the mission and missionaries.
5. I recommend the organization of a branch of this mission in Asuncion, Paraguay. Major Samuel Skousen, a former Argentine missionary, and now an attaché of the United States Government located in this city could be most helpful and direct

the work of the branch. There are at present 14 American members of the Church residing there, all connected with the government. Not all are active, but a good work could be done among them. There is also a native family very much interested who have asked for baptism. It would furnish an opportunity to project the work in that country and under the leadership of Major Skousen would not require an undue amount of attention from the mission president. I would not recommend that missionaries be sent there at the present time, but the organization of the branch would give much encouragement to those who are interested and it could receive some supervision from President Williams. There is fairly good railroad, and other communication from Montevideo. I do not know the exact distance.

6. Literature and other missionary facilities are needed in this mission, as in Argentina.

7. President Williams reports that the cost of schooling in Montevideo for his four children averages about $65.00 per month for a period of nine months of the year. The children attend an American school operated by the Methodist Church. He said this is the only school in which the children can study and receive credit for their studies in the United States. He says his allowance cannot be stretched to cover this additional cost and that his personal funds are not sufficient to enable him to pay it. I recommend that $500.00 per school year be granted to him to cover this item.

IV. BRAZILIAN MISSION

1. I recommend that early consideration be given to the purchase of a mission home in Sao Paulo. The owner of the present rented home is restrained from increasing the rental by the rent controls now in force. If and when the mission president is changed he has given notice he will consider the present month to month tenancy terminated; that he will then exact a greatly increased rental which he has indicated would be three or four hundred percent higher. The house is not nearly large enough for a mission home and office. A better location could

also be secured. I advised the mission presidency to make recommendation.

2. I recommend that as soon as feasible all meetings in German be discontinued and that the Portuguese language only be used in missionary work. All of the young people and most of the old people do all their business in Portuguese. Very few, if any, do not understand Portuguese and the use of German has to a certain extent prejudiced our work.

3. I recommend that better meeting places in better sections of the cities be secured even though higher rentals will be entailed. I do not believe it wise to attempt any building at this time, except possibly in Campin[a]s where there is a very promising branch and where steps are now being taken by the Saints to secure a building lot. They deserve encouragement.

4. I recommend that the missionary effort in Brazil be largely confined to the cities where we are at present maintaining missionaries. In fact I have suggested to President Rex that we withdraw from some distant places and concentrate in a little more compact area. At best transportation and communication are very difficult and an immense amount of time and effort is consumed in visiting the districts and branches, and also in getting missionaries to and from inaccess[i]ble places. I feel we will be better able to prosecute the work in less far-flung areas and watch the results.

5. Immediate attention should be given to plans for providing more literature and missionary facilities. There is a great dearth of missionary help in Portuguese.

6. The transmission of funds to this mission should receive the same consideration as to the other South American missions.

7. It is in this area that the missionaries suffer most from excessive charges for permanent visas. I recommend that we communicate with President Edmunds[7] of Chicago in an endeavor to establish friendly relations with the Brazilian Consulate in that city.

8. I recommend that President Rex[8] be advised to dispose of the new Studebaker automobile as advantageously as possible and secure one of the lighter and cheaper ones.
9. President Rex has invested considerable money in powdered milk in order to supply the missionaries with a safe drink. He represents that he has secured good prices which will be advantageous to the missionaries but I think the practice of maintaining a mission commissary account in foodstuffs is questionable.
10. Attention should be called to the difficulty of administering a mission with a little family and babies in the mission home.

V. CONCLUSION

1. The progress of South American missions should be checked as carefully as possible by close examination of reports by correspondence and by interviewing returned missionaries. The health of the missionaries should be especially observed and checked by inquiries from headquarters. The expense of a visit to the South American missions by one of the General Authorities is so heavy that an annual visit would perhaps not be justified. But if provision could be made so that each mission president during his tenure of office could receive a visit it would probably be very helpful. At least not more than five years should elapse between such visits.

Many of the foregoing suggestions and recommendations need elaboration and undoubtedly some important items have escaped attention. I shall be very pleased to confer with the Presidency on any point.

I propose to file with your office a brief historical sketch of our visit to the South American missions.

Faithfully yours,
Stephen L Richards

Sunday, October 3, 1948

STEPHEN L RICHARDS GENERAL CONFERENCE ADDRESS[9]

*Address delivered at the Sunday afternoon session of the 119th Semiannual General Conference, October 3, 1948, in the Tabernacle.*

I have been deeply moved by this conference, my brethren and sisters, and my inclination would be to spend my allotted time in lending support and sanction to the great messages which have come to us. I have, however, another obligation that I feel I must discharge.

*Report of South American Trip*
My wife and I returned from South America last spring just a day or two too late to attend the April conference. While I have spoken of some of my experiences in a few of the stake conferences, I have thought that I should make a report to the Church on our visits to these missions in the southern continent.

Perhaps it might be well at the outset just to refresh your geographical memories a little. South America is not only south of North America, but it is almost entirely east of the United States, so that during nearly all of the time we spent away we were four hours, or time zones, east of Salt Lake City, and only two time zones west of London. Our travels consumed about eighteen thousand miles, so you see we here at home are a long way from our fellow members in the missions of South America, and because of that difference and the fact that about twenty-two years had elapsed since that country was visited by General Authorities, you will readily understand that we were awaited with a royal welcome.

We left Salt Lake City on the last day of December last year. We spent about two weeks in Washington D.C., and in New York in securing letters of introduction to prominent business people in the south, and also in interviews at the embassies of the countries we intended to visit, where we were introduced through the courtesy of our Congressional representatives. We never did secure time enough to present all of these letters, but we had the satisfaction of making our mission presidents acquainted with some prominent men who may be of some aid in the future.

It was bitter cold when we left New York harbor, with some of the water pipes of the ship frozen, so I assure you it was altogether agreeable, after a few days, to come into a warmer climate. However, we found that you can often get too much of a good thing, and when we reached Rio de Janeiro in the middle of their summer, comparable to our July, in a heat wave more intense than they had had in four years, we longed for the snow and ice we had so recently left. You know you can usually protect yourself against the cold, but you can't against the heat, and I am sure I prolonged my visit to the few air-conditioned offices where I presented letters of introduction, beyond the bounds of strict propriety. I hope it wasn't too obvious. Down in Sao Paulo, the headquarters of the Brazilian Mission, it was a little bit more temperate because that has some elevation above the sea, and Montevideo and Buenos Aires are farther south and in a more temperate zone.

### "Divine Services" Conducted

Soon after we boarded the ship, we were happy to learn that there were seven missionaries aboard, and one member of the Church in the ship's employ. With the assistance of these good folk, on the request of the ship's command, we conducted what were called "divine services" on the two Sundays of the voyage. The missionaries were all splendid young men. I am sure they made an excellent impression. On the way home, on the same ship and a sister ship, we were asked to conduct three more Sunday services, so that I began to feel that I ought to have been put on the ship's payroll. That hope vanished early, however, when it was learned that we didn't preach for hire. The captain, however, rewarded me somewhat by giving me the rather rare privilege of going on the bridge of the vessel with an officer guide to explain the mysteries of automatic steering and radar, and when I was escorted to the huge engine room where I inspected one of the greatest power plants I have ever seen, I felt quite rewarded for my preaching.

We arrived in Buenos Aires, headquarters of the Argentine Mission, in the morning. We could see from the ship's deck the mission president, and his wife, and the missionaries and Saints gathered to meet us. It was noon, however, before we could greet them. The time consumed in getting baggage through customs and in the inspection of visas and securing medical permits, is very considerable, I assure you.

### Inconvenience of Receiving Packages

In this connection I would like to broadcast the counsel throughout the Church to all parents and friends of missionaries in the South American missions, not to send to the missionaries packages at Christmas, or any other time, containing articles which are not essential to them in their work. It often requires many hours and sometimes days of the precious time of missionaries, or the mission staff, to get packages out of customs, and a box of stale cookies which has spent two or three months on the way, even though it carries a lot of love and sentiment from the folk at home isn't worth it. An airmail letter on thin paper with a ten-cent stamp is a far more expeditious and satisfactory message of your affection and encouragement under the circumstances that prevail in South America.

There is a word in frequent use in South America which expresses a quality wholly necessary to peace of mind. It is the word *paciencia* meaning patience. Everybody takes his time about doing things, the government and its agencies, especially. The sooner you learn this the happier you are.

### Hospitable Reception

Well, we finally got through customs to enjoy the welcome and greetings of our patient friends. I will say just a word about our reception at the Laniers Branch of the Argentine Mission in Buenos Aires, because this was typical of the hospitality and greeting of the Saints and missionaries throughout the missions. The Laniers Branch is the largest of all the branches of the Church in South America, and is one of the very few which owns its own place of meeting, which is a very modest one. On this occasion there were gathered about four hundred members of the Church and friends. The hall was crowded. It had been decorated with flowers and streamers, and presented an attractive appearance. An elaborate program had been prepared, with both amateur and professional talent, consisting of speeches, singing, and folk dancing rendered in Spanish and native costume, with some interpretations for our benefit. Children participated liberally. Some of the skits and songs had been specially written, and the whole program represented the expenditure of a large amount of time and effort in preparation. As a climax, Sister Richards was presented with beautiful flowers which grow in profusion in that country. On one occasion the orchids given to her hung from her shoulder almost to her knee. I know the ladies will take note of that.

I was given a beautifully ornamented cake made by some of the good sisters. I am not supposed to eat cake, but I soon discovered that the missionaries have good appetites without many restrictions, and I assure you that none of the cake given to me was wasted.

It was in this welcoming social that we were first made really to feel the sentiment and spirit of our fellow members of the Church in those distant lands. They were respectful and reverent almost to an embarrassing degree. I am not used to having my hand kissed, a custom which is a holdover that some of the older people have kept, from the traditions and practices of their earlier affiliations. They were warm-hearted, and for the most part demonstrative and impulsive. It was apparent that the fellowship promoted by the Church had found a place in their lives, and particularly among the sisters I noted that affectionate regard for each other which we so frequently see at home. It was apparent that nearly all were in humble circumstances, although many were tastefully and somewhat stylishly dressed. Particularly was this true of the girls. They were, however, a little short on the latest fashions. The long skirts had not yet reached them.

### *Many Nationalities Represented*

It was evident that many nationalities were represented, with a preponderance of the brunette people from Spain, Italy, and the Mediterranean countries. There were a few of German and English extraction, but far more from southern than from northern Europe. This group of people which we first met were typical in their racial composition, of the groups we met in all the missions. The stocks from southern Europe prevail. Spanish is the national language in Argentina and Uruguay, and in Brazil, the Portuguese. I talked with a number of families in Brazil who prided themselves on pure Portuguese blood. It so happens, however, that our work in both Argentina and Brazil was begun in the German language, among immigrants from Germany. We still have a few German groups of Saints, where German is spoken, but this practice is being discontinued.

It should be said here, for the information of the Church, that our South American missions do substantially no work among the Lamanite people, and so far as I know, we have no Indian members of the Church in these missions. I met a few Indian boys who were attending school at one of the universities in Argentina who had come from Peru. The missionaries had made friends with them, and they took part on one of our programs. They were small-statured, but seemed intelligent and kindly disposed, and some day perhaps our work may be carried to their country.

### *Distrust in Evidence*

My observation that the Latin Americans are predominantly from the southern European stocks led me to wonder how susceptible these people are to the teachings and influence of the gospel. I recalled that in more than one hundred years we have done little or no missionary work in Spain, Italy, Portugal, and adjacent countries. Perhaps this may be the means, in South America, of some day approaching those countries. I thought I could see in the disposition, customs and practices of these South Americans some of the reasons which have impeded gospel work among them. They are people who have suffered many impositions. They have not been trained and nurtured in the kind of freedoms which northern Europeans and North Americans have enjoyed, in consequence of which, perhaps, they have become by nature suspicious and distrustful. American businessmen told me that after many years of business dealings they were unable to build up that mutual confidence and friendship with native South Americans which may be established in a few weeks or months among our own people. The buildings and homes of the people are indicative of this distrust. Everything is walled in. Even a little home is usually surrounded by a wall six, ten, twelve feet in height, almost unscalable, with a locked gate and sometimes broken glass on top of the wall as a protection against neighbors and others who ought to be counted friends.

All this has a bearing on our missionary work, as you will readily see. Homes are not easily accessible. Interviews are difficult and it takes a long time to build up that confidence which is essential to friendship and mutual understanding. Tracting is attended with difficulties, not only because of walls and locked gates, but because customs are new and strange to our missionaries. During the daytime men folk are not at home, except perhaps for the siesta period, when they are not to be disturbed. This siesta takes a big portion out of a day. Places of business close from twelve to three o'clock, and our missionaries are greatly limited in their opportunities to make contacts. In some sections they were beginning evening tracting in the hope of meeting the families at what would seem to us late hours. I have not heard yet what success attended these experiments.

In the main our missionary work is prosecuted through the medium of *locales*. A *local* is usually a small rented building which serves as a home for the missionaries and a place of meeting in carrying forward Church activities for the groups who attend. One room in the *local* is fitted out to serve as a little church modestly equipped with a pulpit, a small organ and benches. Owing to the housing shortage which prevails in South America as it does with us, it has been very difficult to secure *locales* in good locations of the cities, and we have often been forced to take places in poor localities.

### *Civilization Centers in Cities*

It should be noted that all civilized life in South America centers in the big cities. There is very little agricultural or rural life, as we know it. The vast livestock ranches of Argentina, and the coffee plantations of Brazil are owned by wealthy families who live in the big cities and who dominate the whole agricultural field. The independent farm owner and operator is almost unknown. This situation is material to our missionary work. We do no country work. Our missionaries visit no farm homes so productive of investigators and converts in other countries. They are not allowed, without permits, even to enter the great ranches and plantations. One of the greatest needs apparent in the countries we visited is a division of the lands for a far greater productivity and realization of the vast resources of the countries, and more importantly, for the establishment of an independent, vigorous middle class of landowners and workers.

South America is a land of violent contrasts—the very beautiful and the very ugly; the very rich and the very poor; the very intellectual and sophisticated, and the very ignorant. Of course, countries differ in these respects, but everywhere there is conspicuously lacking that strong middle class which is the backbone of our own and other progressive countries. I saw some indications that this class may be growing. In some industrial centers, such as Sao Paulo in Brazil, when and if it grows, our missionary work will have more assurance of success. It takes humility and intelligence to understand and receive the restored gospel. The aristocracy lack the humility, and the poor and destitute often lack in good measure the intelligence.

### Promising Prospects Among Youth

Our most promising prospects are among the youth in all the countries. They are forward-looking, and they are emerging from some of the distrust and suspicion which has so retarded the progress of their elders. These young people have admiration for many things in America. They learn about us largely through the picture shows. Unfortunately, through this medium they do not always get correct impressions of the best part of our North American life. It's a shame that we have to be advertised by the most effective advertising there is, for our gangsterism, infidelity, frivolity, and cheap wit. These young people, however, see our automobiles, our clothes, our fine homes in the pictures, and they think they would like to have some of these things. They want to learn English and our missionaries capitalize on this desire and teach many of them English. English classes are held in the *locales*. The young people who come in contact with our missionaries develop a great admiration for them—for their fine, clean manhood, their friendliness and their serious work. Mutual Improvement Associations are begun, and gradually the gospel plan unfolds before these people, and they are given an entirely new vision of abundant and rich living with purpose and incentive, even in their poverty.

I saw some branches of the mission made up and carried forward entirely by young people. Of course, there are older people, too, who have proved susceptible to gospel teaching, but in the main I feel that our hope lies with the youth.

South America desperately needs the restored gospel. The nations of that land need, more than anything else, the true concepts of liberty which arise out of a correct understanding of the relationship of man to God and his fellow man. They need a comprehension of justice, equity, and equality. They need to understand more perfectly the dignity of work, and, of course, they need the enlightenment of education. As one man said who gave me a letter of introduction to business associates in South America: "South America needs what the Mormon Church has to offer."

Our missionaries are trying hard to give these things to the people who so sorely need them. Their work is conducted at great expense. It costs more than one thousand dollars in transportation alone to put a missionary in one of these missions and bring him home. Living costs are very high, even in American money, which sells at a premium. The language is difficult, particularly the Portuguese, and many months pass before a missionary can adequately express himself before the people. However, they, our missionaries, carry with them a spirit, and the testimony of truth which, even imperfectly expressed in the language of the people, touches the hearts of many who hear them.

*Elder Richards and President Young at the podium in Argentina. Courtesy of CHL.*

### Missionaries and Saints Faithful

Now I found in all the missions a great enthusiasm among the missionaries for their work. They have developed a love for the people, which lies at the base of all good missionary labors, and they, under the direction of their mission presidents, are organizing and planning to meet the conditions. We also have some very faithful Saints who are great aids in promoting our work. I saw some very good work being carried forward by small branches of the missions—Sunday Schools and Primaries where little children are being taught; priesthood classes where men and boys are learning their duties; Relief Societies and welfare workers are carrying forward commendable projects. Generally, the groups were small and largely dependent upon the missionaries, but there was promise in them.

Perhaps the most stimulating of any exercises I saw were the baptismal ceremonies. We had the privilege of being present at two, one in Argentina and one in the interior of Brazil. Nothing is more encouraging to missionaries and to members of the Church than to see the fruits of their labors and the happiness which comes to those who ally themselves with the work of the Lord. In each service, six to ten were baptized into the Church.

If time permitted, I would tell you some rather interesting aspects of these baptismal services, but it does not. After all, this is the great encouragement to our missionaries. The realization of knowing that they may have been the means of bringing peace—peace of mind and peace to the heart and soul of some one of God's children who has humbled himself

*The Richardses with the missionaries. Courtesy of CHL.*

to seek the truth. I am not able to say how many in South America will respond to the spirit and message we bear, but I am sure we are doing our duty, fulfilling divine command, when we carry the word of our Lord to all lands and peoples.

### Gratitude for Visit

I acknowledge my gratitude to the First Presidency in extending to me the opportunity of making this visit, and I also acknowledge the innumerable courtesies and kindnesses shown to my wife and me by the mission presidents and their wives, the missionaries, and Saints, and friends of the South American missions. It was an unforget[t]able experience. If any good to the noble cause, which I love, shall come of it, I shall be very grateful.

I pray that the Lord may bless our missionaries in all lands and the Saints who are scattered over the earth. I trust that they may all feel as we tried to make them feel in South America, that we are all one in the Church of Christ, that even though we may be widely separated, we can reach out over the lands and the oceans and extend the handclasp of fellowship and good brotherhood to our members throughout the globe. I think this was the message which they, in the southern hemisphere, appreciated more than any other. They wanted to be assured that they were one with us and we with them. The day will come, my brothers and sisters, when the mighty cause with which we have the honor to be associated, will bring to pass that unity in a divided and stricken world. God grant it may come soon I humbly pray, in the name of Jesus. Amen.

### NOTES

1. "Missionary Work in South America Makes Definite Gain," *Church News*, April 17, 1948.
2. Stephen L Richards Final Report to First Presidency after Trip to South America, May 10, 1948, Stephen L Richards Papers, 1921–59, CHL.
3. Frederick S. Williams was president of the Uruguayan Mission.
4. Eduardo Balderas was a Church employee in charge of Spanish translation at Church headquarters in Salt Lake City.

5. L. Pierce Brady was a counselor in the Argentine Mission presidency.
6. Yerba mate is an herbal tea that is very popular in Argentina and parts of South America. It does contain caffeine. The chemicals in it are less harsh than coffee, tea, and green tea.
7. John K. Edmunds was president of the Chicago Stake.
8. Harold M. Rex was president of the Brazilian Mission.
9. Stephen L Richards, in Conference Report, October 3, 1948, 144–51.

EPILOGUE

# LATTER-DAY SAINT MISSIONARY EFFORTS IN SOUTH AMERICA, 1948-2018

### EFFECTS OF THE RICHARDSES' VISIT

Elder Stephen L Richards's 1948 tour marked the end of South America's longest period (twenty-two years) without an official visit by one of the presiding authorities. South American Latter-day Saints and missionaries personally learned from interacting with an Apostle, and Elder Richards's observations and impressions influenced the First Presidency and the Quorum of the Twelve for many years. Indeed, Church leadership took notice and continued to "look southward."

In Uruguay, President Williams created ten branches during 1948. In the Argentine Mission a new mission home was approved. Brazilian Mission president Harold Rex reported that missionary performance increased, the Mutual Improvement Association was organized, and more young adults joined the church. A surge in baptisms revealed the impact the visiting Apostle had on the missionaries. The *Church News* noted: "One month later one of the largest baptismal services in Brazilian Mission history was held in Joinville. The spirit of the work was felt, and many districts held their first baptisms in many months. The district of São

Paulo counted forty baptisms as the year ended."[1] Missionary work then extended to Paraguay with its first convert baptism.[2]

As chairman of the Church's missionary committee, Elder Richards gained a better vision of the Church's needs and operation in South America. In the 1940s, only 7 percent of the missionary force were called to serve in Latin America; the majority of missionaries labored in the United States and Europe. However, the number of missionaries called to Latin America rose steadily during the years following the Richardses' visit, surpassing 10 to 16 percent by the 1970s.[3]

## DEDICATION OF CENTRAL AMERICA

Missionaries were introduced to Central America in 1947. For the next few years, the Mexican Mission assigned missionaries to Guatemala and then to surrounding countries. In 1952 Elder Spencer W. Kimball of the Quorum of the Twelve and Elder Bruce R. McConkie, an Assistant to the Twelve, arrived in Central America to make final preparations to create a new mission. Over the course of a week, Elders Kimball and McConkie visited six Central American countries. Government officials were welcoming and encouraging. On November 15, 1952, Elder Kimball phoned President McKay and received permission not only to create the Central American Mission, as planned, but also to dedicate Central America for proselytizing.[4]

From Guatemala City, Elder Spencer W. Kimball offered a prayer for all of Central America on November 16, 1952. Aspects of the prayer paralleled the prophesied growth foreseen by Elder Ballard when he blessed the South American continent in 1925. Elder Kimball prayed:

> Gracious Father, we thank Thee for the repeated assurance through Thy prophets that these scattered remnants of Israel on this continent, the choicest of all lands, would be brought to the knowledge of Thee and Thy program and be permitted to hear the gospel. . . . Bless, we pray Thee, the missionary work in all the world but today we ask Thy special blessings upon the Lamanite cause and ask that the seed of Lehi in these Central American countries and the gentiles among them may see and hear and understand and have

the courage and fortitude to accept and live the exalting program of Thy divine gospel. . . . Let them [the Saints] blossom as the rose upon the mountains, and let them be converted, "a nation in a day" and let Thy work be glorified and Thy people receive the promised blessings.[5]

With the opening of the Central American Mission, the Church's ensign moved beyond Mexico and was carried as far south as Panama.

## THE FIRST VISIT BY A CHURCH PRESIDENT

David O. McKay, the most internationally traveled of all modern Apostles at the time, became Church President in 1951. He called his longtime friend and associate Stephen L Richards as his first counselor and J. Reuben Clark Jr. as second counselor.

Several years before becoming Church President, President McKay received invitations to visit South America from his son Robert McKay, who served as a missionary in Argentina, and mission president Frederick S. Williams. The opportunity finally came when President McKay announced in 1954 he would journey to London, South Africa, and then Latin America. Six years had passed since Elder Richards's tour, and no Apostles had traveled to South America in the interim. This was the first time a President of the Church would visit South America, whose Latter-day Saint population totaled about two thousand members by the year's end.[6]

President McKay met with Church members in Brazil, Uruguay, and Argentina as well as in other South and Central American countries, including Chile, Peru, Panama, Guatemala, and, later that year, Mexico. President McKay penned his impressions of his trip: "I came to South America with the feeling that there would be plenty of opposition to the Church. I go away feeling that all the people need is a better understanding of the Church and its teachings. These are great countries."[7] After President McKay's trip, the First Presidency and the Twelve began visiting Latin America on a regular basis—almost yearly.

## THE OPENING OF CHILE AND PERU

The opening of Chile began in June 1952, when Billie Fotheringham met with President Stephen L Richards in the Church Administration Building in Salt Lake City. Fotheringham had just accepted a job in Chile and wanted permission to hold church services in Santiago. President Richards gave permission and asked Fotheringham to keep in contact about his experiences.[8] Two years later, President McKay dined with the Fotheringhams during his 1954 tour of South America.

In 1956, just over one hundred years after Apostle Parley P. Pratt visited Chile,[9] formal permission was granted to start missionary work, and two missionaries from neighboring Argentina were assigned to serve there.[10] The Santiago Branch was formally organized on July 5, 1956.[11] Later that year, the first six Chilean converts were baptized.[12]

Peru's beginnings coincided with Chile's. When President McKay visited Peru in 1954, a group of Americans were meeting together, but they were not organized into a branch. The creation of the Lima Branch was authorized July 1956, the same month the Santiago Branch in Chile was organized. Missionaries from the Uruguayan Mission were soon transferred to Peru and arrived in August 1956.[13] Elder Henry D. Moyle of the Twelve also met with government officials and began the process of legal recognition for the Church, which was finalized two years later.[14]

## EXPANDING MISSIONS IN SOUTH AMERICA

President Richards passed away in May 1959. Though he never returned to South America after his 1948 tour, his pioneering efforts were rewarded as growth and progress continued in lands he came to love.

The cause of South America was taken up by Elder Spencer W. Kimball. He ushered in 1959 by spending eleven weeks in South America. Typical of his remarkable work ethic, he traveled thirty-five thousand miles, visited six countries, and held more than one hundred meetings. He recorded that he visited most of the nine thousand members of South America and recommended to the Twelve the creation of new missions along the west coasts of Peru and Chile.[15] He also suggested dividing the Brazilian Mission and believed that stakes were in South America's near future.¹⁶ In his official report in April 1959, Elder Kimball said, "The statement of Horace Greeley, 'Go west, young man, go west' should be changed to 'Go south, young man, go south.'" He then commented in his report to the First Presidency, "We are but scratching the surface in our work in this land."¹⁷

On November 1, 1959, Elder Harold B. Lee of the Twelve formally organized the Andes Mission in Lima, Peru, with Frederick S. Williams translating at the meeting. Williams recorded:

> Elder Lee himself became prophetic, and I, standing at his side as interpreter, felt the deep spiritual context of his word. He stated that the time would soon come when Father Lehi's children would be inspired to accept the Book of Mormon and enter the Church in great numbers. "Soon," he said, "The Pacific Coast of the Americas will become the most fertile proselyting field of the Church."¹⁸

The new Andes Mission president was J. Vernon Sharp, who had served as a young missionary in Argentina during the 1920s and had been present at Elder Ballard's dedication and acorn-to-oak-tree prophecy. Returning to South America more than thirty years later and entrusted with responsibility for the Church's progress in Peru and Chile, President Sharp began building on the aspirations that both Elders Pratt and Ballard had for these countries.

Growth began quickly in Lima, but President Sharp felt divided as he balanced his time with three weeks in Peru followed by three weeks in Chile. In 1960 Joseph Fielding Smith, President of the Quorum of the Twelve Apostles, and Elder A. Theodore Tuttle of the First Council of the Seventy toured the mission and recommended its division, which occurred in 1961 with the formation of the Chilean Mission, allowing Sharp to focus exclusively on Peru.

Continuing on the foundation began in Lima, Sharp started a branch in Cuzco, the ancient Incan capital.¹⁹ President Sharp's successor, Sterling Nicolaysen, worked with Elder Tuttle to engage and understand the indigenous people, who struggled with their identity in a very Spanish- and European-style world.²⁰ Latter-day Saint missionaries also needed to adapt as they learned indigenous languages and worked with unique native cultures. Nevertheless, more than a century after Parley P. Pratt's mission, the Latter-day Saint gospel was beginning to reach the "Lamanites" of South America.[21]

### ELDER A. THEODORE TUTTLE, GENERAL AUTHORITY SUPERVISOR

Back in 1947, President Frederick S. Williams made a request to the First Presidency that a General Authority be "called to live in South America to supervise and coordinate the activity of the various missions after they were established."[22] Elder A. Theodore Tuttle's involvement in the work in South America fulfilled that request. From 1960 to 1965, Elder Tuttle lived in South America with all missions reporting to him as president of the conglomerate South American Mission. Having a General Authority on the ground helped unify and correlate the work of the separate missions. Also, as some missionaries concluded their missions and journeyed home, Elder Tuttle sent them to visit Ecuador and Colombia on fact-finding trips so he could get a report on whether those countries were ready for proselytizing.[23]

On June 28, 1962, the first portion of a seminar for South American mission presidents was held at the Incan ruins at Machu Picchu, Peru, with all six mission presidents, their wives, and Elder and Sister Tuttle in attendance.[24] The great vista and stronghold of the past Incan civilization rejuvenated the leaders, leaving them in awe of the past and determined to shape the future of Latin America in a positive manner. The rest of the seminar took place in Lima. Elder Tuttle's direction and Uruguayan Mission president J. Thomas Fyans's plan called the "Six Steps to Stakehood" gave vision and a concrete path for leaders to prepare districts to become stakes.[25]

Another change in May 1965 showed further administrative development. Along with their other responsibilities, members of the Quorum of the Twelve were assigned as area supervisors to directly oversee missions in each part of the world. Elder Spencer W. Kimball was assigned to South America for the next three years.[26] He worked closely with Elders Tuttle and Franklin D. Richards[27] in touring the countries and prepared to open more.[28]

## DEDICATION OF ECUADOR AND BEGINNINGS IN BOLIVIA, COLOMBIA, AND VENEZUELA

With President George Albert Smith's authorization, Elder Kimball traveled to Quito, Ecuador, and in the early evening of October 9, 1965, dedicated the country for Latter-day Saint missionary work. The rain had just stopped on a hill overlooking Quito, and the missionaries invited an Ecuadorian family visiting the spot to join them, along with two cab drivers. Elder Kimball said of the event: "As these nine Lamanite souls stood before me in the dedication prayer, I seemed to see them standing there representing the Lamanite nations, all Lamanites—the little ones, the youth, the parents and other adults. I seemed to feel a multitude of nations reaching for something heretofore unobtainable, listening for a familiar voice. I seemed to hear the chanting voice of millions, trying to bring back that which was lost; an urgent, plaintive pleading for something lost centuries ago."[29] Recounting what he foresaw, he wrote, "The gospel will eventually work miracles, putting shoes on their bare, calloused feet, food in their hungry stomachs, to make their tiny, diminutive bodies full size, clothes on their burdened backs, homes comfortable and luxurious ones for them."[30]

Elder Kimball noted that in 1964, one thousand missionaries were baptizing one thousand people a month in the seven missions of South America. As part of the trip, he also traveled to Bolivia, where the Church received legal recognition and missionaries at the end of the year.[31] In 1968 former Brazilian Mission president Harold Rex helped start the Church in Bogotá, Colombia, including witnessing Elder Kimball's dedication of that country. Then in 1966 the Church expanded south to Venezuela under the direction of Central American Mission president Ted E. Brewerton.

### THE FIRST STAKES

Elder Tuttle had great hopes that the first stake would be established in Montevideo, Uruguay, and chose to live there as he supervised the work on the continent. He admired the country's stability and felt that its central location between Argentina and Brazil was ideal. He also purchased land for a mission home and what decades later became the Montevideo Uruguay Temple.[32]

In 1964 Elder Kimball proposed to the Quorum of the Twelve that a Uruguayan stake be created, but it was not approved. Elder Kimball told Uruguayan Mission president Fyans, "Some of the Brethren have been quite opposed to the creation of stakes in foreign countries until there is a great maturity on the part of the local people."[33] Not only did the first stake in South America not materialize in Uruguay, but the growth of the country never matched that of Brazil or Argentina, disqualifying Uruguay from being a hub for the Church in South America.

Ever determined to create stakes, Elder Kimball made sure the stronger districts were functioning like stakes during his visits to Argentina, Uruguay, and especially Brazil in 1965. Then in October 1965 he proposed at a meeting of the Twelve that a stake be organized in São Paulo, Brazil. At the time there were about twenty stakes outside North America. To Elder Kimball's delight, the First Presidency approved the measure.[34]

The dam had been opened. In spring 1966 the São Paulo Stake was organized, closely followed that autumn by the Buenos Aires Stake. Elder Kimball returned to Uruguay in November 1967 to organize the Montevideo Stake. Now three of the countries visited by Elder Richards had their first stakes. Peru reached stakehood not long after, in 1970.

### SPECIAL ANNOUNCEMENT

It was during the trips in the 1960s to organize the first stakes in South America, particularly to Brazil, that Elder Kimball recorded an impression about the next major step for the Church. Elder Kimball "felt temples could be built in South America."[35] Just a few years later, he played a pivotal role in the realization of that prompting.

President Kimball arrived in São Paulo in 1975 to conduct an area conference. Almost ten years had passed since he created the first stakes on the continent. He shocked the Latter-day Saints with a special announcement: "Subject to the conditions that exist and your total cooperation, we will build the seventeenth temple of the Lord in this country of South America, and it will be located in São Paulo, Brazil."[36]

With the temple announcement, President Kimball challenged Latter-day Saints throughout the continent to raise money and contribute to the building of the temple.[37] Members of the Church also focused on qualifying to enter the temple by bringing their lives in conformity with the Church's teachings. Later during his time as Church President, Spencer W. Kimball announced additional Latin American temples for Mexico, Guatemala, Peru, Argentina, and Chile, all of which were dedicated in the 1980s.

Christmas Day in 1975 marked fifty years from when Elder Melvin J. Ballard dedicated South America. Statistics as of January 1, 1976, showed Latter-day Saint membership for Mexico at 175,806; Central America at 39,207; South America at 177,860; and the Caribbean at 1,064. The totals for these areas combined was 393,937, or 11 percent of a 3.5 million worldwide Church membership.[38]

### REMOVING BARRIERS

For decades President Kimball and other Latter-day Saint Apostles had prayed about removing the restriction on priesthood and temple blessings for members of African descent, a practice that began in the 1850s in the United States amid racial and cultural conflicts of that era.[39] One of the hallmarks of Spencer W. Kimball's presidency was his announcement in June 1978 that members of all races who are worthy could receive priesthood and temple blessings.

The official telegram came with the announcement on Saturday, June 10, 1978, and Elder Mark E. Petersen stopped to share his thoughts. One man remembered it this way:

> Elder Petersen proceeded to tell us what the process had been like for the preceding several months. He mentioned the long discussions in the upper rooms of the Temple, the question of whether or not [it] was time, their studying of every statement ever given by any of the previous prophets or members of the First Presidency, and the many earnest prayers in sacred places. Then he told us that the world would think that this change was being made for political reasons, to avoid embarrassment for LDS people running for

political office, or to promote proselyting efforts. He said that was not the case, and reminded us of the difficulty in determining who in that country could receive the Priesthood. That struck a chord with me because of similar difficulties we had experienced in Peru and Ecuador to determine who could receive the Priesthood. Elder Peterson told us that the issue of determining who could receive the blessings of the temple in Brazil had motivated the discussions regarding who could hold the Priesthood."[40]

The revelation arrived just months before the São Paulo Temple dedication in October 1978. Brazilians whose lineage previously might have disqualified them from temple attendance no longer had to worry. The announcement threw open the floodgates for continued Church growth in Brazil and even more so in Africa and the Caribbean.

### GROWTH IN THE CARIBBEAN

Latter-day Saint missionaries could now labor among the thirty million people living in the Caribbean, which was highly populated with descendants of African slaves. By the end of 1978, missionaries arrived in the Dominican Republic and Jamaica, and Elder M. Russell Ballard of the Seventy dedicated these lands for their work.[41] Missions covered most of the Caribbean by 1985, except for Cuba. No Caribbean isle of the sea proved more fertile than the Dominican Republic, which grew to one thousand Church members in five years, eleven thousand by 1986, and then to eighty thousand by the time of the dedication of the first Caribbean temple in 2000.[42] As of 2017, there were 135,000 Latter-day Saints in that country alone and more than 20,000 in neighboring Haiti, where a temple was announced in the Church's April 2015 general conference.

### MORE LATINO MISSIONARIES CALLED

Though the maturation of several first-generation leaders was evident by their calls to the presiding councils of the Church, President Kimball was particularly concerned about the calling of native missionaries. In a historic talk to the regional representatives of the Church in 1974, President Kimball requested more missionaries, expressing the need for each country to have a full complement of native missionaries so that other countries could be opened to the Church and its teachings.[43]

In the mid-1970s Elder W. Grant Bangerter of the Seventy worked with local leaders in Brazil to change the perception that Brazilians were precluded from missionary service because their academic obligations could not be interrupted for two years. One poignant moment came as Elder Bangerter heard José Lombardi, the first patriarch in South America, state that a declaration in patriarchal blessings he'd given was that young men were to go on missions. Elder Bangerter raised the vision of priesthood leaders to see that the Lord had already directed their young men to serve missions and that the prophet was calling for their enlistment.[44] In 1978, as the dedication of the São Paulo Temple arrived, only twenty-five hundred of the five thousand Latter-day Saint men in Brazil had been ordained to the Melchizedek Priesthood—a requirement for entering the temple. Elder Bangerter made it a goal for ten thousand men to receive the priesthood.[45] He taught priesthood leaders about the long-term benefits of missionary service, explaining, "If we do not call these native young men and women . . . , there will not be adequate leadership for the rapid growth of the Church, which is now taking place. . . . The calling of local missionaries will provide a fountain of men from which we can draw future leaders."[46]

In a pivotal meeting, a high councilor in the Bosque Stake in Brazil asked all the bishops and elders quorum presidents to get on their knees and pray until the Spirit told them which young men were ready for missions. Then they were to get up and go get those young men and bring them back to be interviewed right then for missions. Through such efforts, Elder Bangerter reached his initial goal of 360 Brazilian missionaries that he had promised President Kimball.[47] A generation of native Latter-day Saints began to answer the call of the prophet, which helped the Church prepare for a time of great growth in the 1980s.

## LATIN AMERICAN GENERAL AUTHORITIES

The Church's 1981 general conference marked the call of the first Latin American General Authority: Argentinian Ángel Abrea of the First

Quorum of the Seventy. The second Latin American General Authority was called in 1985, when Brazilian Helio de Rocha Camargo received a call to the Seventy. The Second Quorum of the Seventy was organized by the end of the decade and added Horacio A. Tenorio of Mexico and Helvécio Martins of Brazil to its ranks. Elder Martins was the first Seventy of African descent.[48]

A need for continued General Authority oversight led to a significant administrative change in June 1984: the announcement of area presidencies in thirteen areas worldwide. Three General Authorities of the Church would reside in a given area with a task to direct the work. Leadership from General Authorities provided decentralization of authority from Salt Lake and more opportunity to lead and train members and to manage the areas of the Church.[49]

### THE LAST REMAINING COUNTRIES

The 1980s saw both successes and setbacks in Central America. Though Guatemala reached forty thousand members by the time of the dedication of its first temple in 1984, several countries like Nicaragua, El Salvador, and Honduras faced considerable internal strife and civil war, disrupting the Church's expansion there. In 1980 North American missionaries were removed from Honduras, but the mission president sent ten missionaries to open up the English-speaking country of Belize, formerly British Honduras, which had gained its independence from England that year.

In 1988 Church President Ezra Taft Benson felt it was time to move into the last remaining countries in South America.[50] On the northeastern tip of the continent above Brazil lay the three Guianas: Guyana, Suriname, and French Guiana, which were colonies of England, Holland, and France, respectively. General Authorities enlisted senior missionary couples to move to these countries.[51] Through their efforts, the Church took root in each one of these three countries, and in 1991 Elder M. Russell Ballard of the Twelve dedicated them, along with Trinidad and Tobago, for missionary work.[52] Thus the Church had a presence in every country in South and Central America except one.

A new century finally brought the Church into the last country in Latin America and the Western Hemisphere that did not have an official Latter-day Saint presence: Cuba. In 2005 a branch of Church members was organized in Havana, and in 2012 Elder David A. Bednar of the Twelve dedicated the country. Efforts have focused on following the government's guidelines, so there are no proselyting missionaries assigned to the country. Instead, conversions have come through members sharing the Church's teachings with friends. These efforts led to the creation of a second branch in 2014.[53]

**CHALLENGES OF GROWTH**

The wave of Latin American growth in the 1980s and 1990s provided huge challenges for the burgeoning Church. President Gordon B. Hinckley told reporters that "the most serious yet exciting challenge was that of managing growth."[54] The Church grew so fast that the long-prophesied mighty oak tree seemed to have developed overgrown boughs and branches in some places. Many stopped attending church. President Hinckley admonished the Saints, "The days are past, the days are gone, the days are no longer here when we will baptize hundreds of thousands of people . . . and then they will drift away from the Church. When you begin to count those who are not active, you are almost driven to tears over the terrible losses we have suffered."[55]

To combat this challenge of retention, President Hinckley assigned Elder Jeffrey R. Holland of the Twelve to serve as an area president in Chile for two years. Over the course of Elder Holland's service, he and his counselors strengthened Church members and challenged them to greater activity, temple attendance, and retention. They consolidated units so priesthood leadership wasn't spread too thin and a stronger foundation could be built.[56] They also trained local leaders to more effectively serve as shepherds for the rapidly growing membership.[57]

Another challenge facing the Church was how to better administer the work. In the 1990s area presidencies faced the daunting task of addressing needs in areas with hundreds of thousands of members. In 1995 President Hinckley released the regional representatives of the Church and created the calling of area authority. Two years later, he made these men Seventies, increasing the Quorums of the Seventy to eight by 2005. By expanding the role of the Seventy to men called to serve in their local region and to coordinate efforts with a group of stakes, the Church could grow but still stay decentralized.

## A TEMPLE-BUILDING PEOPLE

Maturing membership and leadership enabled another expansion in the Church. Feeling inspired while in Colonia Juárez, Mexico, President Hinckley traced a plan for a very basic temple on a piece of paper that he carried with him back to Salt Lake. In the October 1997 general conference, President Hinckley announced a small-temple concept and proposed that temples be built as an experiment with the new design in Colonia Juárez; Anchorage, Alaska; and Monticello, Utah. Further, in the April 1998 general conference, President Hinckley proposed that the Church build thirty-two temples with a goal of having one hundred in operation by the end of 2000, ushering in a frenzy of temple building.[58]

Latin America benefited greatly in this effort. Mexico's temples grew from just one in Mexico City, dedicated in 1983, to nine in 2000, and then to thirteen completed and one announced in 2018. Brazil's temples expanded to eleven by 2018, with three announced and two under construction. Countries that received temples for the first time included Colombia (1999), Ecuador (1999), the Dominican Republic (2000), Bolivia (2000), Costa Rica (2000), Venezuela (2000), Uruguay (2001), Paraguay (2002), Panama (2008), El Salvador (2011), and Honduras (2013). Temples for Nicaragua and Puerto Rico were announced in 2018. Between 2010 and 2018, additional temples were dedicated, were being constructed, or were announced for Peru, Argentina, Chile, Colombia, Ecuador, and Guatemala. And in the April 2016 general conference, a second temple was announced for Lima, Peru, making it the first city in the world outside Utah to have two temples in one city.[59]

Of course, the explosion in temple building was a result of the Church's population growth. At the turn of the twenty-first century, total membership was 2.4 million in South America and 3.5 million for all of Latin America—almost a third of the Church's worldwide population.[60] Three countries passed the mark of one hundred stakes: Mexico (1989), Brazil (1993), and Peru (2013).[61] Mexico reached one million members in 2004, and Brazil followed in 2007.[62]

## SPANISH-SPEAKING UNITS IN THE UNITED STATES

The story of the Church in Latin America would not be complete without mention of the many branches and wards formed for Spanish-speaking members throughout the United States.

Spanish-speaking members first started gathering in the United States in November 1920, when Mexican members started to meet in Salt Lake City. They became known as the Mexican Branch and then the Lucero Ward.[63] In 1936 the Spanish American Mission, which had boundaries from California to Texas, was the only mission of its kind within the United States.[64]

As of January 2016, 780 Spanish-speaking units were present in forty-one of the fifty states, with high concentrations of branches in California, Utah, Arizona, Texas, and Florida. Spanish units were formed usually as part of English-speaking stakes. As of 2018, three all-Spanish-speaking stakes were in California and one in Texas.[65]

With such a large portion of Latin Americans in the United States, Church leaders have organized some events to better celebrate the Latin Latter-day Saint community and pay tribute to their contributions throughout the world. In 2005 Elder M. Russell Ballard of the Quorum of the Twelve hosted a meeting of Latino Saints in the Church's Conference Center in Salt Lake City. The meeting commemorated the 175th anniversary of the Church, and Elder Ballard reflected on the eighty years since his grandfather Elder Melvin J. Ballard dedicated South America. Elder Ballard quoted the acorn-to-oak-tree prophecy and stated, "A miracle has been fulfilled." He explained that the South American Mission had grown to seventy missions on the continent and that Latin America included 5.5 million Church members who attended twenty-eight temples.[66] A celebration of the ninetieth anniversary of Elder Melvin J. Ballard's dedicatory prayer was held in 2015, heralded with a historical marker placed in Tres de Febrero Park in Buenos Aires.

Perusal of the *Church News* in 2015 and any year thereafter shows stories of the members of the Quorum of the Twelve visiting South America frequently—practically every month or two. Never again will the Church see a dearth of apostolic mission tours and visits such as the twenty-two-year span between Elder Melvin J. Ballard's departure in 1926 and Elder Stephen L Richards's arrival in 1948.

## CONCLUSION

Elder Stephen L Richards's apostolic tour as shown through the documents in this book captured a bygone pioneer era. Apostles no longer travel by boat and spend three months doing a single mission tour, but rather travel by airplane or broadcast their messages around the world through communications technology. Gone are the days of counting members by the hundreds. Fledgling branches have been replaced by strengthening stakes that are part of even larger million-member areas of the Church. A mature, global church has emerged.

In 2018 Church President Russell M. Nelson called the first Latin American Apostle, Elder Ulisses Soares. When Elder Soares made his first apostolic trip to South America in 2018, he traveled home to Brazil. Fittingly, his senior companion was President M. Russell Ballard, grandson of Elder Melvin J. Ballard.[67] *Church News* writer Jason Swensen referenced Elder Melvin J. Ballard's 1925 dedication when he described Latin America's growth:

> Almost a century has passed since a latter-day apostle, Elder Melvin J. Ballard, prophesied that South America "is to be a power in the Church."
>
> Since that time, millions, from Colombia to Argentina and several nations in between, have joined the Church. Temples dot the continent. Hundreds of stakes have been formed.
>
> It's tempting to say Elder Ballard's words are fulfilled.
>
> But such a comment would be only a half-truth. The prophecy of South America, according to one of Elder Ballard's apostolic successors, *continues* to be fulfilled. Its true power has yet to be realized.
>
> South America "is the setting for one of the leading extended congregations in the Church and will continue to be so," said Elder Jeffrey R. Holland of the Quorum of the Twelve Apostles. "Much of the present and the future Church growth will focus on all of Latin America."[68]

Indeed, Latin Americans have become an integral part of the maturing Church of Jesus Christ of Latter-day Saints.

## NOTES

1. Joseph M. Heath, "Brazilian Elders Take Stock of Year's Labors," *Church News*, January 12, 1948, 20.
2. See Frederick S. Williams and Frederick G. Williams, *From Acorn to Oak Tree: A Personal History of the Establishment and First Quarter Century Development of the South American Missions* (Fullerton, CA: Et Cetera, Et Cetera Graphics, 1987), 250–51, 253.
3. See Gordon Irving, "Numerical Strength and Geographical Distribution of the LDS Missionary Force, 1830–1974," *Task Papers in LDS History*, no. 1 (Salt Lake City: CHL, 1975), 21.
4. See Spencer W. Kimball, Journal, November 5–16, 1952, CHL.
5. "Elder Spencer W. Kimball Dedicates Land of Central America as a Mission," *Church News*, December 13, 1952, 5, 6, 13.
6. See Kimball, Journal, "Summary of the History of the Argentine Mission."
7. Francis M. Gibbons, *David O. McKay: Apostle to the World, Prophet of God* (Salt Lake City: Deseret Book, 1986), 338.
8. See Billie F. Fotheringham Oral History, interviewed by Gordon Irving, 1996, 12–13, CHL.
9. See F. LaMond Tullis, "California and Chile in 1851 as Experienced by Parley P. Pratt," *Southern California Historical Quarterly* 68, no. 3 (Fall 1985): 291–307.
10. See "Chile," *Deseret News 2013 Church Almanac* (Salt Lake City: Deseret News, 2013), 455.
11. See "Chile," 455; Mark L. Grover, *A Land of Promise and Prophecy: Elder A. Theodore Tuttle in South America, 1960–1965* (Provo, UT: Religious Studies Center, Brigham Young University, 2008), 294.
12. See Carlos Cifuentes, "Official Report of the Santiago Chile Area Conference of The Church of Jesus Christ of Latter-day Saints: Held in the Teatro Caupolicán in Santiago, Chile 28 February and 1 March, 1977," 2, CHL.
13. See Grover, *Land of Promise and Prophecy*, 239–40.
14. See Grover, *Land of Promise and Prophecy*, 240.

15. See Kimball, Journal, Letter to David O. McKay and Council of the Twelve, April 22, 1959.
16. See Francis M. Gibbons, *Spencer W. Kimball: Resolute Disciple, Prophet of God* (Salt Lake City: Deseret Book, 1995), 224, 237.
17. Gibbons, *Kimball*, 223.
18. Williams and Williams, *From Acorn to Oak Tree*, 303.
19. See Grover, *Land of Promise and Prophecy*, 246–47.
20. See Grover, *Land of Promise and Prophecy*, 242.
21. See Williams and Williams, *From Acorn to Oak Tree*, for more information on missionary work in Peru.
22. Williams and Williams, *From Acorn to Oak Tree*, 303.
23. See Grover, *Land of Promise and Prophecy*, 253.
24. See Grover, *Land of Promise and Prophecy*, 1–7.
25. See Grover, *Land of Promise and Prophecy*, 23, 172–75.
26. See Gibbons, *Kimball*, 237–39.
27. Richards was an Assistant to the Twelve. His grandfather, Apostle Franklin D. Richards, was a relative of Stephen L Richards.
28. See Edward L. Kimball and Andrew E. Kimball Jr., *Spencer W. Kimball: Twelfth President of The Church of Jesus Christ of Latter-day Saints* (Salt Lake City: Bookcraft, 1977), 354.
29. Kimball, Journal, October 9, 1965.
30. Kimball, Journal, October 9, 1965.
31. See Grover, *Land of Promise and Prophecy*, 254–56.
32. See Grover, *Land of Promise and Prophecy*, 85–87.
33. Gibbons, *Kimball*, 239; Grover, *Land of Promise and Prophecy*, 180–82.
34. See Kimball and Kimball, *Spencer W. Kimball*, 357.
35. Kimball and Kimball, *Spencer W. Kimball*, 358.
36. Spencer W. Kimball, "Official Report of the São Paulo Area Conference, February 28 and March 1–2, 1975," 2, CHL.
37. See Kimball, "Official Report of the São Paulo Area Conference," 2.
38. See *Deseret News 1978 Church Almanac* (Salt Lake City: Deseret News, 1978), 238, 242–43.
39. See "Race and the Priesthood," The Church of Jesus Christ of Latter-day Saints, https://www.lds.org/topics.
40. Allen E. Litster, email message to Clinton D. Christensen, January 7, 2012. In private possession.

41. See Kevin Mortensen, *Witnessing the Hand of the Lord in the Dominican Republic* (Centerville, UT: DR History Project, 2009), 57–61.
42. See Mortensen, *Witnessing*, 285.
43. See Spencer W. Kimball, "'When the World Will Be Converted,'" *Ensign*, October 1974.
44. See W. Grant Bangerter, *"These Things I Know": The Autobiography of William Grant Bangerter*, comp. Cory W. Bangerter (Provo, UT: BYU Print Services, 2013), 248–50.
45. See Bangerter, *"These Things I Know,"* 309.
46. Bangerter, *"These Things I Know,"* 285.
47. See Bangerter, *"These Things I Know,"* 280, 298–99.
48. See Helvécio Martins and Mark Grover, *The Autobiography of Helvécio Martins* (Salt Lake City: Aspen Books, 1994).
49. See Tad Walch, "LDS Surge in Latin America," *Deseret News*, March 21, 2003.
50. See John Limburg, Suriname Mission History, circa. 2002, 1–2, CHL; Benjamin C. and Ruth H. Hudson Oral History, interviewed by Clinton D. Christensen, August 14, 2003, 7–9, 12–13, CHL; Jacqueline Wortham, Family History and Memories of Jacqueline Josephine Adele Ghislaine Cailteur, 2003, 156, 164–66, CHL.
51. See Jacqueline Wortham, Family History, 156, 164–66.
52. See "Services in 3 South American Countries and Island Republic," *Church News*, March 10, 1990, 3, 10, 13.
53. See Sarah Jane Weaver, "Elder Holland Creates Second Branch in Cuba," *Church News*, June 19, 2014.
54. Sheri L. Dew, *Go Forward with Faith: The Biography of Gordon B. Hinckley* (Salt Lake City: Deseret Book, 1996), 3.
55. Walch, "LDS Surge in Latin America."
56. See *Deseret News 2013 Church Almanac*, 457–58.
57. See Néstor Curbelo, "Conversion and Change in Chile," *Ensign*, October 2014.
58. See Gordon B. Hinckley, "New Temples to Provide 'Crowning Blessings' of the Gospel," *Ensign*, May 1998.
59. More information on each temple may be found at https://www.churchofjesuschristtemples.org/.
60. See *Deseret News 2001–2002 Church Almanac* (Salt Lake City: Deseret News, 2000), 576–81. Statistics are as of December 31, 1999.

61. See "Mexico Marks 100-Stake Milestone," *Ensign*, September 1989; Mark L. Grover, "The Church in Brazil: The Future Has Finally Arrived," *Ensign*, July 2014; Jason Swensen, "Peruvian Saints Celebrate the Creation of the 100th Stake in Peru," *Church News*, July 16, 2013.

62. See Don L. Searle, "One Million in Mexico," *Ensign*, July 2004; *Deseret News 2009 Church Almanac* (Salt Lake City: Deseret News, 2009), 154. Statistics are as of December 31, 2007. See also "Country Information: Mexico," *Church News*, updated January 29, 2010.

63. See Jason Swensen, "Humble Beginnings for Beloved Branch," *Church News*, updated August 15, 2000.

64. See Richard O. Cowan, "Spanish-American Mission Group Still Together after 50 Years," *Deseret News*, March 12, 2010.

65. See Membership information, Church Directory of Organizations and Leaders, CHL. For further study, see also Jessie L. Embry's *"In His Own Language": Mormon Spanish Speaking Congregations in the United States* (Provo, UT: Charles Redd Center for Western Studies, Brigham Young University, 1997).

66. Jason Swensen, "Prophecies Realized in Vibrant Latin America," *Church News*, updated September 22, 2005.

67. See Alex Dantas, "President Ballard and Elder Soares Hold Area-Wide Family Home Evening with Brazilian Saints," *Church News*, August 28, 2018.

68. Jason Swensen, "South American Prophecy Continues to Be Realized," *Church News*, March 3, 2016.

APPENDIX

# TIMELINE OF THE CHURCH IN LATIN AMERICA

Apr. 6, 1830     Church organized in Palmyra, New York.

Oct. 1830     Four Latter-day Saint missionaries, including Parley P. Pratt, called to preach to indigenous peoples of America. They travel and teach in the Midwest on their way to Missouri.

Jun. 27, 1844     Joseph Smith martyred at Carthage Jail. During Smith's lifetime, missionary work commenced in the United States, Canada, the British Isles, parts of continental Europe, the Middle East, Australia, and the islands of French Polynesia.

1847     Brigham Young leads Latter-day Saint exodus west to the Great Basin near the Great Salt Lake in Alta California, Mexican Territory.

Feb. 2, 1848     Treaty of Guadalupe Hidalgo shifts land from Mexico to the United States; Salt Lake City is in US Territory.

| | |
|---|---|
| 1851–52 | Apostle Parley P. Pratt attempts missionary work in Chile and then returns to United States. |
| 1853 | Six missionaries visit Jamaica for a few weeks. Two attempt travel to British Guiana in South America but are prevented by the British government. |
| 1857 | Parley P. Pratt dies at an assassin's hand, never returning to South America and going to Peru as he had planned. His descendants would serve throughout Latin America. |
| 1875 | Book of Mormon extracts in Spanish are published. Missionaries travel to northern Mexico. |
| 1876 | Brigham Young foresees Mexico as the key to preaching the gospel in all of Latin America. |
| Apr. 6, 1881 | Apostle Moses Thatcher dedicates Mexico for the preaching of the restored gospel. |
| 1885–1912 | The Church grows in northern Mexico through the efforts of Latter-day Saint immigrants. |
| 1907–31 | Rey L. Pratt, grandson of Parley P. Pratt, serves as Mexican Mission president and as a General Authority. |
| 1912 | Political problems force Saints from Mexico during times of revolution. |
| 1923 | Assistant Church historian Andrew Jenson and Thomas Page embark on a five-month trip through Latin America. This journey becomes the catalyst for the establishment of a permanent Latter-day Saint presence in South America. They visit Mexico, Guatemala, El Salvador, Nicaragua, Panama, Peru, Bolivia, Chile, Argentina, Uruguay, and Brazil. |

| | |
|---|---|
| Nov. 1925 | Apostle Melvin J. Ballard travels to South America with two Seventies—Rey L. Pratt, who speaks Spanish, and Rulon S. Wells, who speaks German—to meet with members living in Argentina. |
| Dec. 25, 1925 | Melvin J. Ballard dedicates South America for missionary work. |
| Jul. 4, 1926 | During his last meeting in Buenos Aires before returning to the United States, Elder Ballard prophesies that the Church will grow like an acorn to an oak tree, eventually filling South America. |
| 1927 | Frederick Salem Williams (born in Latter-day Saint colonies in Mexico) becomes a missionary in Argentina. |
| 1928 | Missionary work begins in Brazil among German members. |
| 1933 | J. Reuben Clark Jr., a member of the First Presidency and a former US ambassador to Mexico, visits the International Conference of American States in Uruguay at the request of US president Franklin D. Roosevelt. He holds an evening meeting on January 2, 1934, with Church members in Buenos Aires, Argentina. |
| 1936 | The Spanish American Mission is organized for Latinos living in the southwest United States. |
| 1938 | Frederick S. Williams becomes president of the Argentine Mission. |
| 1941 | Williams writes the First Presidency requesting an extended visit to South America from senior Church leaders. World War II interrupts missionary work. |

| | | |
|---|---|---|
| Aug. 1946 | | Following an Argentine Mission reunion in Utah, Williams and others (including Don Smith, nephew of President George Albert Smith) meet with President Smith and his counselor David O. McKay to discuss needs in South America. |
| Sep. 28, 1946 | | Williams sends a report to the First Presidency outlining ideas for expanding missionary work in South America beyond Argentina and Brazil. He also requests that Church leaders visit the continent. |
| Apr. 1947 | | Williams is asked by the First Presidency to open the Uruguayan Mission. |
| Dec. 10, 1947 | | Apostle Stephen L Richards writes to Williams informing him of his appointment by the First Presidency to visit the three South American missions with his wife, Irene, in 1948. |
| 1948 | | Stephen L and Irene Richards visit Argentina, Uruguay, and Brazil—the first apostolic mission tour since Melvin J. Ballard's in 1926. |
| 1952 | | Apostle Spencer W. Kimball and Assistant to the Twelve Bruce R. McConkie visit Central American countries and create a mission. From Guatemala, Elder Kimball dedicates Central America for missionary work. |
| 1954 | | President David O. McKay makes the first visit by a Church President to Central and South America. He tours branches in Brazil, Uruguay, and Argentina and travels to Panama, Guatemala, and Mexico. |
| 1956 | | Apostle Henry D. Moyle travels to Chile and is granted permission to start missionary work there. The Santiago Branch is organized and the first baptisms in Chile occur. |

| | |
|---|---|
| 1959 | Elder Kimball returns to South America and recommends that a new mission be created along the west coast of Peru and Chile. Later that year, Apostle Harold B. Lee organizes the Andes Mission in Lima, Peru. |
| May 1959 | Stephen L Richards, first counselor in the First Presidency, passes away. |
| 1961 | The Chilean Mission is formed. |
| 1961–65 | Elder A. Theodore Tuttle is the first General Authority assigned to live in South America in order to oversee Church development there. |
| 1964 | One thousand missionaries are baptizing one thousand people a month in the seven missions of South America. |
| 1965 | Ecuador is dedicated by Apostle Spencer W. Kimball. |
| 1966 | South America's first stakes are organized in São Paulo, Brazil, and in Buenos Aires, Argentina. Missionary work begins in Venezuela. |
| 1967 | The Montevideo Stake in Uruguay is created. |
| 1968 | Colombia is dedicated by Apostle Spencer W. Kimball. |
| 1970 | Apostle Gordon B. Hinckley organizes the first stake in Lima, Peru. Membership in Peru and Chile reaches almost 12,000 and 15,000, respectively. |
| 1976 | Fifty years after Elder Ballard's prophecy, membership for Mexico, Central America, South America, and the Caribbean reaches 393,937. |

| | | |
|---|---|---|
| Jun. 1978 | | Church President Spencer W. Kimball announces a revelation extending priesthood and temple blessings to all worthy male members of the Church, fueling rapid growth of the Church throughout Latin America and the Caribbean. |
| Oct. 1978 | | The first temple in South America is dedicated in São Paulo, Brazil. |
| Dec. 1978 | | Elder M. Russell Ballard of the Seventy, a grandson of Melvin J. Ballard, dedicates the Dominican Republic and Jamaica for missionary work. |
| 1981 | | Ángel Abrea from Argentina becomes the first Latin American called as a General Authority. |
| 1988 | | Senior missionaries are sent to Guiana, Suriname, and French Guiana—the last remaining countries in South America to receive the restored gospel. |
| 1989 | | The 100th stake in Mexico is organized. |
| 1993 | | The 100th stake in Brazil is organized. |
| 1996 | | Church membership outside the United States exceeds membership within the United States, with 4.7 million international members out of 9.4 million members worldwide. |
| 1997 | | Church President Gordon B. Hinckley's visit to Colonia Juárez, Mexico, sparks plan to create small temples throughout the world. 102 temples are built by end of 2000. |
| 2001 | | President Hinckley announces the Perpetual Education Fund (PEF), from which the first countries to benefit are Chile, Mexico, and Peru. |

| | |
|---|---|
| 2002–04 | Apostle Jeffrey R. Holland is assigned to Chile to consolidate Church units and emphasize convert retention and real growth in a country with over 500,000 members and high rates of inactivity among members. |
| 2004 | Mexico Church membership passes one million. |
| 2005 | The Havana Cuba Branch is organized, the last country in the Western Hemisphere to have an officially established Church unit. |
| Dec. 2005 | Apostle M. Russell Ballard speaks to Latino members in the Conference Center in Salt Lake City and says of his grandfather's acorn-to-oak-tree prophecy, "A miracle has been fulfilled." Elder Ballard states that the South American Mission has grown to 70 missions on the continent, and Latin America consists of 5.5 million members who attend 28 temples. |
| 2007 | Brazil Church membership passes one million. |
| 2013 | Peru's 100th stake is organized. |
| 2015 | A historical marker is placed in Tres de Febrero Park in Buenos Aires, Argentina, to commemorate the 90th anniversary of Melvin J. Ballard's dedication of South America for missionary work. |
| 2016 | The Lima Peru Los Olivos Temple is announced, making Lima the first city outside Utah to receive a second temple. |
| 2018 | South America has 4 million members, 94 missions, 5,545 congregations, and 17 temples. |
| Mar. 31, 2018 | Ulisses Soares, a Brazilian, is sustained as a member of the Quorum of the Twelve Apostles—the first Latin American called as an Apostle. |

# BIBLIOGRAPHY

Alius, John A. "Elder Richards Ends Trip with Tour of Brazilian Mission." *Church News*, April 3, 1948.

Allen, James B., and Glen M. Leonard. *The Story of the Latter-day Saints*. 2nd ed. Salt Lake City: Deseret Book, 1992.

Argentine Mission Manuscript History and Historical Reports. CHL.

Arrington, Leonard J. *Brigham Young: American Moses*. New York: Alfred A. Knopf, 1985.

Atkin, Rebekah. "The Key to Opportunity: Celebrating 10 Years of the Perpetual Education Fund." *Ensign*, December 2011.

Bagley, Will, ed. *Kingdom in the West: The Mormons and the American Frontier*. Vol. 10 of *At Sword's Point, Part I: A Documentary History of the Utah War to 1858*. Edited by William P. MacKinnon. Norman, OK: Arthur H. Clark, 2008.

Ballard, Melvin R. *Melvin J. Ballard—Crusader for Righteousness*. Salt Lake City: Bookcraft, 1966.

Bangerter, W. Grant. *"These Things I Know": The Autobiography of William Grant Bangerter*. Compiled by Cory W. Bangerter. Provo, UT: BYU Print Services, 2013.

Barton, Peggy. *Mark E. Petersen: A Biography.* Salt Lake City: Deseret Book, 1985.

Beck, Wayne M. Papers. In private possession.

Beck, Wayne M., and Evelyn M. Beck Oral History. Interviewed by Gordon Irving, January 17–31, 1974. CHL.

Beecher, Dale F. "Rey L. Pratt and the Mexican Mission." *BYU Studies* 15, no. 3 (1975): 293–307.

Bloomquist, Milton R. Papers. CHL.

*The Book of Mormon.* Palmyra, NY: E. B. Grandin, 1830.

Bray, Justin R., and Reid L. Neilson. *Exploring Book of Mormon Lands: The 1923 Latin American Travel Writings of Mormon Historian Andrew Jenson.* Provo, UT: Religious Studies Center, Brigham Young University, 2014.

Brazil São Paulo North Mission Manuscript History and Historical Records. CHL.

Brazilian Mission Collection, 1946–50, 2005–7. CHL.

Brazilian Mission Manuscript History and Historical Reports. CHL.

Bushman, Richard Lyman. *Joseph Smith: Rough Stone Rolling.* New York: Alfred A. Knopf, 2005.

Campbell, Eugene E. *Establishing Zion: The Mormon Church in the American West, 1847–1869.* Salt Lake City: Signature Books, 1988.

Cannon, Donald Q., and Richard O. Cowan. *Unto Every Nation: Gospel Light Reaches Every Land.* Salt Lake City: Deseret Book, 2003.

Cannon, Hugh J. *To the Peripheries of Mormondom: The Apostolic Around-the-World Journey of David O. McKay, 1920–1921.* Edited by Reid L. Neilson. Salt Lake City: University of Utah Press, 2011.

Carmack, John K. Oral History. Interviewed by John Enslen, February 23, 2010. CHL.

Carroll, Ernest L., Jr. Mission History. In private possession.

Chamberlain, Solomon. Autobiography. 1856. L. Tom Perry Special Collections, Harold B. Lee Library, Brigham Young University.

Cifuentes, Carlos. "Official Report of the Santiago Chile Area Conference of The Church of Jesus Christ of Latter-day Saints: Held in the Teatro Caupolicán in Santiago, Chile 28 February and 1 March, 1977." CHL.

Clark, Kim B. "Learning for the Whole Soul" and "BYU–Pathway Worldwide." *Ensign*, August 2017.

Córdoba [Argentina] Branch General Minutes. CHL.

"Country Information: Mexico." *Church News*, updated January 29, 2010.

Cowan, Richard O. "Spanish-American Mission Group Still Together after 50 Years." *Deseret News*, March 12, 2010.

Curbelo, Néstor. "Conversion and Change in Chile." *Ensign*, October 2014.
Dellenbach, Frederick H. Papers. CHL.
*Deseret News 1978 Church Almanac*. Salt Lake City: Deseret News, 1978.
*Deseret News 2001–2002 Church Almanac*. Salt Lake City: Deseret News, 2000.
*Deseret News 2003 Church Almanac*. Salt Lake City: Deseret News, 2003.
*Deseret News 2004 Church Almanac*. Salt Lake City: Deseret News, 2004.
*Deseret News 2009 Church Almanac*. Salt Lake City: Deseret News, 2009.
*Deseret News 2013 Church Almanac*. Salt Lake City: Deseret News, 2013.
*Deseret News Extra*, September 14, 1852. Mormon Publications: 19th and 20th Centuries. Harold B. Lee Library Digital Collections, Brigham Young University.
Devitry-Smith, John. "William James Barratt: The First Mormon 'Down Under.'" *BYU Studies* 28, no. 3 (1988): 53–66.
Dew, Sheri L. *Go Forward with Faith: The Biography of President Gordon B. Hinckley*. Salt Lake City: Deseret Book, 1996.
Dexter, E. Keith. "Elder Richards Spends Week on Tour of New Uruguayan Mission." *Church News*, March 27, 1948.
*The Diaries of J. Reuben Clark, 1933–1961, Abridged*. Salt Lake City: privately printed, 2010.
*The Doctrine and Covenants*. Salt Lake City: The Church of Jesus Christ of Latter-day Saints, 1921.
*El Siglo Diez y Nueve*, July 27, 1844. In private possession of Fernando Gomez; copy located at Museum of Mexican Mormon History.
"Elder Helvécio Martins of the Seventy." *Ensign*, May 1990.
Embry, Jessie L. *"In His Own Language": Mormon Spanish-Speaking Congregations in the United States*. Provo, UT: Charles Redd Center for Western Studies, Brigham Young University, 1997.
"The First Book of Nephi." *Palmyra (NY) Reflector*, January 2, 13, 1830. CHL.
Folkman, Kevin H. "'The Moste Desert Lukking Plase I Ever Saw, Amen!' The 'Failed' 1873 Arizona Mission to the Little Colorado River." *Journal of Mormon History* 37, no. 1 (Winter 2011): 115–50.
Fotheringham, Billie F. Oral History. Interviewed by Gordon Irving, 1996. CHL.
Furniss, Norman F. *The Mormon Conflict, 1850–1859*. New Haven, CT: Yale University Press, 1960.
Garr, Arnold K. "Latter-day Saints in Tubuai, French Polynesia, Yesterday and Today." In *Regional Studies in Latter-day Saint Church History: The Pacific Isles*, edited by Reid L. Neilson, Steven C. Harper, Craig K. Manscill, and Mary Jane

Woodger. Provo, UT: Religious Studies Center, Brigham Young University, 2008.

———, Donald Q. Cannon, and Richard O. Cowan, eds. *Encyclopedia of Latter-day Saint History.* Salt Lake City: Deseret Book, 2000.

Gibbons, Francis M. *David O. McKay: Apostle to the World, Prophet of God.* Salt Lake City: Deseret Book, 1986.

———. *Spencer W. Kimball: Resolute Disciple, Prophet of God.* Salt Lake City: Deseret Book, 1995.

Givens, Terryl L., and Matthew J. Grow. *Parley P. Pratt: The Apostle Paul of Mormonism.* New York: Oxford University Press, 2011.

Gomez, Fernando R., and Sergio Pagaza Castillo. *Benito Juarez and the Mormon Connection of the 19th Century.* Mexico City: Museo de Historia del Mormonismo en México, 2007.

Gorton, Henry C. Missionary Journal. CHL.

Gray, Tom. "The Treaty of Guadalupe Hidalgo." National Archives. Updated April 25, 2018. https://www.archives.gov/.

Grover, Mark L. "The Church in Brazil: The Future Has Finally Arrived." *Ensign*, July 2014.

———. *A Land of Promise and Prophecy: Elder A. Theodore Tuttle in South America, 1960–1965.* Provo, UT: Religious Studies Center, Brigham Young University, 2008.

———. "The Mormon Church and German Immigrants in Southern Brazil: Religion and Language." In vol. 26 of *Jahrbuch für Geschichte von Staat, Wirtschaft und Gesellschaft: Lateinamerikas* (1989), 295–308.

———. "The Mormon Priesthood Revelation and the São Paulo, Brazil Temple." *Dialogue: A Journal of Mormon Thought* 23, no. 1 (Spring 1990): 39–53.

Grow, Matthew J., Ronald K. Esplin, Mark Ashurt-McGee, Gerrit J. Dirkmaat, and Jeffrey D. Mahas, eds. *Administrative Records: Council of Fifty, Minutes, March 1844–January 1846.* Vol. 1 of the Administrative Records series of *The Joseph Smith Papers.* Edited by Ronald K. Esplin, Matthew J. Grow, and Matthew C. Godfrey. Salt Lake City: Church Historian's Press, 2016.

Hafen, LeRoy R., and Ann W. Hafen, eds. *The Utah Expedition, 1857–1858.* Glendale, CA: Arthur H. Clark, 1958.

Halverson, W. Dee. *Stephen L Richards, 1879–1959.* N.p.: Heritage Press, n.d.

Hammon, Donald Levi Gale. *Levi Byram and Martha Jane Belnap Hammon: Gold Medal Pioneers.* Chapel Hill, NC: Professional Press, 1996.

Harper, Steven C. "The Restoration of Mormonism to Erie County, Pennsylvania." *Mormon Historical Studies* 1, no. 1 (Spring 2000): 3–19.

Heath, Joseph M. "Brazilian Elders Take Stock of Year's Labors." *Church News*, January 12, 1948.

Hinckley, Bryant S. *Sermons and Missionary Services of Melvin Joseph Ballard*. Salt Lake City: Deseret Book, 1949.

Hinckley, Gordon B. "Converts and Young Men." *Ensign*, May 1997.

———. "New Temples to Provide 'Crowning Blessings' of the Gospel." *Ensign*, May 1998.

Hudson, Benjamin C., and Ruth H. Hudson Oral History. Interviewed by Clinton D. Christensen, August 14, 2003. CHL.

Irving, Gordon. "Numerical Strength and Geographical Distribution of the LDS Missionary Force, 1830–1974." *Task Papers in LDS History*, no. 1. Salt Lake City: CHL, 1975.

Ivins, Anthony Woodward. Diary. Anthony W. Ivins Collection. CHL.

Jenson, Andrew. *Autobiography of Andrew Jenson*. Salt Lake City: Deseret News, 1938.

———, comp. *Latter-day Saint Biographical Encyclopedia*. Salt Lake City: Andrew Jenson Memorial Association, 1901–36.

Jessee, Dean C., Mark Ashurst-McGee, and Richard L. Jensen, eds. *Journals, Volume 1: 1832–1839*. Vol. 1 of the Journals series of *The Joseph Smith Papers*. Edited by Dean C. Jessee, Ronald K. Esplin, and Richard Lyman Bushman. Salt Lake City: Church Historian's Press, 2008.

Jones, Daniel W. *Forty Years among the Indians*. Salt Lake City: Juvenile Instructor Office, 1890.

Kimball, Edward L. "Spencer W. Kimball and the Revelation on Priesthood." *BYU Studies* 47, no. 2 (2008): 5–78.

———, and Andrew E. Kimball Jr. *Spencer W. Kimball: Twelfth President of The Church of Jesus Christ of Latter-day Saints*. Salt Lake City: Bookcraft, 1977.

Kimball, Spencer W. Journal. CHL.

Kimball, Spencer W. "Official Report of the São Paulo Area Conference, February 28 and March 1–2, 1975." CHL.

———. "'When the World Will Be Converted.'" *Ensign*, October 1974.

Lee, John D., to Emma B. Lee, December 9, 1876. HM 31214, John D. Lee Collection. Huntington Library, San Marino, CA.

*The Life of Brigham Young*. Salt Lake City: George Q. Cannon and Sons, 1893.

Limburg, John Mathew. Suriname Mission History, circa 2002. CHL.

Litser, Allen E., to Clinton D. Christensen, email, January 7, 2012. In author's possession.

MacKinnon, William P. "'Not as a Stranger': A Presbyterian Afoot in the Mormon Past." *Journal of Mormon History* 38, no. 2 (Spring 2012): 1–46.

Marble, Glenn B. Papers. CHL.

Marsh, Howard J. "An Apostle Tours Argentina." *Church News*, March 6, 1948.

Martins, Helvécio, and Mark Grover. *The Autobiography of Helvécio Martins.* Salt Lake City: Aspen Books, 1994.

McConkie, Bruce R. In "Official Report of the Santiago Chile Area Conference, February 28 and March 1, 1977." CHL.

Mehr, Kahlile B. *Mormon Missionaries Enter Eastern Europe.* Provo, UT: Brigham Young University Press; Salt Lake City: Deseret Book, 2002.

"Mexico Marks 100-Stake Milestone." *Ensign*, September 1989.

"Missionary Work in South America Makes Definite Gain." *Church News*, April 17, 1948.

Mortensen, Kevin. *Witnessing the Hand of the Lord in the Dominican Republic.* Centerville, UT: DR History Project, 2009.

O'Donnal, John Forres. *Pioneer in Guatemala: The Personal History of John Forres O'Donnal, Including the History of The Church of Jesus Christ of Latter-day Saints in Guatemala.* Yorba Linda, CA: Shumway Family History Services, 1997.

Palmer, A. Delbert, and Mark L. Grover. "Hoping to Establish a Presence: Parley P. Pratt's 1851 Mission to Chile." *BYU Studies* 38, no. 4 (1999): 115–28.

Perego, Ugo A. "The Book of Mormon and the Origin of Native Americans from a Maternally Inherited DNA Standpoint." In *No Weapon Shall Prosper: New Light on Sensitive Issues*, edited by Robert L. Millet. Provo, UT: Religious Studies Center, Brigham Young University, 2011.

"Perpetual Education Fund: A Decade of Changing Lives." *Church News*, October 21, 2011.

Piracicaba [Brazil] Branch General Minutes. CHL.

Porter, L. Aldin. "A History of the Latter-day Seventy." *Ensign*, August 2000.

Porter, Larry C. "The Book of Mormon: Historical Setting for Its Translation and Publication." In *Joseph Smith: The Prophet, the Man*, edited by Susan Easton Black and Charles D. Tate Jr., 49–64. Provo, UT: Religious Studies Center, Brigham Young University, 1993.

Pratt, Helaman. Journal, 1875–78. CHL.

Pratt, Parley P. *Autobiography of Parley Parker Pratt*. Edited by Parley P. Pratt Jr. New York: Russell Brothers, 1874.

Price, Richard, and Pamela Price. "Missionary Successes, 1836–1844." *Restoration Voice* 26, no. 14 (November/December 1982).

"Race and the Priesthood." Gospel Topics. The Church of Jesus Christ of Latter-day Saints. https://www.churchofjesuschrist.org/topics.

*Record of the Twelve*. February 14, 1835. CHL. Also available at the Joseph Smith Papers, https://www.josephsmithpapers.org/paperSummary/record-of-the-twelve-14-february-28-august-1835.

Rex, Diania H. *The History of Diania Haycock and Harold Morgan Rex, 1915–2005*. CHL.

Rich, Russell R. "The Dogberry Papers and the Book of Mormon." *BYU Studies* 10, no. 3 (Spring 1970): 315–20.

Richards, Irene. Letters. CHL.

Richards, Lynn Stephen and Annette. Family Papers. CHL.

Richards, Stephen L. Papers, 1921–59. CHL.

Richards, Stephen L. In Conference Report, October 3, 1948.

———. In Conference Report, April 7, 1957.

Richardson, Edwin J. Papers. CHL.

Romney, Thomas Cottam. *The Mormon Colonies in Mexico*. 1938. Reprint, Salt Lake City: University of Utah Press, 2005.

Santos Missionary Record, 1947–59. CHL.

Searle, Don L. "One Million in Mexico." *Ensign*, July 2004.

"Services in 3 South American Countries and Island Republic." *Church News*, March 10, 1990.

Sharp, J. Vernon. Journal. CHL.

Sharp, J. Vernon Oral History. Interviewed by Gordon Irving, December 5–7, 1972. CHL.

Smith, George A. *The Rise, Progress and Travels of the Church of Jesus Christ of Latter-day Saints*. 2nd ed. Salt Lake City: Deseret News, 1872.

Sorrento Branch General Minutes. CHL.

South American Mission Manuscript History and Historical Reports. CHL.

Swensen, Jason. "Humble Beginnings for Beloved Branch." *Church News*, August 15, 2000.

———. "Mexican Colonies Offering Fruits of Leadership." *Church News*, May 11, 2001.

———. "Peruvian Saints Celebrate the Creation of the 100th Stake in Peru." *Church News*, July 16, 2013.

———. "Prophecies Realized in Vibrant Latin America." *Church News*, updated September 22, 2005.

———. "South American Prophecy Continues to Be Realized." *Church News*, March 3, 2016.

Talmage, Jeremy, and Clinton D. Christensen. "Black, White, or Brown? Racial Perceptions and the Priesthood Policy in Latin America." *Journal of Mormon History* 44, no. 1 (January 2018): 119–45.

Taylor, John. Journal. CHL.

"Temple Moments: 'Like a Dream.'" *Church News*, updated October 18, 1997.

Todd, Jay M. "More Members Now outside U.S. Than in U.S." *Ensign*, March 1996.

Tucker, Grant C. Papers. CHL.

Tullis, F. LaMond. "California and Chile in 1851 as Experienced by Parley P. Pratt." *Southern California Historical Quarterly* 68, no. 3 (Fall 1985): 291–307.

———. *Mormons in Mexico: The Dynamics of Faith and Culture.* Logan: Utah State University Press, 1987.

Turley, Richard E., Jr., and Brittany A. Chapman, eds. Vol. 1 of *Women of Faith in the Latter Days*. Salt Lake City: Deseret Book, 2011.

———, and William W. Slaughter. *How We Got the Book of Mormon*. Salt Lake City: Deseret Book, 2011.

Turner, John G. *Brigham Young: Pioneer Prophet*. Cambridge, MA: Belknap Press of Harvard University Press, 2012.

Uruguayan Mission Manuscript History and Historical Reports. CHL.

"The Utah Expedition: Its Causes and Consequences," part 3, *Atlantic Monthly*, May 1859, 583–84.

Walch, Tad. "LDS Surge in Latin America." *Deseret News*, March 21, 2003.

Walker, Sanford S. Mission Papers. CHL.

Weaver, Sarah Jane. "Elder Cook Visits South America." *Church News*, updated December 3, 2015.

———. "Elder Holland Creates Second Branch in Cuba." *Church News*, June 19, 2014.

Whetten, LaVon Brown. *Colonia Juarez: Commemorating 125 Years of the Mormon Colonies in Mexico*. Bloomington, IN: AuthorHouse, 2010.

Whitney, Orson F. Vol. 4 of *History of Utah*. Salt Lake City: George Q. Cannon and Sons, 1904.

Whittaker, David J. "The Bone in the Throat: Orson Pratt and the Public Announcement of Plural Marriage." *Western Historical Quarterly* 18, no. 3 (July 1987): 293–314.

Williams, Corraine S. Oral History. Interviewed by Frederick G. Williams, 1975–76. CHL.

Williams, Frederick S. Oral History. Interviewed by William G. Hartley, 1972. CHL.

Williams, Frederick S. Papers. CHL.

Williams, Frederick S., with J. Vernon Graves, Robert R. McKay, Don Hyrum Smith, Edgar B. Mitchell, and Keith N. McCune. "Proposed Plan for Activating and Extending the Missionary Work in Latin America." September 28, 1946. CHL.

———, and Frederick G. Williams. *From Acorn to Oak Tree: A Personal History of the Establishment and First Quarter Century Development of the South American Missions*. Fullerton, CA: Et Cetera, Et Cetera Graphics, 1987.

Wortham, Jacqueline. Family History and Memories of Jacqueline Josephine Adele Ghislaine Cailteur, 2003. CHL.

Young, Brigham, to Wm. C. Staines, January 11, 1876. Letterpress copybook, 14:125–26. Brigham Young Office Files. CHL.

Young, Walter Ernest Oral History. Interviewed by Gordon Irving and Victor Jorgensen, 1972–73. CHL.

Young, Walter Ernest. *The Diary of W. Ernest Young*. Salt Lake City: n.p., 1973.

# INDEX

## A

Abrea, Ángel, called as first Latin American General Authority, 193
acorn-to-oak-tree prophecy, xxi, 187, 195, 197
*aduana. See* customhouse
American Association of Montevideo, 94–95, 97–98
Anchorage, Alaska, small-temple concept employed in, 196
area authorities, calling of, 195
area presidencies, first announced, 194
Argentina, 2, 85
    Andrew Jenson travels to, xviii
    David O. McKay visits, 185
    German members in, xix–xxi, 9
    Italian members in, 9
    Spanish members in, 9
    Stephen L Richards arrives in, 10–11
    temple announced for, 191, 196

Argentine Mission, xxii, xxiv, xxviii, 9, 18–19, 22, 35, 51, 58, 67, 75, 77, 84, 165–67, 173, 183–84
    Frederick S. Williams called to preside over, xxii
Argualt, Edie (Argentine sister missionary in Uruguay), **93**, 103n43
Arroyo Seco Branch (Uruguay), 83
Asunción (Paraguay), 168

## B

Bahía Blanca Branch (Argentina), 27, 67
Balderas, Eduardo, 166, 181n4
Ballard, M. Russell, 192, 194, 197
Ballard, Melvin J., 35, 187
    assignment to South America, xix
    baptizes German converts in Argentina, xx
    dedicates South America for preaching the gospel, xxi, 191

Ballard, Melvin J. (*continued*)
    lost journals of, xxxvn49
    ninetieth anniversary of dedicatory prayer in Argentina, 197
    passing of, xxiv
Bangerter, William Grant, 193
baptism(s), 28–30, 47, 67, 180
    in Campinas (Brazil), 119–21, **124**, 128, 154n32
    in La Plata (Argentina), **47**
    first in Chile, 186
    first in Uruguay, **90**, 102
    problem of retention following, 195
    surge of, in Brazil, 183
Barbados, early missionaries prevented from traveling to, xiv
Barjollo, Fermin Claudio (Argentine Church translator), 99–100, 104
Beck, Wayne M., 106, 123–26, 141
    and Evelyn M., 154n28, 154n31, 154n32
Bednar, David A., dedicates Cuba for missionary work, 195
Belgrano (Buenos Aires), plan to obtain mission home in, 61, 117, 165
Belize, missionary work begins in, 194
Belo Horizonte (Brazil), 133
Benson, Ezra Taft, 194
Bible
    Latter-day Saint embrace of, 45
    people seen to be ignorant of, 32, 110, 161
Bolivia, xxvii
    Andrew Jenson travels to, xviii
    Church legally recognized in, 189
    missionaries sent to, 189
Book of Mormon
    published in Spanish, xvi
    translation and purpose of, xii
Bosque Stake (Brazil), 193
Brady, L. Pierce, 24, 40, 43, 46, 50–52, 57, 64, 71, 101n8, 167, 182n5
Brazil, vii, xx, 2, 4, **5**, 10, 19, 31, 51, 89, 91, 176–78, 181, 185, 190
    Andrew Jenson travels to, xviii
    David O. McKay visits, 185

Brazil (*continued*)
    effect of 1978 priesthood revelation on growth in, 192
    itinerary of Richardses in, 107–8
    need for Melchizedek Priesthood brethren in, 193
    one million members in, 196
    Stephen L and Irene Richards arrive in, 4–7, 105
    temples in, 192, 196
Brazilian Mission, xxii–xxiv, 53, 81, 160, 169–71, 173
    history of, 103, 129, 153n13
    presidency, **113**
    Spencer W. Kimball recommends dividing, 186
    Stephen L Richards reports on, 169–71
Brewerton, Ted E., 189
Brisas del Hum Hotel (Mercedes, Uruguay), 90
British Guiana, xiv
British Honduras, xviii
Brown, Harold (American Embassy worker in Montevideo, Uruguay), 78, 95, 101n3, 104
Brown, Leonore, 95
Buenos Aires (Argentina), 2, 5, 10, 14, 22, 24, 26, 28, 30, 33, 42–43, 46, 50, 53, 55, 56, 61, 67, 165, 173
    conferences in, 65, 166
    first stake in Argentina, 190
    J. Reuben Clark visits, xxii
    Melvin J. Ballard visits, xx, 35
    number of members in, 12
    university in. *See* Universidad Nacional de la Plata

## C

Camargo, Helio de Rocha, 194
Campinas (Brazil), 107, 112, 113, 119, 122, 126, 128, 133, 154n9, 154n20, 170. *See also* baptisms, in Campinas

Cannon, Sylvester Q., xix
Caribbean, Church in, 191–92
Carroll, Ernest Leroi, Jr., 70n39, 72
Central America
    Church growth in, 191
    dedicated for missionary work, 184
    temples in, 196
"Cerro" (famous hill in Montevideo, Uruguay), 98
Chile
    Andrew Jenson travels to, xviii
    David O. McKay visits, 185
    Jeffrey R. Holland strengthens priesthood leadership in, 195
    opened for missionary work, 186
    temple announced for, 191, 196
Chilean Mission, organization of, 187
Christensen, Dale and Diana, 55, 56
*Christus* statue (Brazil). *See* "Corcovado"
*Church News*, 10, 50, 63, 64, 160–63, 197
    on large baptismal service in Brazil, 183–84
    on ongoing fulfillment of Melvin J. Ballard's prophecy, 198
    on Stephen L Richards's tour of Argentine Mission, 66–68
    on Stephen L Richards's tour of Brazilian Mission, 128–30
    on Stephen L Richards's tour of Uruguayan Mission, 97–99
Church of Jesus Christ of Latter-day Saints, The
    establishes missionary work in Panama, 185
    growth in Argentina, xxii, 2, 9, 12, 23, 65
    growth in Brazil, xxii, 2, 183, 186, 190, 192, 196
    growth in Guatemala, 194
    growth in Mexico, xv
    growth in South America, 196–97
    growth in Uruguay, 2, 75, 80, 183–84, 104n53
    in Cuba, 195
    in El Salvador, 194
    in French Guiana, 194

Church of Jesus Christ of Latter-day Saints, The (*continued*)
    in Guyana, 194
    in Honduras, 194
    in Nicaragua, 194
    in Suriname, 194
    in Trinidad and Tobago, 194
    Latin American journalists favorable toward, 10, 12, 17, 18, 23, 35, 80–82, 133
    one million members in Brazil, 196
    one million members in Mexico, 196
Ciudadela Branch (Argentina), 26
Clark, J. Reuben, Jr., xxii, 1, 80, 185
Coca-Cola, Stephen L Richards explains stance on, 95
Colombia
    Andrew Jenson surveys, xviii
    Church started in, 189
    considered for proselyting, 188
    temple announced for, 196
Colonia Juárez (Mexico), small-temple concept employed in, 196
"Corcovado" (*Christus* statue in Brazil), 4–5, **5**, 145, 156n67
Córdoba (Argentina), 35–36, 41, 62, 73
Coronel Suárez (Argentina), 70n35, 71
Costa Rica, xviii
Cuba, Church organized in, 192, 195
Curitiba (Brazil), 105, 107, 126, 130–31, 133, 136, 139, 141, 155n39, 155n48
customhouse, 11–12, 14, 16, 77, 98
Cuzco Branch (Peru), 187

# D

dedicatory prayers for opening missionary work
    Argentina, xxi, 35
    Brazil, 105
    Central America, 184
    Cuba, 195
    Dominican Republic, 192
    Ecuador, 189

dedicatory prayers for opening missionary work (*continued*)
    French Guiana, 194
    Guyana, 194
    Jamaica, 192
    South America, xxi, 129, 160, 191, 197
    Suriname, 194
    Trinidad and Tobago, 194
    Uruguay, 105
de Jong, Gerrit, Jr., xix, 108, 153n5
Dexter, Keith, 90, 97
Dominican Republic, 192

# E

Easter sermon, on board SS *Argentina*, 148–49
Ecuador, xxvii
    Andrew Jenson obtains information on, xviii
    dedicated for missionary work, 189
    opened for proselytizing, 188–189
    temple announced for, 196
El Salvador, obstacles to Church growth in, 194

# F

First Presidency
    considers sending General Authority on South American mission tour, 75
    letters to Stephen L Richards, 34
Fotheringham, Billie, 186
French Guiana, 194
*From Acorn to Oak Tree*, 76, 100–104
Fyans, J. Thomas, "Six Steps to Stakehood" plan, 188

# G

Gandhi, Mahatma, 13, 18, 20, 70

German members, xix–xx, xxxvn52, 127, 129, 132–33, 135–36, 144, 155n42, 156n60
German language, 129, 135, 170, 176
Gianfelice, Juana, Argentine sister missionary in Uruguay, **93**
gold and green ball, 65, 116, 125, **125**
Gorton, Henry C., 46, 73n77
Guatemala
    Andrew Jenson travels to, xviii
    membership growth, 194
    President McKay visits, 185
    temple announced for, 196
Guyana, xxvii, 194

# H

Haedo Branch (Argentina), 26, **26**
Haiti, 192
Hill of Glory (Mendoza, Argentina), **48**
Hinckley, Gordon B., 195–96
    goal of 100 temples, 196
    and small-temple concept, 196
Holland, Jeffrey R., 195
Honduras
    Andrew Jenson surveys, xviii
    missionaries removed from, 194
    obstacles to Church growth in, 194

# I

Indians. *See* Lamanites; native peoples
Ipomeia (Brazil), 137, 143, 156n60

# J

Jamaica, xiv, xxxiiin15, 192
Jenson, Andrew, visits Central and South America, xvii–iii
Joinville Branch (Brazil), 107, 126, 129, 131, **132**, **134**, 137, 155n42
    large baptismal service held in, 183
Juiz de Forta (Brazil), 133

## K

Kimball, Spencer W., 184
- announces temples for Mexico, Guatemala, Peru, Argentina, Chile, 191
- assigned to South America as member of Twelve, 188
- dedicates Central America for proselytizing, 184–85
- June 1978 revelation on priesthood, 191
- proposes temples for South America, 190
- requests more native missionaries, 192–93
- visits South America, 186
- work ethic of, 186

## L

Lamanites, xii, xxvi, 176
- blessed to blossom as rose, 184–85
- Church progress among, 188
- mission to, xii

language barrier in Latin America, xviii

La Plata Branch (Buenos Aires, Argentina), 43–44, **44**, 46–47, 49, 68, 73–74, 166

La Plata University (Buenos Aires, Argentina). *See* Universidad Nacional de la Plata

Latin America
- barriers to early missionary in, xviii
- size of missionary force in 1940s, 184

Lee, Harold B.
- organizes Andes Mission, 187
- prophesies of Church growth on Pacific Coast of Americas, 187

Lencina, Dora, **45**, 46

Lima Branch (Peru), 186

Liniers Chapel (Buenos Aires, Argentina), 14, 17, **21**, 24, 26, 166, 174

*local* (branch meetinghouse), 48, 58–59, 72n49, 74, 90–91, 177

Lombardi, José (first patriarch in South America), 193

Lucero Ward (Salt Lake City), 197

## M

Machu Picchu (Peru), seminar for mission presidents at, 188

*Madama Butterfly* (opera by Puccini), 23

Maldonado family baptism (Argentina), 28–30, **29**

Malvín Branch (Uruguay), **83**, 83

Marsh, Howard J. (Argentine Mission secretary), 10, **17**, 27
- authors *Church News* report, 66–68
- mission reports of, 17–18, 22, 26–27, 36–37, 40–41, 43, 46, 50, 55–56, 66
- unpublished news article, 20–22

Martins, Helvécio, 194

*mate* (herbal tea), 64, 74n97, 109, 167, 182n6

McConkie, Bruce R., 184

McCune, Alfred William, xiv

McKay, David O., xxv, xxvii, 1
- visit to South America, 185

McKay, Robert, 185

Melchizedek Priesthood
- needed in Brazil, 193
- strengthened in Chile, 195

Mendoza (Argentina), 39, 42, 48, 53, 67, 73

Mercedes (Uruguay), 82, 85, 90–91, 98, 102, 103n37

Mexican Branch (Salt Lake City), 197

Mexican territory, Latter-day Saints settle in, xv

Mexico
- Andrew Jenson visits, xviii
- Church membership in, 191

Mexico (*continued*)
   David O. McKay visits, 185
   gateway to South America, xv
   first temple announced for, 191
   reaches one million members, 196
   temples in, 196
mission homes
   in Argentina, **14**, **15**, 16, 61, 183
   in Brazil, **108**
   in Uruguay, 88, 92, 96, 98–99
Montevideo (Uruguay), xx, 2, 53, 57, 75, 78, 169, 173
   arrival of Richardses in, **77**, 77–78
   Church branches in, 82, 101n11
   first stake organized in, 190
   Irene Richards notes beauty of, 91
   J. Reuben Clark Jr. visits, 80, 101n14
   mission home in, 92
   Richardses travel to, 76
   Richardses visit Congressional Building, 93–94
   Stephen L Richards holds meetings in, 82–89
   Stephen L Richards speaks at American Association of Montevideo, 95–96
   temple in, 190
Monticello (Utah), small-temple concept employed in, 196
Morini's, famous restaurant in Uruguay, 94, 104n46. *See* Ristorante Morini
Moyle, Henry D., 186
Mutual Improvement Association, 47, 86, 91, 114, 121, 126, 177, 179, 183

# N

native missionaries, Spencer W. Kimball requests more, 192–93
native peoples, xii, xiv, xxvi
Nelson, Russell M., calls first Latin American Apostle, 198

Nibley, Charles, xix
Nicaragua
   Andrew Jenson visits, xviii
   obstacles to Church growth in, 194
Nicolaysen, Sterling, 187
Nielsen, Thayle, 141, 156n59
Nirvana Hotel (Montevideo, Uruguay), 92
Nogaro Hotel (Montevideo, Uruguay), 94
Novo Hamburgo (Brazil), 137

# O

Oliver Cowdery, call to preach to native peoples, xii

# P

Panama, xiv
   Andrew Jenson visits, xviii
   David O. McKay visits, 185
   missionary work extends to, 185
Paraguay, xxvii
   Andrew Jenson surveys, xviii
   missionary work begins in, 101n8, 184
Paraná (Brazil). *See* Curitiba (Brazil)
Paysandú (Uruguay), 8, 82, 90, 98, 102, 103n3
*pensiones* (boardinghouses), 58
Pergamino Branch (Argentina), 33–34, 36–37, 166
Perón, Juan, 47, 73n80, 86–87
Peru, xiv
   Andrew Jenson visits, xviii
   David O. McKay visits, 185
   first stake organized, 190
   first temple announced for, 191, 196
   missionary work begins, 186
   second temple announced for, 196
Petersen, Mark E., 191–92
Pink House (Argentine capitol building), 47

Piracicaba (Brazil), 107, 117
polygamy, xiii, 12, 82
Porto Alegre (Brazil), 131, 137, 138, 156n50
Pratt, Orson, xiii
Pratt, Parley P., 186, 187
    first trip to Latin America, xvii
    journey to Chile, xiii
    leaves South America, xiv
    preaches to Lamanites, xii
Pratt, Rey L., xvii, xx
priesthood, restriction on, xxvii–xxviii, 191–92

# R

Rama Florida Branch (Argentina), 22
Ramos Mejía Branch (Argentina), 26, **26**
regional representatives, release of, 195
*Relief Society Magazine*, 64
religious freedom, xviii
revelation on priesthood, xxvii–xxviii, 191–92
Rex, Diania, **106**, 124, **124**, 128
Rex, Harold M., Brazilian Mission president, 106, **106**, 109, **109**, 111, **112**, 123, 135, 141, 182n8, 183, 189
Ribeirão Preto (Brazil), 107, 117, 133
Richards, Franklin D., 188
Richards, Irene
    birth of, xxix
    departs on mission, 2
    keeps record of mission tour, xxx–xxxi, 3
    marriage, xxx
    set apart as special missionary, 2–3
    voice strained by throat surgery, 2, 6, 8
Richards, Lee, 70n43, 72, 117
Richards, Stephen L, **xxix**, 22, 68, **160**
    appointed for South American tour, xxix

Richards, Stephen L (*continued*)
    appreciation of, 117
    arrives in Argentina, 10–11, **11**
    arrives in Montevideo, Uruguay, 77, 77–78
    called as First Counselor to President David O. McKay, 185
    celebrates wedding anniversary, 68
    conferences with members, 120–22, 135
    departs on South American mission tour, 2
    departs Uruguay, 96
    early spiritual doubts of, xxix–xxx
    explains Church doctrine, 19–20
    final report of, 163–71
    gives favorable impressions, 17, 19, 21, 36, 57, 91, 93, 95, 97, 98, 122, 152
    gives priesthood blessing, **45**, 56
    gratitude for visit, 181
    health of, 2, 28, 34, 49, 77, 132, 163
    influence on missionary work, 183–84
    letter from First Presidency, 34
    letters and reports to First Presidency, 10, 22, 23–24, 52–53, 69, 160, 163–71
    marriage, xxx
    meetings with business and government leaders, 2, 9, 22, 33, 43, 87, 92, 95–96, 99, 186
    meetings with investigators, 87, 98, 102n15
    meetings with members, 17–18, 21, 26–27, 33, 41, 83–85, 98
    meetings with missionaries, 24–25, **25**, 27, 35–36, 40–42, 47, 67, 85, 89, 92, 94, 98, 112–13, 115, 118–19, 126–27, 138, 146, **181**
    meetings with mission presidencies, **25**, 50, 56–66, 74n84, 98, 113–15, 140–43, 184
    opinion of South American Saints, 160

Richards, Stephen L (*continued*)
    passes away, 186
    prayer, discussion on, 113
    preaches to 70 investigators at YMCA, 91
    reports on health to First Presidency, 10, 23, 53
    set apart for special mission, 1–2
    speaks to American Association of Montevideo, 94, 95, 97
    travel summary in Argentina, 67–68
Richardson, Edwin J., 28
Río Cuarto (Argentina), 42, 73
Rio de Janeiro (Brazil), **3**, **5**, 108, 126, 133, 136, 144–47
    Irene Richards notes beauty of, 4, 145–46
    Melvin J. Ballard arrives at, xx
    Stephen L and Irene Richards arrive at, xx, 4, 173
Rio Preto (Brazil), 156n60
Ristorante Morini (famous restaurant in Uruguay), 94
Rosário (Argentina), 34, 38, 40, 72, 117
Rotary Club, 14–17, 87, 89, 91, 98, 121, 124

## S

San Nicolás (Argentina), 34
Santiago Branch (Chile), organized, 186
Santos (Brazil), 105, 107, 109, 133, 153n5
São Paulo (Brazil), 113, 126, 133, 139, 140, 143, 154n19, 169, 183
    first South American stake organized in, 190
    first temple in South America, 190, 192
    German members in, 107, 127, 129
    history of Church in, 153n13
    mission home, **108**
    news coverage of Church in, 111–12
    Portuguese members in, 127
    Richardses arrive in, 7, 105, 107–10, **111**

Seventy, expanded role, 195–96
Sharp, J. Vernon (Andes Mission president), 187
*siesta*, 38, 49, 89, 177
sister missionaries. *See* Argualt, Edie; Vogler, Elza J.
"Six Steps to Stakehood," 188
Smith, Don, xxiv
Smith, George Albert, xxiv, 1
Smith, Joseph, Jr., 12
    Mexican newspaper reports death of, xv
    organizes Church of Christ, xi
    translates Book of Mormon, xii
Smith, Joseph Fielding, 187
Smith, Samuel, xii
Soares, Ulisses, called as first Latin American Apostle, 198
Sorocaba (Brazil), 133
Sorrento Branch (Argentina), 35, 40, 73
South America
    Church growth in, 191, 197
    faithfulness of Saints of African descent in, xxvii
    missionaries first called to, xiv
    World War II delays missionary work in, xxiv
Spanish American Mission (United States), 197
Spanish-speaking Church units, 197
Stott, E. Keith, 51
Suriname, 194

## T

Tandil Branch (Argentina), 67
Taylor, John, xvi
temples
    announced for Argentina, 196
    announced for Chile, 196
    announced for Colombia, 196
    announced for Ecuador, 196
    announced for Guatemala, 196
    announced for Peru, 196
    expansion of, in Brazil, 196

temples (*continued*)
   expansion of, in Mexico City, 196
   goal of 100 by end of year 2000, 196
   Gordon B. Hinckley introduces concept of smaller, 196
   proposed for South America, 190, 196
Tenorio, Horacio A., 194
Terminus Hotel, 120, 125
traveling elders, 60, 67
Treaty of Guadalupe Hidalgo, xv
Treinta y Tres Branch (Uruguay), 82, 85, 102
Tres Arroyos (Argentina), 27, 28, 30, 67, 71–72
Tres de Febrero Park, 197
Trinidad and Tobago, 194
Tuttle, A. Theodore, 187–89

## U

Universidad Nacional de la Plata, 54, 74n89
Uruguay, 2, 9, 19, 49–50, 55, 57, 66, 70
   Andrew Jenson visits, xviii
   Church growth in, 75, 190
   David O. McKay visits, 185
   first stake organized in, 190
   *locales* in, 58–59
Uruguayan Mission, 75, 80–81, **81**, 83–84, 95, 97, 104, 168–69, 186
Utah War, xv–xvi

## V

Vaz, Alfredo, 116, 118, **119**, 120, **120**, 121, 123, 154n20
Venezuela, xxvii
   Andrew Jenson visits, xviii
   Church started in, 189
Vogler, Elza J., Argentine sister missionary in Uruguay, 103n43

## W

Wells, Rulon S., xx
West Indies, Andrew Jenson surveys, xviii
Williams, Corraine, 75–76, 92, 95, 102
   memories of Irene Richards, 84–85
Williams, Frederick S., 75–76, 78, 83, 85, 90, 92, 94, 95, 99–100, 181n3, 185, 187–88
   becomes president of Argentine Mission, xxii
   report to First Presidency, xxvi
   requests General Authority visit to South America, xxii, xxviii, 75
   requests to be missionary in Argentina, xxii
   seeks permission to establish printing operation, xxiii
*What of the Mormons?* (book), 99
World War II
   delays General Authority visit to South America, xxiv
   effect on missionary work, 129, 160
   favorable news coverage of Church in era following, 10

## Y

Young, Brigham, xii, xv
Young, Cecile, **11**, 11–12, 27, 35
Young, W. Ernest, 10, 19, 27, **30**, 35, 43, 45, 50–52, 56–57, 67, 70, 74, 117, 154

# ABOUT THE AUTHORS

**Richard E. Turley Jr.** serves as managing director of the Public Affairs Department of The Church of Jesus Christ of Latter-day Saints. Previously he served as assistant Church historian and recorder, managing director of the Church Historical Department, and managing director of the Family History Department.

**Clinton D. Christensen** has worked for the Church History Department since 2001. He earned a BA and MA in English from Brigham Young University and a master of library and information science and archival administration from Wayne State University in Detroit, Michigan. He is part of the Global Support and Acquisitions Division and has spent most of his career collecting Church history in Latin America and the Caribbean.